Cold War Spymaster

Cold War Spymaster

The Legacy of Guy Liddell, Deputy Director of MI5

Nigel West

Frontline Books, London

Cold War Spymaster: The Legacy of Guy Liddell, Deputy Director of MI5
This edition published in 2018 by Frontline Books,
an imprint of Pen & Sword Books Ltd,
47 Church Street, Barnsley, S. Yorkshire, S70 2AS
www.frontline-books.com

ISBN: 978-1-52673-622-2

CIP data records for this title are available from the British Library

For more information on our books, please visit
www.frontline-books.com, email info@frontline-books.com
or write to us at the above address.

Printed and bound by TJ International Ltd, Padstow, Cornwall

Typeset in 11/13pt Ehrhardt by Mac Style

Contents

Acknowledgements

The author acknowledges his debt of gratitude to those who have assisted his research, among them the late Tommy Robertson, Cecil Barclay, Yuri Modin, Oleg Tsarev, Jim Skardon, Jurgen Kuczynski, Ruth Werner, Anthony Blunt, John Cairncross, Dick White, Russell Lee, Arthur Martin, Elvira de la Fuentes, Hugh Astor, Nicholas Elliott, Bob Lamphere, Cecil Phillips, Meredith Gardner, Deke DeLoach, Ray Batvinis, Michael Fox and the others who prefer not to be identified. All offered information and advice at a time when the Treasury Solicitor John Bailey and MI5's legal adviser Bernard Sheldon and then David Bickford were keen to enforce a lifelong duty of confidentiality on serving and former members of the Security Service.

His research was also greatly assisted by Andrew Lownie, Hans-Dietrich Lemmel, Rui Arajo, Oleg Gordievsky, William Tyrer, Peter Stephan Junk and Sebastian Cody.

Author's Note

Many of the documents reproduced in this volume originate from MI5 files and have been redacted during the declassification process. Where possible the redactions have been restored, but where this has not been possible the redaction is indicated thus: [XXXXXXXXXXXXXXXX]

The author has retained the convention of printing codenames in capitals but, for ease of reading, has restored capitalized surnames to ordinary, lower case.

Abbreviations and Glossary

AEC	Atomic Energy Commission
ASA	Army Security Agency (US)
ASIO	Australian Security Intelligence Organisation
B4	MI5's technical surveillance section
B5	MI5's Watcher Service
BIS	British Information Service
BJSM	British Joint Services Mission
BRIDE	Original codename for VENONA
BRUSA	Britain–United States Signals Intelligence Agreement
BSC	British Security Co-ordination
CIC	Counter-Intelligence Corps (US)
CIOS	Combined Intelligence Objectives Sub-Committee
Comintern	Communist International
CPGB	Communist Party of Great Britain
CPUSA	Communist Party of the United States of America
CRO	Commonwealth Relations Office
DB	Director, B Division MI5
DCI	Director of Central Intelligence (US)
DEYOUS	Decipher Yourself
DSIR	Directorate of Scientific and Industrial Research
ENORMOZ	Soviet codename for the atomic bomb project
FPA	Federated Press of America
GCHQ	Government Communications Headquarters
GPO	General Post Office
GRU	Soviet Military Intelligence
INO	Foreign Department of Soviet State Security
IPI	Indian Political Intelligence
ISK	Decrypts of Abwehr Enigma machine-enciphered radio traffic
ISOS	Decrypts of Abwehr hand-ciphered radio traffic
JIC	Joint Intelligence Committee
JSM	Joint Services Mission
KO	KriegsOrganisation
KPD	German Communist Party
MI3	War Office enemy order-of-battle branch
MI5	British Security Service

NCNA	New China News Agency
NKGB	Soviet intelligence service, predecessor to the NKVD, KGB etc
NKVD	Soviet intelligence service
NRA	Nothing Recorded Against
OGPU	Soviet intelligence service
PF	Personal File
RCMP	Royal Canadian Mounted Police
referentura	Soviet intelligence office
rezident	Soviet intelligence station chief
rezidentura	Soviet intelligence station
RIS	Russian Intelligence Service
SD	Sicherheitsdienst
SF	'Special Facilities'
SIS	Secret Intelligence Service
SLO	Security Liaison Officer
SOE	Special Operations Executive
TC	Telecheck
TWIST	Wartime deception committee
UNRRA	United Nations Relief and Rehabilitation Agency
VENONA	Codename for decrypted Soviet cable traffic
XX	Twenty Committee

Introduction

The impact of the declassification and release of the Guy Liddell Diaries covering the period September 1939 to May 1945 would be hard to exaggerate as the then Director of MI5's counter-espionage B Division had entrusted to paper, actually loose-leaf pages in ring-binders, details of virtually every important event that had any intelligence significance during the Second World War. Never intended for a wider readership outside the Security Service's top management, the Diaries offered an astonishing insight into the day-to-day activities of a group of men and women dedicated to detecting and interdicting sabotage, subversion and espionage. Liddell, known as 'DB', had a wide area of responsibility and supervised agents provocateurs, deception operations, sensitive political investigations, and masterminded the countering of Communist-inspired penetration and Jewish terrorism.

The Diaries, of course, speak for themselves, and offer an extraordinary insight into the daily activities of an organization that sought to operate without political interference or direction, and well away from public scrutiny. However, this volume, which covers the entire post-war period until May 1953, is intended to expand on some of the cases that Liddell mentioned, with the advantage of what subsequently has been revealed either by the declassification of other MI5 files, by VENONA, and by access to Soviet archives. Inevitably, from Liddell's perspective, his attention was taken up by a huge variety of investigations, routine liaison and events, but with the benefit of hindsight we can see that there were plenty of episodes that he touched on that have since acquired a special historical significance.

Liddell himself had no expectation that his diaries would be ever read by anyone outside a small group of senior management within MI5, and doubtless would be surprised by their impact. Similarly, he did not have the gift of foresight to help him identify particular topics that were likely to become controversial. A chance encounter with King George VI's private secretary at his club in Pall Mall led to worries about the Duke of Windsor's conduct at a critical moment in the Battle of Britain; an atomic physicist, betrayed by a Soviet defector, negotiations with the deputy *rezident* in Istanbul who wanted £50,000 to betray details of nine moles working for the Foreign Office or tantalizingly unspecified branches of British Intelligence in London; the still-mysterious circumstances of the disappearances performed by Guy Burgess and Donald Maclean in May 1951. This is Liddell's legacy, and amounts to a counter-intelligence goldmine produced by a consummate professional who had spent a lifetime dealing with the complexities of counter-espionage, subversion, penetration and double agents. His knowledge of Communist influence dated back to the Sidney Street siege of January 1911, and before he joined MI5 in October 1931 he had spent eleven years at Scotland Yard's Special Branch. He had been on the scene when the Arcos headquarters in Moorgate had been raided, and had personally debriefed the GRU illegal *rezident* Walter Krivitsky in January 1940. He had introduced J. Edgar Hoover into the subtleties of clandestine surveillance during his visit to Washington DC in January 1937 to indoctrinate the FBI into the Jessie Jordan case, and was the genius behind the introduction of the now famous wartime Double Cross system which effectively took control of the enemy's networks in Great Britain.

Almost completely unknown to the public, apart from his role as an amateur cellist playing regularly at Southwark Cathedral, Liddell died in December 1958 in obscurity, as the security adviser to the British Atomic Energy Authority. In reality, although unnoticed in any obituaries, he was probably the single most influential British intelligence officer of his era.

Cold War Spymaster is intended to examine Liddell's involvement in some important counter-espionage cases, but it is the malign shadow cast by Burgess and Maclean that brought his MI5 career to a premature end and prevented his promotion to the post of Director-General. Liddell's personal circle of friends not only included Burgess and Anthony Blunt, but extended to David Footman, Tommy Harris and Victor Rothschild. Guilty or not, all would be contaminated by their wartime intelligence roles and their relationships with four of the so-called Cambridge Ring-of-Five.

Liddell was a central player in, and a first-hand witness to, a series of extraordinary, interlocking dramas that began at the end of hostilities in May 1945 and can be said to continue to the present day. He had worked with Kim Philby during the war, had employed Blunt as his personal assistant, met Maclean at a dinner party in Washington, DC, and socialized with Burgess who had acted as an intermediary, managing two of MI5's best wartime intelligence sources. Yet when Maclean came under suspicion as the mole responsible for a major haemorrhage of secret cables from the British embassy in Washington in 1944 and 1945, it was Liddell who supervised the investigation. When SIS's David Footman learned that Burgess had fled to France with Maclean in May 1951, it was Liddell he telephoned with the news. When the Welsh academic Goronwy Rees wanted to report Blunt's attempt to silence him, it was Liddell he visited to offer a statement.

Liddell fell into the habit of confiding his thoughts about the day's events to a diary in September 1939, motivated by the wish to preserve a contemporaneous record, much like an unsanitised regimental War Diary, of what had really happened during the conflict. His collection of folders proved such a valuable resource that he continued the practice into the first eight years of the Cold War. His area of responsibilities, to defend the realm, extended across the globe, including the Caribbean, Africa, the Middle East, and reached Rangoon, Singapore and Canberra. He served under three directors-general, one acting D-G and, representing a strand of continuity as well as an institutional memory, earned the confidence of Whitehall mandarins.

There is, however, an element of tragedy in the pages that follow. With the benefit of hindsight, access to recently declassified documents and a more relaxed attitude to the publication of memoirs, we can now see how Liddell was betrayed by Burgess, Blunt and Philby. His inclination, as is now revealed, was to accept the personal assurances given to him by Blunt, and believe that the mounting evidence against Philby could have innocent explanations. He would be proved terribly wrong.

Nigel West

Dramatis Personae

George Aitken	CPGB official and espionage suspect
ALEK	GRU codename for Alan Nunn May
Ismail Akhmedov	Soviet defector in Turkey
Antonio de Almeida	Portuguese banker and Abwehr agent in Lisbon
Herman Amende	Abwehr agent in Madrid
Pavel Angelov	GRU officer at the Ottawa *rezidentura*
Stepan Apresyan	NKVD *rezident* in New York codenamed MAJ
Jane Archer	MI5 officer, née Sissmore
Henry Arnold	Security officer at Harwell
Wystan Auden	Poet and friend of Guy Burgess
Albrecht von Auenrode	Abwehr chief in Lisbon
A.J. Ayer	Friend of Donald Maclean and former SOE officer
BACON	GRU codename for Israel Halperin
Millicent Bagot	MI5 officer
Vladimir Barkovsky	NKVD officer at the London *rezidentura*
Samuel L. Barron	Espionage suspect
Charles Bedaux	French collaborator
Walter Bedell Smith	Director of US Central Intelligence
Cedric Belfrage	NKVD spy in New York
Connie Benckendorff	Former Tsarist naval intelligence officer
Elizabeth Bentley	NKVD agent in New York and defector
Harry Berger	CPGB activist convicted of sedition in 1943
Javier Bermejillo	Spanish diplomat
Ursula Beurton	Married name of Ursula Kuczynski
Derek Blaikie	CPGB member
Rudolf Blaum	Abwehr officer in Lisbon
Anthony Blunt	Art historian and Soviet spy
Wilfred Bodsworth	GCHQ cryptanalyst
Daphne Bosanquet	MI5 officer
Engelbert Broda	Austrian chemist and Soviet spy codenamed ERIC
Hildegarde Broda	Engelbert Broda's wife, later married to Alan Nunn May
BRONX	MI5 codename for Elvira de la Fuentes

Moura Budberg	Connie Benkendorff's mistress and an espionage suspect
Nigel Burgess	Wartime MI5 officer
Len Burt	Special Branch detective
John Cairncross	Wartime GCHQ linguist, SIS officer and NKVD spy
George Carey-Foster	Head of the Foreign Office's Security Department
Bill Cavendish-Bentinck	Chairman of the wartime JIC
CHARLES	NKVD codename for Klaus Fuchs
Johnny Cimperman	FBI legal attaché in London
David Clarke	MI5 F Division officer
CORBY	Codename for Igor Gouzenko
Mark Culme-Seymour	Lunch companion of Donald Maclean
Malcolm Cumming	MI5 officer
Jack Curry	MI5 officer
CURZON	MI5 codename for Donald Maclean
Lady CURZON	MI5 codename for Donald's mother, Lady Maclean
Mrs CURZON	MI5 codename for Donald Maclean's wife, Melinda
Walter Dail	Former Special Branch detective
Patrick Dean	Chairman of the JIC
Dan Delabardelen	CIA station chief in London from 1950
Arnold Deutsch	NKVD illegal *resident* in London
Martha Dodd	NKVD spy codenamed LIZA
Melinda Dunbar	Melinda Maclean's mother
Peter Dwyer	SIS station commander in Washington DC
Jack Easton	Deputy Chief of SIS
EDITH	NKVD codename for Edith Tudor Hart
Ina Ehrlich	Engelbert Broda's second wife and suspected Soviet agent
ELLI	Unidentified Soviet spy in London
ERIC	Soviet codename for Engelbert Broda
Ricardo Espirito Santo	Portuguese banker and Abwehr agent
Trilby Ewer	*Daily Herald* journalist and Soviet spy
Pavel Fedosimov	NKVD officer at the New York *rezidentura* codenamed STEFAN
Aleksandr Feklisov	NKVD officer codenamed CALISTRATUS, alias Fomin, at the New York and then London *rezidenturas*
Judith Fischer-Williams	Jenifer Hart's sister
Robert Fisher	FBI codename for Cedric Belfrage

Bernard Floud	Labour MP and Soviet spy
Peter Floud	CPGB member and espionage suspect
Alan Foote	GRU illegal and defector
David Footman	SIS officer
Klaus Fuchs	Atomic physicist and Soviet spy codenamed REST and CHARLES
Elvira de la Fuentes	MI5 double agent codenamed BRONX
Laurence Gilliam	BBC producer and friend of Donald Maclean
Hubert Ginhoven	Former Special Branch detective
Percy Glading	CPGB official and spy convicted in 1938
GLAN	Soviet codename for Vladimir Barkovsky
Ann Glass	MI5 officer
Gustav Glück	Art historian and espionage suspect
Harry Gold	Courier for Klaus Fuchs and Soviet spy convicted in 1950
Jacob Golos	NKVD illegal *rezident* in New York until 1943
GOMER	NKVD codename for Donald Maclean
Oleg Gordievsky	KGB officer who defected in 1985
Paul Gore-Booth	British diplomat in Washington
Anatoli Gorsky	NKVD *rezident* in Washington, alias Gromov
Igor Gouzenko	GRU cipher clerk in Ottawa who defected in 1945
Israel Halperin	GRU agent in Canada codenamed BACON
Alexander Halpern	SIS officer and espionage suspect
Derek Hamblen	MI5 SLO in Canberra
Stuart Hampshire	Wartime cryptanalyst and espionage suspect
Paul Hardt	Alias of Theodore Maly, NKVD illegal *rezident* in London until 1937
Tommy Harris	Art dealer and former wartime MI5 officer
Jenifer Hart	NKVD spy in the Home Office
Jack Hewit	Wartime MI5 agent
Bernard Hill	MI5's Legal Adviser
Roger Hollis	MI5 officer
Georg Honigmann	Lizzie Friedmann's third husband
Oswald von Hoyningen-Huene	German ambassador in Lisbon
David Hubback	Husband of Judith Fischer-Williams
Claire Isaacs	CPGB member and espionage suspect
Kemball Johnston	Wartime MI5 officer
KASPAR	MI5 codename for Josef Lemmel
Rolf Katz	Comintern agent and Czech journalist alias André Simon
Eric Kessler	MI5 agent codenamed ORANGE

Ivone Kirkpatrick	Permanent Under-Secretary at the Foreign Office
Filipp Kislitsyn	NKVD officer at the London *rezidentura*
Hanna Klopstock	CPGB member and espionage suspect
James Klugmann	CPGB member and NKVD agent
Maxwell Knight	MI5 B Division officer
Semyon Kremer	GRU officer at the London *rezidentura*
Walter Krivitsky	GRU defector interviewed in London in 1940
Boris Krotenschield	NKVD *rezident* in London, alias Boris Krotov, codenamed BOB
Jurgen Kuczynski	Wartime KPD leader in England
Marguerite Kuczynski	Wife of Jurgen Kuczynski
Ursula Kuczynski	GRU agent
Freddie Kuh	*Chicago Sun* journalist and Soviet spy
Konstantin Kukin	NKVD *rezident* in London from 1943
Fyodor Kulakov	GRU cipher clerk in the Ottawa *rezidentura*
Mickey Ladd	Assistant Director, FBI
Isabel Lambert	Donald Maclean's lover
Bob Lamphere	FBI special agent
Sir Alan Lascelles	King George VI's private secretary
Russell Lee	MI5 officer
Josef Lemmel	MI5 agent codenamed KASPAR
LIZA	NKVD codename for Martha Dodd
Karl von Loesch	Hitler's interpreter
Gordon Lunan	GRU agent in Canada
James MacGibbon	NKVD spy in Washington
Bobby Mackenzie	Regional Security officer at Washington embassy
Alan Maclean	British diplomat and Donald's brother
Donald Maclean	British diplomat and NKVD spy codenamed GOMER
Melinda Maclean	Donald Maclean's wife
Nancy Maclean	Donald Maclean's sister, and former MI5 secretary
Roger Makins	Foreign Office diplomat
Theodore Maly	NKVD illegal *rezident* in London, alias Paul Hardt
John Marriott	MI5 B Division officer
Arthur Martin	MI5 B Division officer
MARY	Soviet codename for Lizzie Philby
Peter Matthews	Foreign Office News Department
Alan Nunn May	British physicist and Soviet spy codenamed ALEK

Stewart Menzies	SIS Chief
Hugh Miller	MI5 officer
Cyril Mills	MI5 officer in Ottawa
Ken Mills	MI5 officer in Gibraltar
Helenus Milmo	Wartime MI5 officer, barrister and Philby's interrogator in 1951
Graham Mitchell	MI5 officer
Vasili Mitrokhin	KGB defector
Charles Moody	CPGB member and espionage suspect
Kenneth Morton Evans	MI5 officer
Pyotr Motinov	GRU officer at the Ottawa *rezidentura*
William Murrie	Deputy Under-Secretary, Home Office
Maurice Oldfield	SIS officer
Henriquetta de Oliveiro	Abwehr postbox in Lisbon
ORANGE	MI5 codename for Eric Kessler
Geoffrey Patterson	MI5 SLO in Washington DC
Vitali Pavlov	NKVD *rezident* in Ottawa
PEACH	MI5 codename for Kim Philby
Rudolf Peierls	Atomic physicist and espionage suspect
Vladimir Petrov	NKVD *rezident* in Canberra and defector
Edouard Pfeifer	Edouard Daladier's chef de cabinet
Kim Philby	SIS officer codenamed SÖHNCHEN by the NKVD and PEACH by MI5.
Angela Pilley	CPGB member and espionage suspect
Barty Pleydell-Bouverie	Former SOE officer in Washington
Peter Pollock	Guy Burgess' lover
Vladimir Pravdin	NKVD officer in the New York *rezidentura*, codenamed SERGEI
Ronnie Reed	MI5 B Division officer
Goronwy Rees	Oxford academic and Soviet spy
Patrick Reilly	Foreign Office Adviser to SIS
REST	NKVD codename for Klaus Fuchs
Andrew Revai	Hungarian journalist and Soviet spy
Trudie Rient	Espionage suspect in New York
James Robertson	MI5 B Division officer
Vasili Rogov	GRU officer at the Ottawa *rezidentura*
Erna Rosenbaum	Donald Maclean's psychiatrist
Tess Rothschild	Second wife of Victor Rothschild, wartime MI5 secretary
Victor Rothschild	Former wartime MI5 officer
Hans Ruser	Abwehr defector from Lisbon
Walter Schellenberg	Sicherheitsdienst officer
Erich Schröder	SD Chief in Lisbon

Dick White	Director MI5's B Division
Esther Whitfield	SIS secretary and Kim Philby's lover
Lish Whitson	FBI officer
Hugh Winterborn	MI5 B Division officer
Peter Wright	MI5 officer
Anatoli Yakovlev	NKVD officer at the New York *rezidentura*, real name Yatskov, codenamed ALEKSEI
Pavel Yerzin	NKVD officer at the London *rezidentura*
Courtenay Young	MI5 officer
Kenneth Younger	Wartime MI5 officer and later Labour MP
Nikolai Zabotin	GRU *rezident* in Ottawa
Robin Zaehner	Wartime SIS officer and espionage suspect
Vasili Zarubin	NKVD *rezident* in Washington alias Zubilin

Guy Liddell.

The Duke of Windsor.

Kim Philby.

Donald Maclean.

Guy Burgess.

Anthony Blunt.

Portraits courtesy of Nicola Loud

Chronology of Events

1940

30 January	Liddell interviews Walter Krivitsky in London.
1 August	The Duke of Windsor departs Lisbon aboard the *Excalibur*.
15 August	The Duke of Windsor sends a coded telegram to Ricardo Espirito Santo from Bermuda.
15 August	The Duke of Windsor disembarks from the *Lady Somers* in Nassau.

1945

30 May	Bill Cavendish-Bentinck raises the case of Carl von Loesch with Liddell.
24 August	Tommy Lascelles approaches Liddell over von Loesch's Reich Foreign Ministry archive.
5 September	Igor Gouzenko defects in Ottawa.
4 September	Konstantin Volkov visits the British consulate-general in Istanbul.
11 September	Kim Philby briefs Liddell on the Gouzenko case.
13 September	Volkov delivers a letter to the British consulate containing the terms for his defection.
14 September	Philby asks Liddell to send Hollis to Canada to supervise the Gouzenko case.
15 September	Gouzenko reveals the existence of a spy in London.
17 September	Volkov's letter is received in the Foreign Office pouch in London.
19 September	Stewart Menzies assigns the Volkov case to Philby.
26 September	Philby departs London but is delayed en route.
	Volkov is flown out of Istanbul.
28 September	Philby arrives in Istanbul.
2 October	Liddell is shown an intercepted letter from Engelbert Broda addressed to Alan Nunn May.
21 November	Roger Hollis interviews Gouzenko in Canada.
25 November	Hollis reports on his interview with Gouzenko.
30 November	Elizabeth Bentley makes formal statement to the FBI.

1946

15 February	Jim Skardon interviews Alan Nunn May who confesses.
22 May	The secret protocols to the 1939 Molotov–Ribbentrop Pact are published.

28 June	Klaus Fuchs returns to England.
7 September	Fuchs attends a rendezvous at Mornington Crescent.
October	Henry Arnold reports suspicions about Fuchs to MI5.

1947

March	Philby is posted to Istanbul.
17 September	Ursula Kuczynski is interviewed by Skardon and Michael Serpell at her home in Great Rollright.
8 December	Liddell sends 'entirely negative' report on Klaus Fuchs to the Ministry of Supply.

1948

January	Colonel Badham summaries the case against Fuchs.
20 February	Guy Burgess denounces Andrew Revai to Liddell.
May	Engelbert Broda returns briefly to England.
November	Donald Maclean is posted to Cairo.

1949

March	Alan Nunn May tells MI5 his recruiter he is no longer in the country.
August	Klaus Fuchs is identified as a spy in the VENONA traffic.
7 September	Fuchs is placed under surveillance by MI5.
12 October	Fuchs approaches Henry Arnold at Harwell about his father.
November	Burgess is reported to the Foreign Office following his indiscretion in Gibraltar.
December	The Soviets change their cipher system.
21 December	Skardon interviews Fuchs for the first time.

1950

January	Maclean is reported for drunken remarks at a party given by Hugh Slater.
2 January	Liddell briefs the Prime Minister on the Fuchs investigation.
24 January	Fuchs makes a formal confession.
2 February	Fuchs is arrested.
8 February	Liddell links Engelbert Broda to Klaus Fuchs.
27 February	Ursula Kuczynski returns to Germany.
2 March	Percy Sillitoe briefs the Prime Minister on the Fuchs conviction.
16 June	David Greenglass identifies his recruiter to the FBI as his brother-in-law Julius Rosenberg.
17 July	The FBI arrests Julius Rosenberg.
11 August	Ethel Rosenberg is arrested by the FBI.
November	Fuchs identifies Ursula Kuczynski as his Soviet contact.

1951

18 April	Home Office Warrant granted on Tatsfield 352.
23 April	Maclean is placed under B5 observation.
1 May	Liddell seeks a telecheck on Maclean.
	Maclean lunches at the Travellers Club.
2 May	Maclean lunches with his mother at Iverna Court.
3 May	Maclean lunches at the Travellers Club.
4 May	Maclean lunches with Peter Floud at the Victoria & Albert Museum.
7 May	Burgess docks at Southampton and is driven to London by Anthony Blunt.
8 May	David Footman lunches with Guy Burgess at the Reform Club.
	Maclean lunches with his sister-in-law Harriet and her husband Jay Sheers at the Café Royal.
9 May	Maclean lunches at the Travellers Club.
	Maclean meets Philip Toynbee at The Victoria pub.
11 May	Maclean lunches at the Travellers Club.
	Burgess dines with David Footman at the Reform Club.
15 May	Burgess and Maclean lunch at the Reform Club.
	Maclean visits Freddie Ayer and spends the night with Isabel Lambert.
	Burgess dines with Peter Matthews at the Reform Club.
16 May	Maclean lunches at the Garrick Hotel with Mark Culme-Seymour and Laurence Gilliam.
	Burgess lunches with Peter Pollock at the Reform Club.
	Philby reads Martin's telegram in Washington.
17 May	Maclean lunches with Melinda at Scott's, Piccadilly.
21 May	Burgess dines with David Footman at the Reform Club.
23 May	Burgess lunches with Blunt at the Reform Club.
24 May	Burgess and Maclean lunch at the Reform Club.
	Burgess dines with Peter Pollock at the Reform Club.
25 May	Burgess and Maclean embark on the *Falaise* at Southampton.
7 June	Skardon interviews Melinda Maclean.
12 June	Philby flies back to London.
14 June	Philby is interviewed by Dick White.
15 June	Sillitoe confers with Walter Bedell Smith in Washington.
2 November	Liddell dines with Hilda and Tommy Harris.
7 December	Prime Minister Churchill orders Philby's interrogation within a week.
12 December	Philby is interrogated by Helenus Milmo.

1952

4 March	John Cairncross is identified as a spy.
15 April	John Cairncross resigns from the Civil Service.
December	Alan Nunn May released from Wakefield Prison.

1953

19 June	Ethel and Julius Rosenberg are executed at Sing Sing.
August	Melinda Maclean visits Tommy Harris in Mallorca.
11 September	Melinda Maclean disappears from Geneva.
October	MI5 identifies Engelbert Broda as Alan Nunn May's likely recruiter.

Chapter I

The Duke of Windsor

On 24 August 1945 Guy Liddell described an encounter with the King's private secretary, Sir Alan Lascelles, who had expressed anxiety about a cache of microfilmed secret documents from the Reich Foreign Ministry which had been recovered on 14 May from Muhlhausen in Thuringia where they had been buried by Karl von Loesch, one of Hitler's interpreters.[1]

Loesch had disclosed the existence of the material to a British officer, Colonel Robert C. Thomson, who, with his American colleague Gardner C. Carpenter, was also a member of the Combined Intelligence Objectives Sub-Committee (CIOS). The organization's purpose was to find the scientists and technicians who had worked on the Reich's advanced industrial projects and recover their equipment. Although the Foreign Ministry's archive was slightly out of CIOS's ambit, it would turn out to be of immense political value.

Before the war Thomson had been a Foreign Office interpreter, qualified in French, German, Spanish, Russian and Polish, and had travelled the world as a King's Messenger, one of the elite couriers employed to carry sensitive documents to and from diplomatic missions overseas. Thomson's role in Germany was to trace and recover the Reich's technical treasures before they fell into Soviet hands, which had brought him to the Schönberg estate in Thuringia where, under von Loesch's direction, he had visited a property occupied by the US 5th Armored Division, to find a pine forest and dig up a metal canister containing microfilms of the records of former German and Japanese embassies and consulates at Tsingtao, Chefoo, Hankow, Yokohama, Vienna, Berlin and Hamburg, and the Manchurian legation to Rome and, more significantly, microfilm copies of Foreign Minister Joachim von Ribbentrop's secretariat covering the period March 1938 to June 1943. The find, amounting to 9,725 pages, was of enormous political and historical importance because the microfilm included the only documentary evidence of the secret supplementary protocol to the 1939 Nazi–Soviet Pact made between Molotov and Ribbentrop. For years the Soviets had denied the existence of any such pact, but Loesch's treasure trove included two treaties that defined Soviet and German 'spheres of interest in Eastern Europe'. The first agreement, signed on 23 August 1939 as a secret protocol, or annex, to a non-aggression pact signed the same day, assigned Latvia and Estonia to the Soviets and Lithuania to the Germans. A second protocol, signed on 28 September 1939, transferred Lithuania to the Soviet sphere.

As von Loesch, formerly a racing driver, explained to Thomson, his mother had been English and he had been born in London in 1880. He held the SS rank of *Untersturmführer*, and had been questioned by the Gestapo following the 20 July 1944 plot to assassinate Hitler. He had fallen under suspicion because of his links to the plotters, but he had survived interrogation at Hagenberg Castle, near Linz.

While most of the records of the Foreign Ministry, the Auswärtiges Amt, amounting to 400 tons, had been stored in a pair of castles, at Degenershausen and Meisdorf in the Harz mountains, inside the designated Soviet zone, the top-secret archive had been entrusted to von Loesch who had been ordered to supervise its destruction. Instead, Loesch had handed Thomson a letter addressed to Duncan Sandys, Winston Churchill's son-in-law who was then Minister of Works, explaining that he had been up at Oxford with him. Soon afterwards he was interviewed by Bill Cavendish-Bentinck, then Chairman of the Joint Intelligence Committee (JIC). Evidently, during this encounter von Loesch had expressed his desire to travel to London, and Cavendish-Bentinck discussed this with Liddell, who noted on 30 May 1945:

> Bill Cavendish-Bentinck rang me up about the case of Carl von Loesch who was formerly attaché to Ribbentrop's dienststelle in this country. He has come into possession of the secret archives of the German Foreign Office. They had been photographed and at the last moment it was decided to burn them. Von Loesch managed to bury them and the SD who were doing the job merely burned the empty boxes thinking they were burning the archives. The films are now in this country and von Loesch's presence is required to elucidate them. He is by birth a British subject. I explained to Cavendish-Bentinck that if we once got him here we might not be able to get him out again and he might be an embarrassment. He is going to find out whether by virtue of his service in the German Army von Loesch loses his British nationality, or whether he would be liable to prosecution as a renegade. In actual fact, we should not proceed against a character of this kind but his presence here might cause difficulties.

On 1 June 1945 Cavendish-Bentinck wrote a memorandum for the Foreign Office regarding von Loesch's wish to come to England:

> We have decided not to bring over to this country Karl von Loesch who provided us with these microfilms. If he was landed in this country he could remain here and could apply for a writ of habeas corpus. On the ground that he is a natural born British subject. We could counter this by warning him that in this case he is a traitor and that a noose will be placed round his neck, but it would be inconvenient and might give rise to publicity. He will be further questioned in Germany.

Soon after the meeting with Cavendish-Bentinck, von Loesch was allowed to move from the Russian zone into the American zone, and was granted the privileges of possessing a car, a motorcycle and a motorized bicycle, and sufficient fuel to run them. At a time of severe restrictions and petrol rationing, these were unusual concessions made to an SS officer, and would be the source of considerable friction between the military component of the British documents team led by Thomson, which consisted of five officers and eleven other ranks, and the group of seven civilians headed by Carpenter. The principal cause of the tension was a volume of 450 pages which, having been taken by the US Counter-Intelligence Corps (CIC) to Marberg Castle, would be referred to privately as 'the Windsor file', one section of the Ribbentrop most-secret records which were excluded from the copying process underway at Marburg so both Allies could share the windfall.

Frustrated by Thomson's obfuscation, the Americans arrested Loesch on 17 August, on the authority of a new directive about the treatment of Nazis issued the previous month, and placed him in solitary confinement. When interrogated by the head of the CIC in Marburg, Loesch admitted having been a Nazi since joining the Party in 1933, and it was concluded that Thomson had given him access to US Army gasoline and had advised him not to mention his SS status. Outraged, Carpenter commented to General Eisenhower's senior political adviser Robert Murphy that 'I cannot but believe that with respect to von Loesch he is acting on instructions from above.'

Thomson arranged for part of Loesch's cache to be flown to the Secret Intelligence Service's (SIS) technical branch at Whaddon Hall, in Buckinghamshire, where a copy was made of all the microfilms. Crucially, they were found to contain both correspondence and records of conversations between Hitler or Ribbentrop and leading foreign statesmen, and some of the content would have explosive implications, especially for the British monarchy. Having been declared authentic on 31 May by the Foreign Office's historical adviser, Ernest Llewellyn Woodward, the British government sought to prevent copies reaching the French or the Soviets who, under the terms of the four powers occupation, were entitled to see all captured documents. On 23 May Cavendish-Bentinck advised that 'we should hold hard as regards informing the French and Soviet Government of the discovery', adding that 'the Soviet Government have never informed us of any discovery that they have ever made and I do not see why we need show such zeal in informing them'.

Finally, under some pressure, the Foreign Office reluctantly agreed that the von Loesch material should be given to the US State Department, but insisted that it should not be shown to the US military government in Germany. Murphy then protested to his British counterpart, Sir Ivone Kirkpatrick, which led the British ambassador in Washington, Lord Halifax, to lobby Edward Stettinius when they met in San Francisco on 31 May at the inauguration of the United Nations. Stettinius acquiesced, and the embassy in London was instructed the very next day to drop Murphy's complaint. Murphy himself would not become aware that he had been outmanoeuvred for another ten days, when he was informed during a visit to London.

Although the Soviets would always deny the existence of the secret protocols, there was corroboration found in the handwritten notes of Dr Paul Otto Schmidt, Hitler's senior interpreter. Whereas Schmidt's papers were limited to his original draft notes or memoranda on discussions with foreign statesmen, the value of von Loesch's version is that they were the final, retyped papers seen by Hitler. However, when the less sensitive Schmidt documents were scheduled to be sent to London, Murphy, convinced that there was evidence of 'conspiracy and a gross negligence or both' intervened to block the transfer, and on 22 June Cavendish-Bentinck minuted:

> When I was at SHAEF last week Mr Murphy again complained to me with some vehemence that copies of the Top Secret German documents found by Colonel Thomson were being withheld from him. I suspect that Mr Murphy thought that I was responsible for this ... Mr Murphy was not satisfied and maintained that he was entitled to a copy of these and any other German documents found in Germany which he might desire. My impression of Mr Murphy, to whom I took rather a dislike, was that he could not find this grievance he would look for another.

Just when the British felt that the Windsor file had been suppressed, General Eisenhower stepped in unexpectedly, and in September demanded that 'the original documents dealing with relations between Great Britain and Germany between June and December 1940' should be sent to SHAEF. An order signed by General Edward C. Betts secured the file, but when Thomson attempted to obtain its return he learned that he had been pre-empted by the Foreign Office which had recovered it from John Winant, the ambassador in London. Indeed, the Foreign Office had extracted an undertaking from the new Secretary of State, James Byrnes, that the Windsor file would not be mentioned at the Nuremburg trials, and the British embassy was told by Dean Acheson in October 1945:

> The British Government is assured, however, that the Department of State will take all possible precautions to prevent any publicity with respect to the documents in its possession relative to the Duke of Windsor without prior consultation with the British Government.

Meanwhile, as the American occupation authorities demanded access to the von Loesch collection, Guy Liddell was consulted by Buckingham Palace:

> I saw Tommy Lascelles at the Travellers Club last night. He asked me to go back with him after dinner and take a look at certain papers on which he wanted advice. These papers were in fact German Foreign Office telegrams which

had been found at Marburg. Presumably they were microfilms which Karl von Loesch had taken out of their boxes and buried in the ground. The order was finally given to have them destroyed but in fact the SD unwittingly had destroyed only the boxes. The telegrams in question were dated about June– July 1940 and sent by Eberhard von Stohrer and Oswald von Hoyningen-Huene, the German ambassadors in Madrid and Lisbon respectively, to Ribbentrop. There were also some from Ribbentrop to the ambassadors and one either to or from Otto Abetz. The fact that Abetz had something to do with the scheme subsequently revealed in the telegrams might suggest that Charles Bedaux was behind the whole thing. The telegrams showed that the Germans had made a very determined effort to lure the Duke of Windsor back into Spain from Portugal and to prevent him from taking up the post that had been offered to him in the Bahamas. The Germans never appeared in the picture but through the Spanish Foreign Minister and the Spanish Minister of the Interior they sent agents to the Duke who was staying in Lisbon as the guest of Esperito Santo Silva, the head of the bank of that name which of course is known to us as an agency for the transmission of funds to German agents. Various statements are attributed to the Duke by these agents which are not of a very savoury kind. Although it seems doubtful that the Duke was scheming for his own restoration it is fairly clear that he expressed the view, which I understand he has expressed elsewhere, that the whole war was a mistake and that if he had been King it would never have happened. He clearly rather felt himself in the role of mediator, if his country had finally collapsed, but he did not think the moment opportune for any sort of intervention. He seemed to believe that he understood the German people far better than anyone else. The Germans went to very great lengths to persuade him not to embark for the Bahamas and Walter Schellenberg, who was in Lisbon at the time, was reporting to the ambassador and organising acts of intimidation such as the sending of anonymous letters with bouquets of flowers to the Duchess warning her that the offer of the appointment in the Bahamas was merely a plot by the British to do away with him.

The Duchess's maid was allowed to go to Paris to collect things from the Duke's flat and the Germans intended to get the Spaniards to delay her return for as long as they could. Meanwhile Walter Monckton was sent out to persuade him to leave at the earliest moment, a matter in which he was ultimately successful. Before the Duke left he fixed up, according to the telegrams, some kind of code with Esperito Santo Silva in order that he might fly back to Portugal from Florida if his intervention was required. It was further stated that about 15 August a telegram had been received from the Bahamas by Esperito Santo asking whether the moment had arrived. My advice to Tommy was to check up as far as possible the telegrams, some of which would be verifiable from records; this would enable him to get some sort of appreciation of the reliability of the reports which were ultimately reaching the Germans. I warned him that in our experience agents in Spain and Portugal had throughout the war shown a strong tendency to report to their masters precisely what they thought their masters would like to hear. Apart from this, the information in the telegrams had probably been subjected to translation into two or three different languages where there was generally a fairly wide scope for error. On our side we could, if he liked, interrogate Walter Schellenberg who was under our control at Camp 020 on the part that he had played in Lisbon. This might of course lead to him pouring out the whole and the information would become available to the interrogator. I explained that the interrogators had to deal with highly confidential matters and that we could I thought ensure absolute discretion. He agreed that this should be done. The other enquiry that we could make would be to take a look at any telegrams sent to the Banco Espirito Santo around 15 August 1940 since in the light of our personal knowledge we might find the code telegram referred to. I explained that we had been interested in this bank for other reasons and that there might be a record in our files. I gather that Censorship obtained during the early days of the war a telegram from Madame Bedaux to the Duchess in the Bahamas which seemed to be of a singularly compromising nature. There were a lot of blanks in this telegram but the sense of it seemed to be that the question of either the Duke's mediation or of his restoration was discussed at some previous date and Madame Bedaux was anxious to know whether he was now prepared to say yes or no.

I gather that the Duke is coming here on a short visit to his mother in the near future and that he will ultimately settle at Cap d'Antibes, although various jobs for him have been under consideration, such as the Governorship of Madras and ambassador in Washington *etc* for all of which he would seem to be singularly unsuited. Ernest Bevin is *au fait* with all the information given above and is endeavouring to recover the copies and films of the telegrams in question since, if by any chance they leaked to the American press, a very serious situation would be created.[2]

Thus, according to Lascelles, the concern was not so much the nature of the Duke's indiscreet remarks about the wisdom of war with Germany, but the detail of what, if anything, was stated in a coded telegram on or about 15 August 1940, a date known as 'Black Thursday' because, at the height of the Battle of Britain, the Luftwaffe had planned 'Eagle Day', when German bombers had concentrated their raids on airfields in a strategy intended to eliminate the RAF's ability to defend British airspace. First the radar stations at Rye, Dover and Foreness were put out of action, and then the attack, with fighters and bombers operating from bases in France and Norway, hit the RAF airfields at Manston and Marlesham Heath. The German tactic had been to draw the air defences to the south, and then strike at airfields in Northumberland, Durham and Yorkshire.

By the end of the day the RAF War Diary recorded 161 enemy aircraft had been shot down, with a further 61 'probables' and 58 damaged, for the loss of 34 RAF interceptors and 18 pilots killed or missing. The fierce air combat that day was regarded as a turning-point in the conflict, so the idea that this was also the day that the Duke, from the safety of Nassau, was contemplating defeat, was especially offensive. However, according to Liddell, Lascelles had not been absolutely certain about the exact date, 15 August, which was actually two days before the Duke had arrived in Nassau to take up his new role as governor. In the meantime he had lodged for five days at Government House in Hamilton after his arrival in Bermuda on 8 August, and had undertaken the remainder of the voyage down to the Bahamas on 13 August aboard a Canadian cargo ship, the RMS *Lady Somers*, docking at New Providence early on the morning of Saturday, 17 August.

Whereas much of what the Duke reportedly had said was no surprise, and not particularly damaging, the existence of a coded telegram addressed to a known German intermediary, the Portuguese banker Espirito Santo, which contained a reference to a pre-agreed arrangement for his restoration, could only be regarded as hideously incriminating. The accompanying commentary, if any, would also be highly relevant because a casual reader might not appreciate the banker's true role, nor understand his notoriety within Britain's tiny counter-espionage community.

Portugal's largest bank was owned and run by Ricardo Espirito Santo and his two brothers. He was the son of the bank's founder, José Maria do Espirito Santo e Silva, and had taken over from his elder brother in 1932, the year that his close friend, the economics professor and Minister of Finance, Antonio de Oliveira Salazar, was appointed prime minister. For the rest of his life Ricardo remained associated with the dictator Salazar and his regime, and he was also linked to the German minister *en poste* since 1934, Baron von Hoyningen-Heune, whose mother had been English, and to the legation's Abwehr representative, the Viennese aristocrat Albrecht von Auenrode, and to the local Sicherheitsdienst (SD) chief, Erich Schröder. In addition, the wily SD counter-intelligence expert Walter Schellenberg had been sent to Lisbon on a mission to lure the Duke back to Spain, perhaps by arranging his abduction while attending a shooting party near the border.

Of these Germans, only Schellenberg underwent post-war interrogation at the hands of the British, but the focus of his interviews was not the Duke of Windsor, but the extent to which he had successfully penetrated British intelligence networks.[3] However, the Windsor file indicated that he at least had been held in some respect by the ambassador in Madrid, Eberhard von Stohrer. British knowledge of von Auenrode's activities and the internal structure of the Lisbon KriegsOrganisation (KO) would remain somewhat a mystery, and largely dependent on a defector, Hans Ruser, until October 1946 when Rudolf Blaum, the KO's administrative officer, underwent a lengthy interrogation in Germany.[4] For their part the Americans recruited a former Madrid KO agent, Hermann Amende, who proved a valuable source of information on local Abwehr personalities.

In 1940, when the Duke was staying in Portugal between his arrival from Spain on 4 July and his departure on the American liner SS *Excalibur* on 1 August, bound for Bermuda, he was the guest of Ricardo Espirito Santo at his palatial villa, Boca do Inferno, near the picturesque fishing village of Cascais, west of Lisbon. Ricardo's wife, née Mary Cohen, whom he had married when she was sixteen, was the daughter of a well-known financial trader in Gibraltar. The Espirito Santo bank would be placed on the Allied blacklist in 1943 because of its trade with the Axis, specifically its close relationship with the Deutsche Bank, and in 1944 would be directly implicated in German espionage, acting as a conduit for an Abwehr spy in London tasked to collect information about plans for the imminent Allied invasion.

When Lascelles met Liddell he wanted to know about the content of the Duke's alleged 15 August telegram, and whether it could be verified by other sources. In reality, of course, MI5 had no such records, and it is doubtful that Imperial Censorship had retained a copy of the communication, but the revelation that the Duke had conspired with a known agent of the Nazis to communicate in a code would have been quite enough for any prosecution under the 1940 Treachery Act. No wonder, when Churchill was consulted about the von Loesch archive by Clement Attlee, who feared 'that the publication of these documents might do the greatest possible harm'. Churchill had replied on 25 August 1945 'I earnestly trust it may be possible to destroy all traces of these German intrigues'.

In fact the Foreign Secretary, Ernest Bevin, who called the Windsor file 'a hot potato' had advised Attlee on 13 August that 'we should try to persuade the United States Government to co-operate with us in suppressing the documents concerned' and advised that 'a disclosure would in my opinion do grave harm to the national interest'.

The von Loesch microfilm attracted further attention when Harry Truman's new administration decided to release the full details of the Ribbentrop–Molotov pact, which were published on 22 May 1946 simultaneously by the *St. Louis Post-Dispatch* and the *Manchester Guardian*. The Kremlin denounced the publication as a forgery, but nothing was mentioned about the third volume of the material, the Windsor file. As for von Loesch, he underwent denazification successfully in 1947 in Stuttgart, where he would remain.

When the Windsor file was eventually made available by the US National Archive, there were three items which attracted attention, and one in particular referred to a message received from the Duke in Bermuda on 15 August 1940. The first message, from Baron von Hoyningen-Huene was dated 2 August and addressed to Ribbentrop personally:

With reference to your telegram No. 442 of July 31.

(1) In accordance with the telegraphic instruction which arrived shortly before midnight, I immediately got in touch with our confidant the

Duke's host, the banker Ricardo do Espirito Santo Silva, who happened to be at the Ducal couple's farewell reception at a hotel here. After the end of this affair he visited me at my residence, where we discussed thoroughly possible further courses of action. I would note at this point that the person concerned is an unobjectionable individual, who has never denied his friendly attitude toward Germany and whose discretion is beyond question. The confidant promised to give the message to the Duke in the course of the morning.

(2) Every effort to detain the Duke and Duchess in Europe (in which connection I refer particularly to Schellenberg's reports) was in vain. Their departure took place this evening. The decision of the Duke was influenced during the last few days especially by his close friend, Sir Walter Monckton, who had come to Lisbon expressly for the purpose of indicating to the Duke the serious objections which existed to a further postponement of his departure. Monckton told the confidant verbally that while the Duke was no doubt the most popular man in England, the whole of England today still stood behind Churchill.

(3) On the other hand the message which was conveyed to the Duke made the deepest impression on him and he felt appreciative of the considerate way in which his personal interests were being taken into account. In his reply, which was given orally to the confidant, the Duke paid tribute to the Fuhrer's desire for peace, which was in complete agreement with his own point of view. He was firmly convinced that if he had been King it would never have come to war. To the appeal made to him to co-operate at a suitable time in the establishment of peace, he agreed gladly. However, he requested that it be understood that at the present time he must follow the official orders of his Government. Disobedience would disclose his intentions prematurely, bring about a scandal, and deprive him of his prestige in England. He was also convinced that the present moment was too early for him to come forward, since there was as yet no inclination in England for an approach to Germany. However, as soon as this frame of mind changed, he would be ready to return immediately. To bring this about there were two possibilities. Either England would yet call upon him, which he considered to be entirely possible, or Germany would express the desire to negotiate with him. In both cases he was prepared for any personal sacrifice and would make himself available without the slightest personal ambition. He would remain in continuing communication with his previous host and had agreed with him upon a code word, upon receiving which he would immediately come back over. He insisted that this would be possible at any time, since he had foreseen all eventualities and had already initiated the necessary arrangements. The statements of the Duke were, as the confidant stressed, supported by

firmness of will and the deepest sincerity, and had included an expression of admiration and sympathy for the Fuhrer.

Huene

This telegram, apparently based on a conversation held with Ricardo Espirito Santo soon after he had left the Duke on his final night in Lisbon, did not amount to anything particularly incriminating as the Duke and doubtless his supporters could claim that this was nothing more than exaggerated bluster and unreliable hearsay, perhaps with Espirito Santo telling the minister what he probably wanted to hear. However, the key point was the assertion that the banker had agreed a codeword which was to be employed as a clandestine signal to summon the Duke back from the Bahamas when the time was right for his intervention.[5]

The second telegram, from von Stohrer in Madrid and dated 3 August, was addressed to Ribbentrop and reported on the efforts made to dissuade the Duke from leaving Lisbon, serving to confirm what had already been reported to Berlin:

The Spanish Minister of the Interior just informed me that his confidential emissary had just telephoned to him from Lisbon, using phraseology which had been agreed upon, that on the day of their departure he had spent a considerable time with the Duke and Duchess. The Duke had hesitated even up to the last moment. The ship had had to delay its departure on that account. The influence of the legal adviser of the Duke, Sir Walter Turner Monckton, was again successful, however, in bringing him around to leave. The confidential Emissary added that the Duke had clearly perceived that it would have been better to have remained here so as to be able to step in at the decisive moment. The Duke believed, however, that it might be possible for him to do this from the Bahamas. For this purpose an arrangement was reached concerning which the confidential agent did not wish to say anything over the telephone. Schellenberg, who has just returned from Lisbon, is reporting about all his numerous and extremely circumspect measures taken to prevent the departure. His account in respect to the influence of Sir Walter is in accord with the reports of the Spanish confidential agent. Schellenberg also made certain arrangements which ought to make possible resumption of relations with the Duke. Stohrer

Stohrer's confidential emissary was a Spanish diplomat, Javier Bermejillo, who had been acquainted with the Duchess when he had been attached to the Spanish embassy in London before the war, and the ambassador's telegram merely confirmed that Schellenberg's mission to prevent the Duke from embarking on *Excalibur* had failed. According to document 265, Schellenberg himself had transmitted several messages via Madrid over the previous few days:

ie, on July 18. 'Reports tram Schellenberg had been transmitted via Madrid as telegrams Nos. 2547 of July 27 (B15/B002601), 2550(7) of July 28 (8680/ E036166-57), and 2588 of July 31 (B15/B002614-15) ie, August 1. The Ambassador in Spain reported In telegram No. 2632 of August 2, received at 1:25 pm., August 2, that Schellenberg had just telephoned from Lisbon that the Duke and Duchess had sailed the previous evening on the American steamship *Excalibur* (B16/B002629).

These telegrams, which were not reproduced, simply documented Schellenberg's daily reporting through Madrid, but the final record in the series was damning:

In telegram No. 884 of August 15 (B16/B002665), the Minister in Portugal reported: 'The confidant has just received a telegram from the Duke from Bermuda asking him to send a communication as soon as action was advisable. Should any answer be made?' No answer to this telegram from Lisbon has been found.[6]

This record, as it appears in the Windsor file, superficially, and read in isolation, does not seem to be particularly significant, but when 'the confidant' is identified as Espirito Santo, and the context is the secret codeword agreed between the two men, it becomes obvious that the Duke on some date before 15 August, is alleged to have sent his contact a plea from Bermuda, just before his departure on 13 August, reminding him of their secret arrangement. Thus, if the von Loesch material is to be believed, the Duke's action served to corroborate the worst interpretation which could be placed on his position as described a fortnight earlier by Hoyningen-Heune.

The sentiments attributed to the Duke by the German minister in Lisbon would be reflected by reports submitted to the Spanish foreign ministry by Bermejillo, and then corroborated by an account of a dinner at Government House by the Governor of Bermuda, Lieutenant General Sir Denis Bernard, who had been outraged by his guest's remarks. The political opinions expressed by the Duke centred on an anti-Semitic, anti-Communist viewpoint, blaming Anthony Eden for the war, accompanied by an assertion that if he had been King, the conflict would have been avoided. Certainly General Bernard regarded the comments as disloyal, but they were not inconsistent with the Duke's previous, and subsequent, indiscreet observations. However, the Duke's incautious remarks were far removed from an overt act of treachery, a light in which his telegram to Espirito Santo could have been seen.

From MI5's perspective, any link with the Espirito Santo Bank was to be considered highly compromising, as its wartime counter-espionage specialists had become quite familiar with the Lisbon channel. For example, on 8 March 1944 Liddell recorded in his diary that the Germans had found an ingenious method of circumventing Imperial Censorship's scrutiny of outgoing cables:

One of B1(a)'s agents has received a plain-language code which is to indicate the sector of the coast at which the Second Front will be opened. The telegrams containing this code are supposed to come from the Guaranty Trust Company to the Banco Espirito Santo, and the code lies in the amount of money demanded. I gather that the reaction of the bank would normally be to tell the client to send his own telegram. However, there might well be cases where the bank would perform this service. There is, on the other hand, no possible machinery at present in force for preventing anyone sending a telegram to a bank in Lisbon which purports to come from a bank in this country. This is quite a serious matter since Censorship does not provide against such a contingency. Telegrams of the kind described would probably be sent on without question.

The B1(a) agent in question was Elvira de la Fuentes, codenamed BRONX, who had been writing letters in secret ink, supervised by her case officer, Hugh Astor, to her Abwehr contact in Lisbon since November 1942.[7] The mail had been posted to a certain Henriquetta de Oliveiro at a cover-address in Lisbon.

By April 1944 the Peruvian bridge-playing lesbian socialite had mailed sixty such communications from her flat in Mayfair's Clarges Street, but the postal service was slow, taking up to three weeks for delivery, and as D-Day approached the anxious Germans had entrusted her with an ostensibly innocuous, but faster, method of passing information, by sending coded telegrams to the Espirito Santo's general manager, Antonio de Almeida. Payments of particular sums indicated the location of the landings on pre-agreed sectors of the European coast, and the pretext reflected the reliability. Thus a dentist's bill meant certainty, whereas a doctor's suggested rather less reliability. A request for immediate settlement meant an invasion within a week, whereas 'urgent' implied with a fortnight, and 'quickly' in a month. So, on 29 May, just days before OVERLORD, she sent the bank a request: 'Send £50 quickly. I have need of a dentist.' This was to be interpreted as a prediction with certainty of an invasion in the Bay of Biscay in a month's time. If the demand had been for '£70 for my medicine, if possible', the message meant an invasion in northern France was probable on an unknown date.

MI5 had three reasons for believing that this technique was not only effective, but was accepted fully by the enemy. Firstly, when the D-Day landings began, the garrisons in and around Bordeaux remained *in situ* and did not move north to counter-attack the invaders. Indeed, the 2nd SS Panzer Division *Das Reich* was transferred from Toulouse to reinforce Bordeaux. Secondly, the Kriegsmarine concentrated its U-boats in the Bay of Biscay, and not in the English Channel, thereby reducing the threat to the Allied armada by an estimated thirty submarines; and thirdly, the Abwehr had called upon BRONX to repeat the exercise in March 1945, with much the same code, in anticipation of further Allied landings in Denmark, Norway or northern Germany.

While the bank telegram system had provided the Abwehr with an apparently quick and safe method of one-way communication, to enhance the exchange of letters, the involvement of such a senior Espirito Santo bank official as Almeida was regarded as proof positive that the whole bank, from the top down, was acting as an Axis surrogate. Antonio de Almeida, who had trained as a civil engineer, had attended the same school in Lisbon as José Ribeiro Espirito Santo and they had remained friends for life. He had joined the bank in 1915 and helped build the branch in the Avenida dos Aliados where he lived in a third-floor flat directly above the bank premises. After the war he and his wife Olga remained very friendly with the Germans, often traveling to Baden-Baden and St Moritz, and the time of his death in October 1968, at the age of 77, he was the bank's deputy chairman.

The complicity of the Espirito Santo bank in an ingenious chain of communication would not have come as a surprise to Liddell, bearing in mind B Division's wartime experience of the Lisbon conduit and its manipulation by BRONX, but the involvement of the Duke with the Nazis, and his treasonous telegram, would have had a profound impact on public opinion in Britain and the United States, if it had become widely known. In the event, Buckingham Palace's close interest in the Reich Foreign Ministry's Windsor file, and Lascelles' approach to Liddell, would remain secret long after the unnoticed death of von Loesch in Stuttgart in January 1951, or indeed the death of the Duke at his Paris home in May 1972.

Chapter II

CORBY

MI5's first major post-war counter-espionage investigation was precipitated in September 1945 by the unexpected defection of Igor Gouzenko, a cipher clerk employed at the Soviet embassy in Ottawa. Aged 27, and accompanied by his wife Svetlana, Gouzenko had been in Canada since June 1943, but had come to the end of his posting to Canada and was scheduled to return to Moscow under the cloud of an adverse report from his GRU *resident*, Colonel Nikolai Zabotin. Instead of going home, the young Russian applied for political asylum with the offer to the Royal Canadian Mounted Police (RCMP) of documentary proof, on 109 sheets of paper, of the GRU's local network, an organization that had also penetrated the Manhattan Project in the United States.[1]

Gouzenko later explained that he had not planned his defection in detail, but nor had it been entirely spontaneous. He had discussed the idea with his pregnant wife, but had seized the moment when, very unusually, he had been alone in the first-floor *referentura* that evening, the members of the *rezidentura* being absent attending a National Film Board of Canada movie screening. Usually the cipher clerk, codenamed KLARK, had been shadowed by his replacement Lieutenant Fyodor Kulakov, but on this occasion he had been left on his own. Slipping out of the building, he went home to his wife and infant son Andrei, determined not to return to face disciplinary action in Moscow.

Among the material removed from the GRU *rezidentura*, which appeared to compromise no less than eighteen agents, were references in eight separate telegrams, all dated 1945, to a spy codenamed ALEK who was also identified by his real name, Dr Alan Nunn May, a young, unmarried Trinity Hall, Cambridge-educated physicist who had been posted to the Chalk River reactor in 1943. He was scheduled to return to London imminently and take up a teaching position at King's College, London.[2]

Liddell first became aware of the case on 11 September 1945 when he was briefed by SIS's Kim Philby. In the temporary absence of the Security Liaison Officer (SLO) in Canada, Cyril Mills, all communications from Ottawa were channelled through the SIS station commander in Washington, Peter Dwyer.

Kim Philby came over with a series of telegrams received from the Western Hemisphere on the subject of Russian espionage. The gist of the story is that there has been for some considerable time a Russian espionage organisation under a Colonel or General Zabotin, the Soviet military attaché in Ottawa.

The Russians have succeeded in planting agents in External Affairs, the High Commissioner's office and also in the atomic bomb circles. This information has come to light owing to one of Zabotin's subordinates bring in a whole heap of documents to the RCMP. For some reason or other the informant has been held with the documents, which disclose the presence of at least sixteen agents who have been identified. The principal agent connected with the atomic bomb is a Cambridge physicist sent out to Canada in 1942, named Alan Nunn May. We had great difficulty in identifying this man as his initials were given as A.L. May and he did not appear to have been vetted especially for Tube Alloys. The documents in Ottawa indicate that May is to make contact with some Soviet agent over here, very detailed instructions being given as to how, when and where the meeting is to be effected. The question arises now whether in view of the disappearance of the agent from Soviet circles in Ottawa, the meeting will in fact take place, and whether it would be better to search and interrogate May after confronting him with the agent in Ottawa or whether he should be thoroughly searched and frightened on arrival here, or whether he should be let through on the assumption that the meeting will take place sooner or later and that we shall thereby unearth a Soviet network in this country. The whole case has got on to a very high level. There is a series of telegrams running between Norman Robertson of External Affairs and Sir Alexander Cadogan, another between Malcolm MacDonald and Mechtig of the Dominions Office, and another between Security Co-ordination and SIS. Finally, Jumbo Wilson [Field Marshal Sir Henry 'Jumbo' Wilson, Chief of the British Joint Staff Mission, Washington DC] and Lord Halifax [British Ambassador, Washington DC] have weighed in. As usual with these high levels, it is extremely difficult to get down to brass tacks, and to get the right action taken. We here are in the unfortunate position of being in possession of only a number of somewhat corrupt telegrams whereas if we were in Ottawa knowing the full circumstances in which the agent had come in plus the contents of the documents we should be in a far better position to come to the right conclusion. The whole thing of course is wrapped up in about four layers of cotton-wool as it concerns the atomic bomb. Most people have not realised quite that an atomic bomb has been dropped in Japan and the world now knows quite a lot about it. I am going to consider the matter and we will have a further meeting tomorrow.

The complete picture was far from clear, but the most immediate issue was whether May should be interviewed while he still in Canada, or be allowed to travel back to London where he was under instructions to re-establish contact with his Soviet controller at a rendezvous arranged for the corner of Great Russell Street and Museum Street on three alternative dates in October.

When Liddell enquired about the vetting procedure which May had undergone in 1943, as he had been checked by the Tube Alloys project when he had joined the Cavendish Laboratory from a radar research project at Bristol in early spring 1942, no trace had been found, and the same happened when a new 'look-up' was made in the registry files. In fact May had been a well-established Communist Party member, having joined in 1936, and would travel to Canada by ship, the SS *Bayano*, in January 1943. By then May had held one clandestine meeting in a London café with a Soviet diplomat, arranged through a Communist Party of Great Britain (CPGB) contact at Cambridge, and a briefing session with Douglas Springhall, the CPGB's National Organizer. It had been Springhall who had given him his instructions for holding a rendezvous with another Soviet in Montreal, after he had acquired an apartment for himself in a location that would make hostile surveillance difficult.

Three days later, on 14 September, Philby asked Liddell to send Roger Hollis to Canada to handle Gouzenko, and this he did. In fact Hollis made two journeys to Ottawa, the second being towards the end of October 1945. However, by the time Hollis had arrived on his first mission, the RCMP had informed Liddell that Gouzenko, now codenamed CORBY, had disclosed the existence of a Soviet asset occupying a high position within British intelligence in London, codenamed ELLI. When questioned by the RCMP on 15 September CORBY revealed some clues about ELLI:

Alleged Agent in British Intelligence
CORBY states that while he was in the Central Code Section in 1942 or 1943, he heard about a Soviet Agent, in England, allegedly a member of the British Intelligence Service. This agent, who, was of Russian descent, had reported that the British had a very important agent of their own in the Soviet Union, who was apparently being run by someone in Moscow. The latter refused to disclose his agent's identity even to his headquarters in London.

When this message arrived it was received by a Lt. Colonel Polakova who, in view of its importance got in touch with Stalin himself by telephone.

Various candidates were considered for this mole, including Captain Ormond Uren, formerly of SOE's Hungarian Section, who had been imprisoned for espionage in 1943, but the consensus was that ELLI was an entirely new, and hitherto unsuspected, GRU agent.[3] Meanwhile, Philby had been in touch with his Soviet controller at the London *rezidentura* and reported on the disaster:

Gouzenko, cipher clerk of the Zabotin organisation, has been given the codename CORBY. MI5 has established four planned meetings of May with his London contact. These meeting were fixed for 7, 17 and 27 October and 7 November. Neither May nor any of his contacts appeared at these meetings. In London they are of the firm opinion that May, as well as other agents from the Zabotin network, were warned of the impending danger. According to MI5, May has not put a foot wrong from the time he arrived in England.

He did not establish any suspicious contacts. He does not show any signs of being afraid or worried and continues to work quite normally on his academic research. Bearing this in mind, MI5 came to the conclusion that May was a tough customer who will not break down under questioning until he is confronted with fresh and convincing evidence. The matter was postponed indefinitely for serious political considerations. It is not only a question of friendly relations with the USSR, but also of the future control over atomic secrets.

Attlee intends to discuss the CORBY case with Truman and Mackenzie King. The interested departments (MI5, FBI and RCMP) fear that the decision will be contradictory or such that it cannot be carried out since (1) it will require the simultaneous arrest of all the suspected persons in the United Kingdom, Canada and the USA (this exceeds the possibilities of the RCMP which can only cope with six of them); (2) it will require the arrest and questioning of the suspects without any publicity (this is, in practice, also impossible since relatives and friends will start enquiries etc); (3) it will require the arrest and subsequent trial of the suspects (the available evidence is not sufficient and the case may have to be dropped). The arguments prepared by the Foreign Office for Attlee show an increasing tendency to take energetic steps. They argue in favour of arrest and interrogation and, where possible, prosecution of the suspects, the recall of Zabotin and the Soviet Ambassador in Canada and a sharp protest to the Soviet Government. They don't insist particularly on wide publicity of this case but are of the opinion that fear of publicity should not stop us from taking action. Some indications show, however, that the Canadians and Americans are less enthusiastic about this and may resist the Foreign Office.

While there is no evidence that Hollis actually met Gouzenko in September 1945, who was accommodated at a safe-house accompanied by two Russian-speaking RCMP officers, John Leopold and Melvyn Black, he certainly conducted a personal interview on Wednesday 21 November, as he reported to Liddell on 25 November:

A. I paid a brief visit to CORBY on Wednesday. He makes a very good impression as regards his honesty and truthfulness.
B. I dealt particularly with 'ELLI' case, the position of which is as follows:

1. Corby himself deciphered 2 telegrams from Soviet Military Attaché in London, one stating ELLI was now going over to DUBOK method and the other that British Military Attaché in Moscow would not give name of British agent there.
2. LIUBIMOV told him in 1943 that ELLI was a member of high grade intelligence committee, that he worked in British counter intelligence.

> CORBY thinks that LIUBIMOV mentioned the number 5 in connection with committee.
>
> 3. KOULAKOFF in 1945 told CORBY that a high grade Soviet agent was still working in United Kingdom. He did not specifically say that this agent was ELLI and appeared unwilling to discuss matter. CORBY did not press it.
>
> 4. CORBY told me that he did not know that the two incidents of the theft of the papers from Military Attaché in London and attempt to Telephoto his office were reported by ELLI.
>
> 5. I tried to get some further indication of the nature and scope of information supplied by ELLI: for instance I asked whether he supplied information on German war dispositions, political matters etc. CORBY said that he did not know and refused to be led in these matters and I think it is quite clear that he knows nothing more about ELLI than information given in previous paragraphs

The molehunt for ELLI effectively stalled, as no further information about the culprit emerged, apart from some corroboration from another GRU defector, Ismael Akhmedov, who had been based in Istanbul but had decided to remain in the West in May 1942. However, the SIS expert sent to interview him in 1945 was Kim Philby, who reported that Akhmedov was of minor importance with nothing of interest to disclose, so he was overlooked for several years. He did not emerge from hiding until 1948, and in October 1953 gave evidence to the Senate Internal Security Subcommittee under the alias 'Ismail Ege'. He waited until 1984 before writing about his experiences in an autobiography, *In and Out of Stalin's GRU*.[4] Philby's assessment of Akhmedov's value was largely correct, except that he also referred to a spy in London codenamed ELLI. According to a post-war MI5 summary of Soviet espionage cases, Akhmedov had spoken 'of a GRU female agent in the United Kingdom, known as MARY, and of a girl or woman named ELLI. The unidentified ELLI lived in London in 1940 and is of considerable interest since it has been alleged that she was in some way connected with the British intelligence services.'

At the time, Philby had been dismissive of Akhmedov's contribution, unaware of quite who ELLI and MARY might have been. Doubtless he would have been aghast if he had realized that MARY was the codename assigned to his first wife, Lizzie Friedmann.

While the molehunt for ELLI was in its very earliest stages, and Alan Nunn May had returned to London, he was placed under discreet surveillance by MI5, but was warned by a contact not to attend the arranged rendezvous scheduled for three alternative days near the British Museum in October 1945. The message went undetected by MI5, but on 2 October Liddell was informed by his subordinate John Marriott about a link between May and a well-known Austrian physical chemist, Engelbert Broda, who had come to England as a refugee in April 1938, was employed at the Cavendish Laboratory and also happened to be a leading Communist.[5]

Broda would not be mentioned again by Liddell, but his suspicions were completely justified. Broda was not only himself an experienced Soviet spy, codenamed ERIC, but he was also having an affair with Edith Tudor Hart, a notorious Comintern agent and, incidentally, the woman responsible for recruiting Kim Philby while he was married to Lizzie Friedmann. Curiously, it would later emerge that Broda had been involved with Klaus Fuchs, and had acted as an intermediary for him with the Soviet embassy.

Although MI5 would not grasp the significance of the link between May and Broda for some years, it was absolutely pivotal. Born in 1910 in southern Austria to a family with Jewish antecedents, Broda was educated in Berlin where he joined the KPD as a student, and was arrested at a Communist demonstration in Vienna in June 1931. In September 1935 he married another Communist, Hildegarde Gerwing, from a Jewish family in Aachen, and together they travelled widely, including to the Soviet Union where he stayed for about nine months between 1935 and 1936. Finally, they moved as refugees to London in March 1938 and lived in a flat in Highgate Road. Broda would become active in the Austrian émigré community and, as a fervent undisguised Marxist active at the Austrian Centre at 126 Westbourne Terrace came under MI5's scrutiny. In July 1938 a Special Branch report noted:

A group of the Austrian Communist Party composed principally of refugees who have come to England has been functioning in London for several months and meeting at regular intervals. Mrs Edith Tudor Hart has now been delegated by the Central Committee of the Communist Party of Great Britain to act as a liaison between the Central Committee and this group and to assist in its control. The leader of the group is Engelbert Broda, an Austrian whose address is kept secret from all, even Mrs Tudor Hart, who only knows his telephone number and communicates with him by that medium. Until last week this was Primrose 3456; since then it has been Paddington 5443.

At that stage MI5 was unaware that Edith Tudor Hart, née Suschitsky, was an experienced Comintern agent whose best friend, also from Vienna, was Lizzie Friedmann, married since 1934 to a journalist, Kim Philby.

Broda was interned in October 1939 but was released in December, after just ten weeks. He was then detained again in July 1940 and sent to a camp at Huyton, but was freed after thirteen weeks. In December 1941, when MI5 received a request from the Directorate of Scientific and Industrial Research (DSIR) for a permit to employ Broda, it was explained that Broda was 'an active member of the Central Committee of the Austrian Communist Party of the which party he was Cell Leader in Vienna' but DSIR's director, Sir Edward Appleton, decreed that 'the exigencies of this Department do override objections on security grounds to Mr Broda's employment on the work for which his services are desired'.

In these circumstances, a few days before Christmas 1941 Broda reported at the Cavendish Laboratory in Cambridge to work for another Austrian Jew, Hans von Halban, and a French scientist of Russian origin, Lev Kowarski, and was indoctrinated into the Tube Alloys project at a crucial moment, just a fortnight after the Americans had embarked on what would become the Manhattan Project. In moving to Cambridge, leaving his wife to work as a nurse at Stoke Mandeville Hospital in Buckinghamshire, Broda largely removed himself from MI5's immediate purview but MI5's Regional Security Liaison Officer, Major Dixon, was alerted by Millicent Bagot to what she described a delicate case:

> In view of the nature of his work I am anxious that Broda should not be aware that he is the subject of suspicion, but if you should obtain any information to show that he is taking part in any political activities I should be grateful if you could let me know immediately.

Thus Broda was fully involved in the development of a British nuclear weapon when May joined the team in early 1942 from the physics department at Bristol University. May had joined the CPGB in London in 1936, having graduated from Cambridge, where he had been a contemporary and friend of Donald Maclean, and had visited the Soviet Union in the same year, so was easily persuaded to begin attending the weekly meetings of a local cell of Communist scientists. He and Broda thus became colleagues and would work together until May was posted to Montreal in January 1943, making the transatlantic voyage on the SS *Bayano*, and it was during this period that both men became spies, and May began an affair with Broda's wife Hilde.

It is now known, from Soviet archives, that Broda first made contact with the NKVD *rezidentura* at the embassy in London in 1942. At that time the NKVD had been alerted to the Cabinet decision to develop an atomic weapon by John Cairncross, then working in the Cabinet Office, who had obtained a copy of the MAUD Report and given it to his contact. In December 1942 the *rezidentura* reported that Edith Tudor Hart, codenamed EDITH, had passed a detailed report on atomic research in Britain and America, a project the NKVD had codenamed ENORMOZ:

> EDITH sent us a detailed report through MARY on the results and status of work on ENORMOZ, both in England and in the USA. ERIC had given her this report on his own initiative to pass to the FRATERNAL [CPGB]. The materials will be sent out in the near future. According to additional information that has been gathered ERIC who since January 1942 has been Professor Halban's assistant in a special division (devoted to ENORMOZ) of the central laboratory on explosives in Cambridge – is completely informed

about all the work being done on ENORMOZ both in England and in the USA. He has access to American materials on ENORMOZ that the English had received as part of an information exchange.... ERIC is a long-time COMPATRIOT [Communist] who understands the need for such work.

Having obtained Moscow's approval, the *rezidentura* then reported on the next stage of Broda's cultivation and recruitment. The unnamed scientist intended to send the material to the CPGB but it had been relayed to Anatoli Gorsky, working under attaché cover at the embassy, who had asked Moscow for permission to establish direct contact with this scientist and when approval had been given, he requested his contact to meet the scientist again and ask him to agree to a meeting with a Soviet intelligence officer.

We instructed EDITH to conduct a preliminary conversation with him and get him to agree to meet our comrade. During the conversation between EDITH and ERIC the latter was initially hesitant and said that he had to think about it and does not see any need to meet with someone because he has already written down everything he knows about ENORMOZ. Later in the same conversation ERIC's attitude changed, and he said that he hopes the person he meets is not an Englishman, because English comrades are generally very indiscreet. And, in the end, once EDITH had told him that everything had been properly arranged, ERIC said that he would be glad to meet our comrade.

The meeting took place in January 1943 at a London Tube station, and after the usual signs and passwords had been exchanged, the scientist was judged to be straightforward and friendly, although obviously nervous. He verified all the arrangements for the meeting and it lasted more than an hour and a half, during which nothing was called directly by its name, but 'ERIC knew with whom he had agreed to co-operate' concluded the *rezidentura*. The officer assigned to handle the source was Vladimir Barkovsky, codenamed GLAN, who remembers that when he met his new source for the first time he had been asked whether he understood nuclear physics and, upon receiving an unsatisfactory reply, the scientist said that he wanted his contact not to be just a transmitting channel, but to understand what it was all about. He urged the intelligence officer to study *Applied Nuclear Physics* by Ernest Pollard and William Davidson, and Barkovsky took his advice, and was grateful to ERIC for insisting on this as the American textbook turned out to be a great help to him in running his source. 'He told me, "we'll go through the book together, and then it will be considerably easier for you to deal with me". I also did not see any other way out. I was completely swamped with work, but I started poring over the textbooks.'

The *rezidentura* submitted a detailed report of Barkovsky's first encounter with Broda:

ERIC met GLAN cordially and carried himself with great ease and friendliness, although it was obvious that he was nervous. He carefully verified all of the rendezvous terms. At the outset of the meeting, ERIC said that he had only been notified of the meeting the day before and therefore was unprepared for a serious discussion about ENORMOZ. Because GLAN's primary objective was to strengthen ties with ERIC, obtain his direct consent to work with us, and determine the course of this work. GLAN did not press him for information rightaway and instead set about achieving the aforementioned objectives. The first conversation with ERIC lasted over an hour and a half. As a result of the conversation ERIC gave his full consent to work with us. During the conversation, nothing was called by is proper name but ERIC knows who it is he agreed to work for. ERIC reports that in their field of work the Americans were significantly ahead. As part of a technical information exchange, their laboratory received bulletins from the Americans on the progress of work on ENORMOZ in America. Owing to the nature of his work, ERIC has access to these bulletins, and the information he gives us reflects American achievements in this field as well as English ones.

ERIC passed on the secret material to which he had direct access and, being of a daring nature and something of an adventurer, he took what was kept in the safes of his colleagues. Barkovsky recalls how, when the scientist told him about this opportunity, and brought him the impression of a doorkey, a duplicate was required. It was too dangerous to have this work done in a local shop, and it would take too long to send the impression to Moscow, as the wartime diplomatic bag had to be sent via the United States and the Far East and took months to reach Moscow. However, as a young man Barkovsky had been a sixth-grade fitter, and he did the job himself and made a duplicate that fitted perfectly:

> As a result of the decision taken by us we manufactured a copy of the key for ERIC and worked out arrangements for meetings so that we can contact him three times a week in London without prior notification. As a result we managed to remove from ERIC all the available American materials and other interesting materials on ENORMOZ.

This episode corresponds to a report sent to Moscow from the *rezidentura* in 1944:

> One of ERIC's colleagues went to Canada for a while and gave him his personal key to the library containing reports on ENORMOZ. We made ERIC a copy of the key and arranged contact terms that allowed us to contact him in London three times a week without any prior arrangement. In accordance with these terms, on arriving in London on one of the agreed upon days, ERIC was supposed to mark a page of a phone book inside a designated phone booth. After entering this phone booth at a fixed time and

finding the mark he had made, we would go out to meet him at the appointed place and time. As a result, we were able to receive from ERIC all available American reports of the second batch, as well as other interesting materials on ENORMOZ. ERIC continues to work willingly with us, but he still balks at even the slightest hint about material assistance. We once gave him more than he asked to cover his expenses. He was displeased by this and said that he suspects we want to give him a certain kind of help. He asked us to give up any such thoughts once and for all. In such circumstances, we fear that any gift from us as a token of appreciation for his work will make a negative impression. ERIC is completely selfless in his work with us and extremely scrupulous when it comes to anything that could be seen as payment for his work.

ERIC's importance as a source is confirmed by a reference to him in an internal NKVD memorandum entitled *On the composition of the agent network for ENORMOZ of the First Directorate of the NKVD of the USSR (as of August 1945)*:

during the period of his co-operation with us he supplied an enormous quantity of most valuable, genuine documents in the form of official American and British reports on the work on ENORMOZ and, in particular, on the construction of uranium piles.

Describing ERIC's relationship with the NKVD, Barkovsky noted in a letter to the Centre that he had been motivated by ideology, and was scrupulous when it came to money:

ERIC as before works for us with enthusiasm, but still turns down the slightest hint of financial reward. Once we gave him more to cover his expenses than he had asked for. He showed his displeasure and stated that he was suspicious of our desire to give him financial help. He asked us to stop once and for all our attempts to do so. In view of this we fear that any gift to him as a sign of gratitude for his work would have a negative effect. ERIC is completely unselfish and extremely scrupulous in regard to anything that might appear as 'payment' for his work.

Barkovsky recalled ERIC as a young physicist and CPGB member who volunteered information from inside the British atomic research programme, but also had access to data from the United States, and was able in 1943 to assert that 'the Americans are far ahead'. He was 'a person who had come to us by himself, without any recruitment. He wanted to help and correct the injustice'.

In his opinion, justice lay in preventing Russia's allies from knowing very important work of a defence nature. At our first meeting he began explaining something to me with much enthusiasm, but I had only the slightest idea about the structure of the nucleus … He not only gave me technical data, but explained the sense of it, so that I could comprehend what we were discussing. I prepared my own glossary that proved to be extremely useful. All the terms were new ones that no one had ever heard of before. And these people did not cost the treasury one pound. They were our kind of people, brave people with initiative who considered that giving aid to the Soviets was a moral and political duty. Understandably this pertains, I hope, not only to atomic scientists.

Barkovsky described ERIC as 'extremely well-informed about the most diverse aspects of the work that was being done by the English in that area. He is the person with whom I worked. He was an excellent person and it was very pleasant to work with him. I remember him with gratitude. He was two years older than me.'

During this period, when Broda was passing hundreds of documents to Barkovsky, Roger Hollis in F Division was recording his concerns about Broda, and in May 1943 noted:

As we cannot be told the nature of the work for which Broda is required we can only state that we know of Broda's connection with the Communists, and mention the definite risk that any information which he gets will be given to the Communists.

A further note in Broda's file, added in July, stated that 'He now knows a considerable amount of the more secret aspect of the work. DSIR is very anxious about Broda' and several days later stated 'I agreed that we should keep a careful watch for any references to Broda's work during our investigations upon the Communist Party's espionage activities'.

MI5 kept tabs on Broda through a source recruited inside the Austrian Centre, codenamed KASPAR. He was a Jewish Austrian writer, Josef Lemmel, who had arrived in London from Vienna aged 59, and was recruited by B5(b)'s Claud Sykes, formerly an academic, German translator and author in 1933 of *Richtofen: The Red Knight of the Air*. In 1930, while acting as one of Max Knight's agents, codenamed M/S, he had penned *The Secrets of Modern Spying* under the pen-name Vigilant.[6]

Although not a Communist, Lemmel was an ardent anti-Nazi and, while acting as the Centre's librarian, with his wife Renate became close to Edith Tudor Hart, providing first-hand, eyewitness accounts of his contact with her, and in November 1945 generated this report to F Division:

On 3rd November a Conference of Scientists for the promotion of Austrian Science took place at Burlington House under the auspices of the Association of Austrian Engineers, Chemists and Scientific Workers. The whole conference was stage-managed by Dr E. Broda, and it is said in Austrian Communist circles that the object of this meeting was to establish contact with scientists engaged on atomic energy research. Although I have no definite proof, I have always suspected Broda of being engaged in scientific espionage, and according to Edith Tudor Hart he has for some time occupied himself with secret scientific research at Cambridge connected with atomic energy. She stressed Broda's importance to the party in view of his qualifications and connections. In view of the intimate relations existing between Edith Tudor Hart and Broda, it must be presumed that she is well-informed of her lover's activities. As Chairman of the Association of Austrian Engineers, Dr Broda maintains close contacts with Austrian and foreign engineers and scientists and with Austrian students in the provinces, through whom he links up with British Communist student circles. Although outwardly the above conference appeared above board and non-political, I learned that secret meetings took place afterwards at which Dr Broda presided. At the official Conference Professor (Sir D'Arcy) Thompson took the chair, and speeches were made by Professors Blackett, Donnan, Hogben and Karl Przibram.

During this period, when Broda had split from his wife but used the excuse of visiting his son in London to meet his Soviet contract every two or three weeks, he drew further attention to himself, unintentionally, when he wrote to May upon his return from the United States in September 1945. Unaware that May's mail was being intercepted, he wrote:

Dear May, I am glad to hear you are back safely. Will you come to Cambridge some day or may I look you up in London? I shall love to see you. Yours, E. Broda.

This was innocent enough, but MI5 was very conscious that the Soviets were likely to warn May that he had been compromised by Gouzenko's defection and this connection was considered highly suspicious. Indeed, this intercept was considered so significant that it was shown to Liddell by John Marriott on 2 October:

John Marriott showed me an intercept saying that Engelbert Broda, an atomic physicist in Cambridge who is known to be a Party member, is in touch with Nunn May whom he is anxious to see.

At this point MI5 was quite convinced that Broda had engaged in espionage, even if there was no direct evidence, and certainly none on which to justify an arrest or prosecution. One of MI5's best-informed sources was KASPAR, who reported on 10 November 1945:

Although I have no definite proof, I have always suspected Broda of being engaged in scientific espionage and according to Edith Tudor Hart he has for some time occupied himself with secret scientific research at Cambridge connected with atomic energy. She stressed Broda's importance to the Party in view of his qualifications and connections. In view of the intimate relations existing between Edith Tudor Hart and Broda it must be presumed that she is well-informed of her lover's activities.

May was finally interviewed on 15 February 1946, and confessed during a second interview with Len Burt five days later. What prompted the limited admission that he had passed information to a Soviet diplomat in Canada was May's fear that he might be extradited to Ottawa to answer charges or, worse, that he might be handed over to the American authorities to risk a possible death sentence. In those circumstances he was willing to admit to MI5 an offence in Canada, but would not acknowledge any offences in England before his departure, nor name any of his co-conspirators. He was arrested on 5 March and news of this was the subject of a report from Lemmel, codenamed KASPAR:

On 8th, at about 7 p.m., in the presence of [XXXXXXX] Edith Tudor Hart answered the door bell, and had a conversation with the caller which lasted for about ten minutes. She then returned rather irritated and [XXXX] that a man had just called, introducing himself as Mr Francis, and enquired about Alexander Tudor Hart who he thought was living at her place. When she told him that Tudor Hart was not staying with her, and that she know his whereabouts either, as it was none of her business, the man pretended to be surprised, and tried in a very clumsy way to start a conversation with her, asking her if she was Alexander's sister. She stopped him by saying that she was not his sister, but his ex-wife, as she had realised that the caller was nothing more than a snooper, not an ordinary one, but a special one, judging by his Oxford accent. Edith seemed rather worried, and incident must be in some way connected with Broda, or with one of his friends who might have got into trouble with the police. She then wondered whether she would be forced to give evidence against Broda, and accused of being too careless. 'When a man is involved in such a business as he is' she added, 'he ought to be careful and not endanger his friends by writing to or visiting them.' The following Wednesday, the 13th, early in the morning, Broda came up from Cambridge by the first train, and told her that a man had been caught by his landlord in the act of trying to get into his room. Broda suggested that this might have been a general check-up added: 'all of our people are all right, don't get alarmed, don't write and don't phone.' A note was added: Any discussion about intelligence work or even the mention of anything of the sort is now strictly prohibited.

Lemmel may have been encouraged to concentrate on Broda and Edith Tudor Hart, because on 10 April he submitted another report:

> Broda is still very careful, refrains from meeting people and using the telephone. He is in contact with Ilona Suschitzky, wife of Wolfgang Suschitzky, Edith Tudor Hart's brother whom he knows from Moscow. She is active at the Austrian Centre.

The precise role played by Ilona Suschitsky (née Donat) who was of Hungarian birth is uncertain, but she lived in Moscow between 1931 and 1936 where she had taught in a school and stayed at the Hotel Lux with her lover, Hans Goldschmudt.[7] In September 1946 KASPAR was still enjoying access to Tudor Hart and Broda:

> According to Broda, the Russians have already solved the problem or are near the solution. Broda states that, contrary to the Anglo/American method, the Russian scientists have found a way of releasing atomic energy through the combination of [XXXXXXX] four hydrogen atoms to helium which proves to be much cheaper and more efficient.

Lemmel would remain in England, running a travel agency, until 1962 when he returned to Vienna where he published an 'autobiographic novel', *The Indestructable*, in 1981. He died in July 1980, his role as KASPAR unknown to anyone outside MI5. His book drew of many of his own experiences, such as his temporary internment at Mooragh on the Isle of Man, and his constant but unsuccessful political struggle, as a Christian social democrat, against the Communists.

Once again, MI5's interest was fixed on an important target, although no-one realized it at the time. Born in Vienna in 1908 to William Suschitzky, a radical socialist who advocated birth control and sex education and owned a bookshop in the working-class district of Petzvalgasse, Edith had trained as a Montessori kindergarten teacher and in 1925 had travelled to England to work as a teacher. Two years later she was back in Vienna, and studied photography under Walter Peterhans at the Bauhaus in Dessau. In 1931 she had been deported after she had been spotted at a CPGB rally.

In 1933, at the height of the political repression, she married Dr Alex Tudor Hart, a left-wing Cambridge-educated medical practitioner, at the British consulate, and moved to Brixton in south London, and then to the Rhondda Valley.[8] As well as an active member of the banned Austrian Communist Party, she was also a Soviet illegal who had completed two undercover missions, to Paris and London, in 1929.

Upon their return from South Wales, Alex Tudor Hart joined the Republican forces in Spain as a surgeon, while his wife opened a studio in Acre Lane in South London and began to specialize, after the birth of her son Tommy in 1936, in child portraits. It was during this period, while active in the Workers' Camera Club, contributing to *Picture Post* and organizing the Artists against Fascism and War exhibition, that she maintained contact with her friend from Vienna, Lizzie Friedmann, who was by then separated from Kim Philby, and liaised closely with Bob Stewart of the CPGB, who was himself acting as a clandestine link between the CPGB headquarters and the Soviet embassy. In March 1938 a Leica camera originally purchased by her was discovered in a police raid on the home of Percy Glading, who was subsequently convicted of organizing the Woolwich Arsenal spy-ring, but when questioned by Special Branch detectives she simply denied any involvement. At that moment MI5 had no reason to be suspicious of her, nor any reason to believe that, as a talent-spotter in June 1934, she had cultivated Kim Philby and introduced him to Arnold Deutsch for recruitment as the source codenamed SÖHNCHEN (SONNY). In 1940 she was divorced from Alex, and had acquired a substantial MI5 file which listed her aliases as Betty Gray and Edith White.

After the war Edith worked as a commercial photographer and briefly for the Ministry of Education, but her mental condition deteriorated and she suffered a breakdown, her son Tommy already having been institutionalized with schizophrenia, an illness he was thought to have developed during the London Blitz. She also had an affair with his psychoanalyst, Donald Winnicott of the Tavistock Institute, who would then treat her for a psychiatric illness involving persecution mania. According to the family, Edith was escorted to the hospital by her sister-in-law, Ilona, on the instructions of her Soviet handler, and would not be forgiven for the act. Later Edith opened a small antiques shop in Bond Street, Brighton, where she was traced by MI5 following Anthony Blunt's confession in April 1964, but was deemed not to be a threat. She died of liver cancer in May 1973 aged 64, her remarkable espionage role largely undiscovered, despite an interview with MI5 conducted in February 1947 in which she reportedly acknowledged having been in contact with the Soviets in Austria and Italy back in 1932 and 1933, but made no incriminating admissions, and apparently maintained silence about Lizzie and (by then) Lizzie's ex-husband. She was also unhelpful in December 1951 when she was interviewed again at her ground floor flat in Abbey Road by Skardon, on the pretext of a background check on Lizzie Friedmann's new partner, the German journalist and editor of the *Berliner Zeitung* Georg Honigmann. Originally from Frankfurt, Honigmann had been the Berlin correspondent for *Voss* until 1933 when he had come to London, later to be appointed head of Reuter's European service.

During a lengthy period of surveillance on Edith the Watchers never spotted any incriminating activity, apart from fare-dodging on the bus to Golders Green. After her encounter with Skardon he reported that 'This woman prevaricated from one end of the interview to the other.' She admitted having known Friedmann but insisted that she had long resigned from the Communist Party. MI5 had hoped that she might be panicked by the incident, in which she claimed not to recognize Philby's photo, into contacting him but she did not rise to the bait.[9]

As a celebrated photographer, Edith enjoyed a wide range of contacts within British society, and her expertise as a recruiter is confirmed in a letter dated 8 October 1936 from the London illegal *rezidentura* to Moscow Centre noting a recent significant success:

EDITH. Through EDITH we obtained SOHNCHEN. In the attached report you will find details of a second SOHNCHEN who, in all probability, offers even greater possibilities than the first. Edith is of the opinion that [name deleted] is more promising than SOHNCHEN. From the report you will see that he has very definite possibilities. We must make haste with these people before they start being active in university life.

When, three months after his confession in April 1964, Anthony Blunt was asked about Tudor Hart he told his MI5 interrogator, Peter Wright, that

Edith Tudor Hart was a close friend of Lizzy Philby and he had always believed that it was Tudor Hart who first recruited Kim Philby. He thought Philby's recruitment preceded that of Burgess. Certainly Tudor Hart was involved in the whole affair and, as source out, was probably 'the grandmother of us all'. He thought Tudor Hart would know of his involvement although he had never met her.

* * *

Alan Nunn May, having entered a guilty plea, was sentenced to ten years' imprisonment, some of which was spent at Camp Hill, the prison on the Isle of Wight which, coincidentally, also accommodated Douglas Springhall. In August 1953, following his early release from Wakefield prison in December 1952, benefiting from the statutory one-third remission for good behaviour, he married Hildegarde Broda, her husband Engelbert having moved to Vienna in April 1947. The circumstances of Broda's departure was duly reported by Lemmel:

According to Mrs Tudor Hart, Broda has just returned from a visit to Rome. He flew to Rome about 3 weeks ago where he contacted a certain woman called Ada Drakovitch, Jugoslav, employed by UNRRA [the United Nations Relief and Rehabilitation Agency]. Broda was in touch with this woman about 10 years ago in Belgrade when he visited Jugoslavia on orders from the Party. From what Tudor Hart said it would seem that Ada Drakovitch is employed by the Russian intelligence.

Thus, having expressed his wish to his British employers to return to Austria, Broda had discovered in September 1946 that two sisters, Ina Ehrlich and Vera Stein, with whom he had been acquainted years earlier, were living in Rome, and had corresponded with Ina. According to MI5's research, she had been born in 1902 in Zagreb, and so was eight years older than Broda, but a comment added to an intercepted letter in February 1947 observed 'She would clearly not object to marrying Broda'. Accordingly, Broda had flown to Rome on 3 March and returned to London eight days later to settle his affairs. He flew back to Italy on 22 April and the couple were married the following month, moving to Vienna.

Ina was a poet, translator and author of stories for Jewish children, but in 1941 she had led a left-wing women's organization and forced to flee to Dalmatia. During her marriage, as Ina Jun Broda, she published poems, essays, and translated Serbo-Croat and Italian texts into German. In 1950 her *Der Dichter in der Barbarei* gave an account of her experiences during the Nazi occupation and in 1958 she published *Die schwarze Erde*, an anthology of Yugoslav partisan poetry.

Broda, who risked a return to Britain only once, briefly in May 1948, later explained to his family that her first husband and child had been murdered by the Croatian Ustaše during the German occupation, and that she had then joined Tito's partisans. However, the marriage was not a success, and ended in divorce in June 1953. Broda died in October 1983, followed later the same year by Ina, never having commented publicly about his espionage.

May also exercised great reticence about his activities, apart from his official statement in which he had admitted having passed classified information to a Soviet diplomat, Pavel N. Angelov, who had called at his apartment on Swail Avenue for the first time in April 1945, having telephoned at his laboratory to make an appointment. When the two men had met, Angelov had used the *parole* 'Greetings from Alek' to confirm his *bona-fides*. Thereafter May took papers home at the weekend 'several times' and left them overnight with Angelov so he could copy them in time for their return on Monday mornings. On one occasion May had supplied samples of Uranium-233 and U–235, which had been considered so important that the assistant military attaché, Colonel Pyotr Motinov, had carried them to Moscow by air.

Alan Nunn May died in January 2003, having completed the manuscript of an autobiography which during his lifetime he had feared to publish because he believed it contained information that might have led to other criminal charges. To his stepson, Paul Broda, he denied that he had ever known Donald Maclean at Trinity Hall, and stated that Engelbert had not played any role whatever in his espionage. As for the precise identity of the individual who acted as an intermediary in 1942, when he began contact with the Soviets, MI5 concluded that Broda had been the most likely candidate, a view expressed in a minute entered on his MI5 personal file in October 1953:

Engelbert Broda might well have been the person who recruited Nunn May for the Russian Intelligence Service. You will remember that one of Nunn May's few admissions was that he was recruited for the RIS [Russian Intelligence Service] only a very short while before he left this country for Canada and that the individual who recruited him was no longer within reach in March 1949 when Nunn May said this Broda was no longer in the country.

Chapter III

Klaus Fuchs

T he name of Klaus Fuchs first appeared in Liddell's diaries on 8 December 1947 when he recorded a meeting at which those gathered had lamented the attitude adopted by the Ministry of Supply which had found MI5's 'entirely negative' information about him unwelcome. Although he does not mention the outcome of the deliberations, the decision was made in Fuchs' favour, thus allowing the scientist further access to the most highly classified documents concerning the development of an independent British nuclear weapon.

Considered a brilliant theoretical physicist by his colleagues, the German-born Fuchs had been proposed for a permanent position at the atomic research establishment at Harwell following his return from the United States where he had played a significant role in the development of the atomic bomb at Los Alamos.

Fuchs next came to MI5's attention in August 1949 as a candidate for the spy identified in the VENONA traffic as the source of a leak from the Manhattan Project in 1944 and 1945.[1] One clue to the reference in one of the decrypted Soviet messages which suggested that the agent, codenamed REST and then CHARLES, had a sister in the United States, and the two best suspects were Fuchs and his colleague Rudolf Peierls. Fuchs was further implicated because his sister's name and address had been found in the address book of Dr Israel Halperin, one of the Soviet agents implicated by Igor Gouzenko. Halperin, the Professor of Mathematics at Queen's University, was a Canadian born in Westmount, Quebec, of Russian immigrant parentage who during the war had served as a major in the Canadian Army, attached to the Directorate of Artillery. After graduating from the University of Toronto he had studied at Princeton. In the documents provided by Gouzenko he was codenamed BACON.

Halperin had been acquitted of the charges arising out of Gouzenko's revelations, and although he had never met Fuchs, he did know his sister, Kristel Heinemann, and had mailed magazines and newspapers to Fuchs while the scientist had been interned in Canada in 1940. When Halperin had been arrested, Fuchs' name and current address in Edinburgh had been found in his address book which also contained details of between 140 and 160 American citizens. His behaviour, combined with the evidence provided by Gouzenko, persuaded the Canadian Royal Commission on Espionage to denounce him as a GRU agent, but there was insufficient evidence to carry a criminal prosecution, so Halperin had returned to his teaching post, and died in 2007 at the age of 96, having been acquitted on charges of breaching the Official Secrets Act.

Another of the detainees, D. Gordon Lunan, described Halperin as one of 'three gifted people orbiting in the upper reaches of contemporary scientific knowledge but down to earth on social and humanitarian issues'. When first pitched by Lunan, who 'approached him more frankly than the others', he was 'anxious to be of help' and was considered by Lunan to be 'enthusiastic and politically experienced'. However, his initially optimistic opinion that Halperin 'is definitely keen and will be helpful', as he wrote to Major Vasili Rogov on 28 March 1945, proved unfounded, and documents purloined by Igor Gouzenko, dated 5 July 1945, showed that he was 'unwilling to take any risk in obtaining material which he is convinced is already obtainable'.

He is himself curious about the Chalk River plant and the manufacture of uranium. He claims that there is a great deal of talk and speculation on the subject, but that nothing is known outside of the small and carefully guarded group completely in the know. He emphasized that he himself is as remote from this type of information as I am myself.

Evidently Halperin had been pressed to supply atomic information, but his access had been limited to improving existing ordnance and perfecting proximity fuzes for artillery shells. 'He only gives oral information, but this does not answer our demands,' complained Rogov in a handwritten memorandum removed from his briefcase by Gouzenko. 'It has become very difficult to work with him, especially after my request for Ur-235. He said that as far as he knows, it is absolutely impossible to obtain it.'

I asked him what is taken into consideration in the construction of the very large plant (Chalk River, near Petawawa, Ontario), in the general opinion the principle of production of which is based on the physical properties of the nucleus; with regard to his expression of opinion that it is impossible to get Uran 235, he replied that he does not know. He believed that the project is still in the experimental stage.

Under cross-examination by the Royal Commission after his detention, Halperin proved unco-operative, refused to answer any questions and dismissed his lawyer. Although he was completely compromised by the content of seven separate documents removed from the embassy *referentura*, Lunan eventually refused to give evidence against him, having first agreed to do so, an offence for which he was later imprisoned, but then was freed.

The connection between Halperin and Fuchs was noticed in time to increase suspicions, but it was not until 31 October, when Liddell notes that Fuchs had been in touch with Henry Arnold, the security officer at Harwell, that preparations were made for his interrogation. The other candidates, Rudolf Peierls, Frank Kearton and one other, had been eliminated by 8 November.[2] Once the focus was on Fuchs, there were numerous discussions about how he should be dealt with, until 21 December when Jim Skardon held his first interview. Liddell briefed the Prime Minister on 2 January, but the big breakthrough was achieved at their fourth encounter on 24 January when Fuchs asked to see Skardon again and confessed to having been an active Soviet agent between 1942 and February 1949.

Fuchs' signed statement, made voluntarily and without a formal caution, was deemed admissible and was the foundation of the prosecution case which was presented at the Old Bailey on 22 February, eliciting a plea of guilty, and Fuchs was sentenced to fourteen years' imprisonment. On the afternoon of 2 March Percy Sillitoe briefed the Prime Minister on the case but, as he disclosed a fortnight later, the version of events that he had described to Attlee was quite wrong. At a meeting at Leconfield House on 17 March 1950 Sillitoe declared that

at that time he had not seen the file. Had he done so he would have been extremely apprehensive, and had an enquiry been ordered he felt that he would probably have lost his job and the department would have been split from top to bottom. He then criticised the action during the earlier stages of the enquiry. He drew attention in particular to a minute by T.A. Robertson which had expressed the view that Fuchs might well be a spy, and also to one by Michael Serpell expressing the view that both Fuchs and Rudolf Peierls might well be spies.

Alas, Liddell did not identify precisely who had attended the D-G's gathering, but it would not have included Robertson, who had resigned at the end of August 1948 when he had been passed over for promotion by Dick White. At the conclusion of the meeting, at which various participants stoutly defended MI5's conduct of the investigation, Liddell records that:

The D-G subsequently made it clear to Dick White that he did not wish to imply in any of his remarks that the brief which had been put up to him when he visited the Prime Minister was in any way intended to be inaccurate or misleading.

That somewhat abbreviated interpretation of what had occurred does not entirely reflect what other witnesses have recalled about the same episode, which is that a very public rebuke of Dick White's briefing, which had been relayed to Attlee, had amounted to a flat lie. Furthermore, White had been so stung by the criticism that he had contemplated resignation, although he would be persuaded to change his mind by Liddell and Hollis.

The scale of the deception can be determined by a very similar review provided by White to the prosecuting authorities shortly before the trial. On that occasion MI5, represented by White, Skardon and the Security Service Legal Adviser Bernard Hill, had conferred with the Attorney-General Sir William Shawcross and the Director of Public Prosecutions Sir Theobald Mathew. During their deliberations Shawcross had challenged White and suggested that the judge was very likely to ask how Fuchs could have been employed on a top-secret project at Harwell when he had been known to be a Communist since 1942.

This, of course, was not only the nub of the issue, but the fatal flaw in MI5's performance. In response, White had asserted disingenuously that there had never been any evidence that Fuchs had been a member of the CPGB, and that the information concerning his KPD membership had emanated from the Gestapo in Kiel, and had not been confirmed by any police reports after he had settled in England.

The truth, of course, was very different, as Sillitoe only learned after he had actually read the Fuchs file. In fact Fuchs had been investigated twice, in 1943 and again 1947, before he was compromised by VENONA. In 1933 the Bristol police had been involved in Fuchs' unsuccessful attempts to renew his German passport, and had received a report about his KPD activism from Kiel. However, the police had reported to MI5 that 'during his stay in this city Fuchs is not known to have engaged in any communist activities'. Thus the true position was much worse than Shawcross had imagined, and that MI5 had been aware of Fuchs' communism for a full decade before his name came up in 1943 when he underwent a security check in relation to his work with the Ministry of Supply on the Tube Alloys project.

The first investigation was prompted in November 1943 by a request from the DSIR which reported that Fuchs had received his certificate of naturalization on 30 July 1942, and asked if there was any objection to his departure to the United States. Both Michael Serpell and Millicent Bagot had been dismayed by this news, but neither had been indoctrinated into the Manhattan Project and therefore were unaware that Fuchs, now carrying a new British passport, was to be employed in New York and then Los Alamos on developing the Anglo–American atom bomb. Nor had they been consulted by MI5's C3 regarding his naturalization application which had been supported by a report from the Birmingham police: 'The Chief Constable is assured that if Fuchs still has any interest in politics it is not an active one and that he has not been known to associate with communists in this District.' At that time Daphne Bosanquet of F2(b) had obtained a Home Office warrant to intercept Fuchs's letters, but none were found, and in the absence of any adverse information, no objection to Fuchs' application had been made, and he thus became a British citizen.

Fuchs sailed to Newport News, Virginia on the RMS *Andes* with the rest of the British Scientific Mission and would remain there until he flew back from Newfoundland at the end of June 1946. In his absence F Division passed his file to the travel control branch, D Division, which received a request from Michael Perrin who sought confirmation of Fuchs' status because he was to stay on in the United States rather longer than had been intended originally.

This is a very important matter vis-à-vis the Americans and I want to be sure that we do not slip up in any way. I know that you people have had at one time slight doubts about some of Fuchs' connections, and I should be much obliged if you could let me know the present position as quickly as possible.

MI5's response in January 1944 would be based on David Clarke of F Division who allegedly thought that Fuchs 'is rather safer in America than in this country, and that for that reason he is rather in favour of his remaining in America where he is away from his English friends'.

Thus MI5 acquiesced in Fuchs' extended stay in the United States, still in ignorance of his role in the Manhattan Project, and he did not come back to MI5's attention until October 1946 when, working at Harwell on the development of an independent British plutonium bomb, he was the subject of a report by the facility's security officer, Henry Arnold. Although Arnold's suspicions were dismissed, Michael Serpell had drawn a parallel with Alan Nunn May and highlighted Fuchs' known connection with Hans Kahle, with whom he had been interned between July 1940 and January 1941 at Camp L, on Quebec's Plains of Abraham, and Peierls, whose wife was Russian. Serpell strongly recommended that Fuchs should undergo a thorough investigation. His view was supported by Jane Archer who also suggested that both Fuchs and Peierls should be prevented from working on any atomic energy project. However, F Division's director, Roger Hollis, concluded that 'I can see nothing in this file which persuades me that Fuchs is in any way likely to be engaged in espionage or that he is any more than anti-Nazi.'

Despite Hollis' reservations, a second Home Office warrant was imposed on Fuchs and Peierls, but the interception was terminated in April 1947 and no further action was taken until later the same year when the question of Fuchs' permanent establishment was raised. The result was advice from Colonel Badham in January 1948 which summarised the position, mentioning the Gestapo accusation and his later association with Kahle. This information was considered by the Ministry of Supply which in August explained that 'the slight security risk' posed by Fuchs was outweighed by the advantages.

That was the position, with the Ministry of Supply making the final decision, before VENONA implicated the physicist in August 1949, thus sparking off the third and final investigation which resulted in his confession and his imprisonment in March 1950. During the period Fuchs had been under intense MI5 surveillance, from August 1949 until his arrest, the Watcher Service had failed to uncover anything more incriminating than his tawdry affair with Erna Abrahamsohn, the Austrian-born Jewish wife of his next-door neighbour and colleague, Professor Herbert Skinner, who was deputy head of Harwell and director of the General Physics Department. When Fuchs and Mrs Skinner slipped away in the middle of January 1950 to spend three nights together at the Palm Court Hotel in Richmond, while her husband was in Liverpool, the episode was reported in his Personal File (PF).

When Sillitoe had given Attlee an account of the case on 3 March there had been no mention of the recommendations made years earlier by Serpell, Robertson and Archer and if the full truth had emerged it is hard to imagine how MI5 could have avoided some kind of inquiry which might even have resulted in a wholesale reorganization or the removal of the officers, principally White, Hollis and Liddell, who had failed to act on the most explicit warnings.

Even MI5's post-conviction investigation into Fuchs failed to uncover the full details of his espionage in England before he travelled to the United States, and it would later emerge that he had been introduced to the GRU *resident*'s assistant, Semyon Kremer, by the KPD leader Jurgen Kuczynski in April 1941.[3] It is believed that Fuchs held covert meetings with Kremer four times, and handed over around 200 pages of notes about his work on the Tube Alloys project until the contact was broken when the GRU officer was recalled to Moscow immediately after the German invasion of the Soviet Union in June 1941.

Fuchs' statement concerning his post-war espionage provided MI5 with plenty of leads to follow up. In his efforts to re-establish contact with the Soviets in England after his return from the United States, Fuchs had attended a rendezvous at Mornington Crescent Tube station on the first Saturday in September 1946 but had failed to make contact. In fact the *rezident*, Konstantin Kukin, fearing hostile surveillance, had instructed a subordinate, Pavel Yerzin, to observe Fuchs at a distance, but he never spotted him. Kukin, of course, had been directed by Moscow to suspend all operations while the fall-out from Gouzenko's treachery had been assessed fully.

Unaware of the panic caused by the defection in Ottawa, Fuchs had been dismayed at his apparent disconnection and had asked a pair of pre-war CPGB friends, Angela Pilley and then Angela Tuckett, to convey a message. This approach was rebuffed by the CPGB, or so he believed, prompting him to try and repeat the steps he had taken originally taken to contact the GRU in April 1941. However, he discovered that Kuczynski had returned to Germany, so he spoke to his wife Marguerite at their home in Hampstead and, having consulted the refugees' leader in London, Hans Siebert, this resulted in a meeting with Hanna Klopstock on 19 July 1947 in Richmond Park. She had instructed him to visit the Nag's Head in Wood Green on the evening of 27 September, and this was where he met a member of the London *rezidentura*, later identified as Aleksandr Feklisov.

Undeterred, Fuchs then attended that meeting and was given detailed instructions on a dead-letter box at 166 Kew Road, where he was instructed to toss a magazine, *Men Only*, onto the garden lawn with his message written on page 10. The occupants were known CPGB members; Charles Moody, who had been implicated in the Woolwich Arsenal case in 1938, his wife Gerty, and her sister Claire Isaacs. The latter pair had been in trouble for distributing subversive, anti-war literature to troops in 1935.[4] All three suspects were interviewed by Jim

Skardon, but they denied any knowledge of Fuchs' drop arrangements, so this aspect of the case remained unresolved. Moody, however, had accumulated a large MI5 file dating back to August 1931, and had been linked in the past to George Aitken, the CPGB's propaganda director who had attended the Lenin School in Moscow in 1927 and served as the political commissar to the XVth International Brigade during the Spanish Civil War.

MI5 also interviewed Angela Tuckett, a formidable veteran CPGB campaigner, to obtain her recollection of Fuchs' testimony that he had been in contact with her in December 1946 or January 1947. A qualified solicitor and a CPGB activist, Tuckett had known Fuchs in Bristol when he had been working at the university between 1933 and 1937. She had joined the staff of the *Daily Worker* in 1942 and at the time of her interview with MI5, which she reported to King Street and Moscow, she was assistant editor of *Labour Monthly*.

The one person Fuchs seemed anxious to protect, as Liddell recorded in his diary on 8 February 1950, was the intermediary who had originally introduced him to the Soviets:

He has refused to give us the name of the person who introduced him to the Russian agent in this country; he pleads that this man is a good fellow at heart and that he did not know that Fuchs was going to have more than one visit, or that he was going to hand over documents, that he is now out of the country and that he would not like to prejudice his chances if at some future date he wanted to enter this country as a refugee. We think this man may be Engelbert Broda, who is in Austria.

Although Liddell suspected Broda had played the role of intermediary, it had actually been Jurgen Kuczynski, leader of the wartime émigré KPD in London. Kuczynski had put Fuchs in touch with Kremer in 1941 and, coincidentally, Kremer had appointed Jurgen's sister to handle Fuchs. Astonishingly, Jurgen had no idea, until years later, that Ursula had ended up running Fuchs. She only told him after she took up permanent residence in Germany in February 1950.

Warned by various sources that MI5 was in pursuit of what appeared to have been a very comprehensive confession from Fuchs, the NKVD attempted to undertake a damage-limitation exercise and adopt the appropriate countermeasures, but Moscow was reluctant to grasp that its own communications system had incriminated Fuchs. The Soviets were reeling from the impact of the defection of Gouzenko, which had coincided with the FBI's access to Elizabeth Bentley, who had worked at the assistant to Jakob Golos, the NKVD illegal *rezident* in New York, and was thought to have compromised up to eighty members of his network. Compounding the catastrophe was the knowledge that the FBI was questioning Fuchs' New York contact, Harry Gold.

An emergency audit conducted by Moscow suggested that a widening group of people had been in a position to incriminate Fuchs, among them Hans Siebert,

Ursula Beurton, Angela Pilley, Hanna Klopstick and Angela Tuckett. For Kukin, the dilemma was to balance the risk of contacting Fuchs to tell him to be more circumspect. Without guidance, Fuchs had embarked inadvertently on a course that was likely to undermine his own security, but thus far the people he had approached, directly or indirectly, had been considered reliable, even if they were not formally NKVD agents. Early in 1950 Moscow, still reluctant to even refer to the cipher breaks disclosed by Philby, concluded the post-mortem:

British Counter-intelligence started investigations into the Fuchs case in September 1949 on the basis of the following warnings: a) information from the FBI on a leakage of atomic secrets from the USA to the USSR in the period 1944–45; b) information from Canadian Counter-intelligence on the discovery of Fuchs' name in the diary of one of the suspects in the May case; Study of documents on Fuchs' past, especially those in the Gestapo archives, revealed his membership of the German Communist Party. Earlier vetting of his political reliability, when he was accepted for scientific research work at Birmingham University in 1941, and his behaviour after his return from the USA had given no grounds for suspicion. When, in the USA, he was sent to Los Alamos, he was not vetted at all. The investigation carried out in 1949 convinced MI5 that Fuchs was responsible for the leakage of information from the USA, although that did not dispose of any direct evidence against him and therefore no action was taken. But it was Fuchs himself who hastened events. On 12 October 1949, Fuchs approached the security officer at the Harwell atomic research centre, Henry Arnold, and informed him that his father had accepted an offer from the GDR authorities of a professorship at Leipzig University and that this decision would affect his position at the research centre. Arnold did not give an answer straightaway and on 20 October Fuchs again asked him how matters stood. MI5 decided to use these developments to question Fuchs. The interrogation took place in December 1949 and was conducted by an MI5 officer, William Skardon. Fuchs admitted his membership of the Communist Party in the past, but completely denied being a spy. Skardon played on Fuchs' loyalty to his English friends and colleagues and appealed to his feelings of gratitude towards Britain which had given him shelter and provided him with his life's work. These tactics evidently worked and called forth in Fuchs a psychological conflict. At the end of January, he made a full confession of his work for Soviet Intelligence and told everything he knew. On the basis of Fuchs' confession, MI5 established certain specific facts: the name of the man who brought Fuchs in contact with the Soviet representatives, Jurgen Kuczinsky; the name of the first Soviet representative, the secretary of the military attaché, Simon Kremer; the name of the member of the German Communist Party who put him in touch with a Soviet representative in 1947, Hanna Klopstock; the approximate number of meetings and arrangements for contacting representatives of Soviet Intelligence in Britain and the USA, as well as in Paris.

As for Fuchs himself, he had admitted that he had been handled initially by a woman he had met first in a Birmingham café in October 1942, and thereafter held a regular rendezvous with her in the Oxfordshire market town of Banbury every three or four months.[5] They had met a total of six times. As Fuchs never learned her name, he could not, or would not, identify her photo to his MI5 inquisitors, but in fact Skardon and Serpell had already met her. On 13 September 1947 they had visited Ursula Beurton at The Firs, her ramshackle cottage in Church Lane in the village of Great Rollright, because she had been named as a GRU illegal by a defector, Alan Foote.[6] At that encounter Beurton simply confirmed that she had not been in touch with the Soviets since her arrival in England in 1941 and declined to co-operate further. She had reported this encounter to Moscow immediately, and another identical encounter in April the following year, but MI5 never linked her to Fuchs until long after she had fled to East Germany on 27 February 1950, three weeks after the newspapers had announced Fuchs' arrest. Fuchs would not acknowledge to MI5 that Beurton had been his contact until November 1950, by which time she was well out of reach.

The NKVD should have been alerted in September 1949 by Kim Philby that some of Moscow's ciphers had been successfully attacked in the United States, and that the FBI was closing in on a British scientist who had fallen under suspicion. Philby had entrusted the message to Burgess because he had only learned the information on the day before he had been scheduled to embark on his transatlantic voyage to take up his appointment in Washington DC, and was not due to be in contact for some months, but his co-conspirator had failed to pass on the vital warning, with catastrophic consequences.

In retrospect, the Fuchs investigation was not exactly MI5's finest hour, but the organization survived, even if there were some who knew the scale of the failures, and were surprised at the lack of any adverse consequences. For example, on 16 February 1950, Liddell recorded an encounter with the FBI:

I spent the evening with Lish Whitson and Johnny Cimpemnan. Rather significantly, Lish asked me who was going to be the scapegoat here for the Fuchs affair. I said that as far as I knew there would be no scapegoat – in fact, I could see no reason why there should be one. In similar circumstances, without previous knowledge, we should probably act in exactly the same way that we have in this case. I referred to all the excitement that was going on in the United States and said that I thought it would be a pity if it had any lasting effect on Anglo-American co-operation.

Chapter IV

Konstantin Volkov

O n 27 August 1945 the Soviet vice consul in Istanbul, Konstantin Volkov, wrote an unsigned letter to his counterpart in the British consulate-general, seeking an interview. That encounter took place on 4 September when Volkov, accompanied by his very nervous wife Zoya, turned up unexpectedly at Sir Charles Barry's elegant building, formerly the embassy, without an appointment and was seen by Chantry Page, who did not speak Russian, and the first secretary, John Reed, who acted as interpreter. Reed's grasp of the language was far from complete, but he had spent two years at the embassy in Moscow during the war and so was competent. Indeed, Volkov refused, on security grounds, to allow a locally-employed linguist to act as his translator.

At that meeting Volkov identified himself as the local deputy *rezident* who, until June 1943 had worked at the NKVD's 3rd (British and Scandinavian) Department at the organization's Moscow headquarters, and set out the terms for his defection which, he said, had been prompted by a bitter quarrel with his ambassador. Just over a week later, on 13 September, he delivered an unsigned letter, written on a Cyrillic typewriter, in which reiterated the details. John Reed's translation, was sent in the diplomatic pouch to the Foreign Office in London on 17 September:

> Further to our conversation I have the honour to report to you that, on the basis of the conditions which are described below, I can hand over to the special British intelligence service all the documents listed below of the Intelligence Directorate of the NKGB of the USSR of which I have been an employee since the autumn of 1936:
>
> 1. List of 314 agents of the Intelligence Directorate of the NKGB in Turkey. This list includes active agents and also agents on ice. On some agents there are official descriptions.
> 2. List of employees of military and civilian intelligence services of Great Britain known to NKGB. List includes about 250 official and secret employees of mentioned service of whom there are descriptions.
> 3. List of materials: in some cases there are duplicates or photocopies which were given to us by NKGB agents who are employees of the British intelligence organs and Ministry of Foreign Affairs of Great Britain. Judging by the cryptonyms there are nine such agents in London. This list is of extreme importance since it gives opportunities to establish the NKGB agents in the most important institutions. It is known to me, for

example, that one of the NKGB agents fulfils the duties of the chief of an otdel (department) of the English counter-intelligence Directorate in London. Another works in the apparat of British consulate in Istanbul.

4. Copies of materials of personal files and special dossiers of English intelligence.

5. Photostats and translations of instructions from English intelligence, in particular, London's correspondence with General Hill.

6. Copy of the assessment of the leadership of the Middle East Department of Intelligence Directorate of NKGB on materials of English intelligence organs in Iran.

7. Detailed data about some NKGB agents in Palestine, Balkan countries and Iran. Their cryptonyms and contacting arrangements.

8. Full list of officials of Intelligence Directorate of NKGB in Moscow, their addresses and their business and home telephones. Also the addresses of the garages and car numbers of Intelligence Directorate of NKGB.

9. Addresses of some safe apartments of Intelligence Directorate of NKGB in Moscow.

10. Recruitment material on a Captain (probably now a Major) of the counter-intelligence service of the NKGB, on a secretary of the Chief Directorate of the People's Commissariat of Oil Industry and on a woman employee for errands in one of the divisions of special assignments in Moscow. All three persons can be used in the interests of the English service.

11. Two genuine identity cards of officers of Intelligence Directorate of NKGB in Moscow for 1945 which give right of entry to all operational, archival and other business premises of the NKGB, NKVD and counter-intelligence directorates of People's Commissariat of Defense and People's Commissariat of Navy. They could be used as samples.

12. Samples of stamps and commandant's seals of two directorates of NKGB which provide opportunities to get passes and take packages of official documents out of building of NKGB of USSR.

13. Samples of official forms and registration cards of Intelligence Directorate of NKGB. They can be used for getting information from the operational registry section of Intelligence Directorate and other special directorates in Moscow. Through these forms one can establish all NKGB agents throughout the world.

14. Keys of two offices of operational sections of Intelligence Directorate of NKGB in Moscow where secret documentation on Middle East is kept.

15. All possible documents describing financial state and operational possibilities of some rezidenturas of NKGB of USSR.

This list can be extended by other documents which I pass you on the spot. Among these are:

1. Copies of telegrams sent to Moscow and sent to ambassador. Their value, apart from content, lies in that they allow the deciphering of all cipher telegrams sent by consulate-general and perhaps incoming telegrams.
2. List of officers of Intelligence Directorate of NKGB, People's Commissariat of Defense and People's Commissariat of Navy working under cover of legal missions in Turkey, their cryptonyms and functions in the rezidentura. Also an incomplete list on Iran and Egypt.
3. Several keys to offices, safes and entrance doors of consulate-general.
4. Notes on conversations of the leadership of consulate-general with visitors and other official documentation.
5. In particular I can describe the structure of political and military intelligence of USSR in Turkey and also of intelligence Directorate of NKGB in Moscow.
6. I can also present a detailed report on the structure of military counter-intelligence in units of the Red Army, their competence and methods of work.
7. I can also give explanations about NKGB operations carried out against English secret officials in Moscow (Hill, Barclay) and about sources of obtaining samples of English diplomatic and military ciphers in Moscow.[1]

The terms for the transfer of these materials to you are the following;

1. Secrecy about all my proposals. No reports on this subject to be sent by radio or telegraph.
2. All consultations with your leadership should be carried out directly and not through intermediaries.
3. Loss of my work and position should be properly compensated by giving me at least 50,000 pounds sterling. I give this figure as a minimum taking into account the importance of my material and the consequences all my relatives in the USSR will inevitably face.
4. Granting me asylum and full guarantees of security.
   I request that you inform me about your decision (positive or negative) before 25 September or – at the latest – 1 October 1945.
   You can invite me for negotiations through my consular telephone, naturally with proper precautions (better if such a call could be made in the form of an official or personal invitation and only on behalf of the consulate which would not arouse suspicion).
   In conclusion, I assure you that through your person the Government of Great Britain that my present contribution and modest participation will bring nearer the day of just revenge in the interests of the people of the mighty British Commonwealth, for the sake of freedom-loving and suffering humanity. Your sincere friend.[2]

copy

TOP SECRET.

With reference to our conversation, I have the honour to inform you that on the conditions stated below I can place at the disposal of the British Special Service numbered documents of the Intelligence Service of the People's Commissariat of State Security (N.K.G.B.) of the U.S.S.R., an official of which I have been since the autumn of 1936:

1. A list of the agents of the N.K.G.B. Intelligence in Turkey numbering 314 men. The list shows both active and reserve agents; including the official, descriptions (characteristics) of special agents.

2. A list of the known regular N.K.G.B. agents of the military and civil Intelligence in Great Britain and their agents. In the list are noted about 250 known and less well known agents of the above-named service with their characteristic details.

3. A list and, in certain cases, duplicates and photostats of the material handed over to us by the agents of the N.K.G.B. who are our collaborators in the English Intelligence Service and the Ministry of Foreign Affairs in Great Britain. Judging by the clichés, the number of such agents in London could be nine. This list is of exceptional interest because it provides a possibility of identifying the agents of the N.K.G.B. in exceptionally important British institutions. I know, for instance, that one of the agents of the N.K.G.B. is fulfilling the functions of the head of a Section of the British Counter-Espionage Service in London and that another is working within the British Consulate at Istanbul.

4. Copies of the material of the papers and special dossiers of the British Intelligence.

5. Photo clichés and translations of important material of the British service and in particular of the correspondence between London and General Hill.

6. Copy of the (?) conclusion of the Direction of the Near Eastern Section of the N.K.G.B. dealing with the material of the British Service in Iran.

7. Detailed information in connection with certain agents of the N.K.G.B. who are in Palestine, the Balkans and Iran, their photographs and connections.

8. A full list of the agents of the Intelligence Service of the N.K.G.B. in Moscow, their home addresses and the numbers of their official and private telephones. Also the addresses of the garages and motorcars of the N.K.G.B. service.

9. The addresses of certain kanspirativnich (sic) flats of the service of the N.K.G.B.

10. Recruiting material (sic) about the captain, now probably major, of the counter-espionage service of the N.K.G.B., of the secretary of the head of the People's Commissariat of the petrol industry and a member of the management of one of the divisions of special significance in Moscow. All these three people could be used in the interests of the British Service.

11. Two original identity documents of officers of the Intelligence Service of the N.K.G.B. in Moscow in 1945 giving the right of access to all operational, xxkaxvxkxxxxxxxxxxxxxxxxxxxxxxxx

archive....

archive and other services of the N.K.G.B. organisation, N.K.V.D. and counter-espionage organisation of the People's Commissariats of Defence and of the War Fleet of the U.S.S.R. These identity papers can be used as examples.

12. Examples of the stamps and executive seals of two services of the N.K.G.B. authorising the giving of certificates and passes and right of taking out of the N.K.G.B. building in Moscow packages and parcels of service documents.

13. Copies of blank Service forms and of all sorts of account-ing forms of the Intelligence Section of the N.K.G.B., the latter can be used for obtaining by the method used in the N.K.G.B. any documents in the operational accounting section of the Intelligence Section and other special organisations in Moscow. Copies of the above mentioned blank forms will give you the possibility of finding out the agents of the N.K.G.B. in all the countries of the world.

14. Keys of two cabinets of the operation section of the Intelligence Section of the N.K.G.B. in Moscow where the secret documents for the Near East are kept.

15. There are also all kinds of documents about the financial organisation and the operational possibilities of the separate bureaux of the N.K.G.B. of the U.S.S.R.

This list of material in my possession can be supplemented by a number of documents which I have the possibility of giving you here on the spot. The letter include copies of the cypher telegrams sent and despatched from Moscow, the value of which, that is to say of their contents, consists in the possibility of decyphering all further telegrams sent out from the Consulate General and perhaps of the incoming ones. (2) A list of the regular officers of the Intelligence of the N.K.G.B., of the People's Commissariats of Defence and of the Fleet of the U.S.S.R. working under the cover of legal Soviet representatives in Turkey, their clichés and the functions of each of those in residence, also a full list for Iran and Egypt. (3) Certain clichés of cabinets, safes and doors of entry into the Consulate. (4) Written records of conversations of the head personnel of the Consulate General with visitors and other Service documents. (5) In particular I can furnish the struc-tural plan of the political and military intelligence units of the U.S.S.R. in Turkey and also of the direction of the N.K.G.B. in Moscow. (6) At the same time I can copy a detailed document about the distribution of the organs of the military counter-espionage in the units of the Red Army, their methods of work. (7) In addi-tion to which I can give explanations about the measures taken by the N.K.G.B. in connection with the English Secret Service in Moscow (Hill and Barclay) and also about the sources from which we have received copies of British diplomatic and military cyphers in Moscow.

The conditions under which all the above mentioned material can be handed over to you are as follows:

One. The maintenance of absolute secrecy about my proposal. The non-despatch of any report about the present question either by your radio or by telegraph.

Two. All agreements with your management must be conducted directly and without the participation of any third parties.

Three. The loss of my post and situation must be worthily com-pensated by an immediate payment to me of at least £50,000 sterling. I consider this sum as a minimum considering the importance of the material and evidence given to you as a result of which all my relatives living in the territory of the U.S.S.R. are doomed.

Four.....

Four. The offer to me of a refuge and also a guarantee of full safe-conduct. I beg you to communicate to me your decision either provisionally or definitely by the 25th September or at latest by the 1st October, 1945.

You could call me up for conversations on one of the Consulate telephones, naturally only if all necessary precautions are observed. If the call is absolutely essential, it would be best if it were couched in the form of an official and personal invitation which should originate from the Consulate, thus not causing any suspicion.

In conclusion I assure you, and in your person the Government of Great Britain, that my present approach represents the proof of my sincere affection for the interests of the mighty fraternity of the British peoples and for freedom loving and suffering humanity.

Yours sincere friend

(Unsigned)

В дополнение к нашему разговору, имею честь

сообщить Вам, что на указанных ниже условиях я могу пе-

редать в распоряжение специальной английской службы всю

перечисленную документацию Разведывательного Управления

Наркомата Государственной Безопасности СССР, сотрудником

которого я являюсь с осени 1936 года.

1. Список агентуры Разведуправления НКГБ в Турции
   на 314 человек./ В списке учтена, как действую-
   щая, так и законсервированная агентура. На отдельных агентов имеются официальные характеристики/

2. Список известных НКГБ кадровых сотрудников военной и гражданской разведок Великобритании, также
   как и их агентуры. В списке значатся около 250
   гласных и негласных сотрудников поименованной
   службы, на которых указаны характеризующие их
   данные.

3. Список материалов,/ а в отдельных случаях ,- их
   дубликаты и фото-копии/, переданных нам агентами
   НКГБ, являющимися сотрудниками английских развед.
   органов и Министерства Иностранных Дел Великобритании.

   / Судя по кличкам, таковых агентов в Лондоне
   насчитывается -9 /

   Этот список представляет исключительный интерес,
   дает возможность установить агентуру НКГБ в чрез-
   вычайно важных Британских учреждениях. Мне, например,
   известно, что один из агентов НКГБ исполняет обязан-

ности начальника отдела английского контр-разведывате. -
ного Управления в Лондоне, а другой работает в аппарате
Британского консульства в Стамбуле.

4- Копии материалов дел-формуляров и специальных досье
английской разведки.

5- Фото-клише и переводы руководящих материалов английской
разведки, в частности переписка Лондона с генералом УИЛЛ.

6- Копия заключения руководства Ближне-Восточного Отдела
Разведуправления НКГБ по материалам английских разведорга-
нов в Иране.

7- Подробные данные в отношение некоторых агентов НКГБ, нахо-
дящихся в Палестине, Балканских странах и Иране,/ их клички
и условия связи/.

8- Полный список сотрудников Разведуправления НКГБ в Москве,
их домашние адреса и №№ служебных и домашних телефонов.
Также адреса автогаражей и №№ автомашин Разведуправления
НКГБ.

9- Адреса некоторых конспиративных квартир Разведуправления
НКГБ в Москве.

10- Вербовочный материал на капитана/ теперь, очевидно-
майора/ контр-разведывательной службы НКГБ, секретаря
Главка Наркомата Нефтяной Промышленности и сотрудницы
для поручений в одной из дивизий специального назначения
в Москве. Все эти три лица могут быть использованы в
интересах английской службы.

11- Два подлинных удостоверения личности офицеров Разведуправления НКГБ в Москве на 1945 год, дающих право про-
хода во все оперативные, архивные и другие служебные

-2-

помещения НКГБ, НКВД и контр-разведывательных управлений

Наркомата Обороны и Наркомата Военно-Морского Флота СССР.

Эти удостоверения могут быть использованы в ка-

честве образцов.

12- Образцы штампов и комендантских печатей двух управлений

НКГБ, дающих возможность выписки справок и пропусков на

право выноса из здания НКГБ СССР пакетов служебной доку-

ментации.

13- Образцы служебных бланков и всевозможных учетных карточек.

Разведуправления НКГБ. Последние могут быть использованы

для получения установленным в НКГБ порядком любых справок

из оперативно-учетного отделения Разведуправления и других

специальных управлений в Москве.

Наличие указанных выше бланков даст вам возможность

установить агентуру НКГБ по всем странам мира.

14- Ключи от двух кабинетов оперативных отделений Разведупр-

ления НКГБ в Москве, где хранится секретная документация

по Ближнему Востоку.

15- Имеются еще всевозможные документы, характеризующие фи-

нансовое состояние и оперативные возможности отдельных

резидентур НКГБ СССР.

Этот список располагаемых мной материалов может

быть дополнен за счет документов, которые я имею возможность пере-

дать вам здесь на месте. К числу последних относятся:

1- Копии отправленных в Москву и послу шифртелеграм,

ценность которых, /помимо содержания/, заключается

в возможности дальнейшего расшифрования всех исхо-

дящих из генконсульства шифртелеграммы/ а может быть и
входящих/.

2- Список кадровых офицеров Разведуправления НКГБ. Наркомата
Обороны и Наркомата Военно-Морского Флота СССР. работаю-
щих под прикрытием легальных Советских представительств
В Турции / их клички и функции каждого в резидентуре/.
   Также- не полный список по Ирану и Египту.

3- Несколько ключей от кабинетов. сейфовж и входных дверей
генконсульства.

4- Тетради записей бесед руководства генконсульства с посе-
тителями, также как и другая служебная документация.

5- Специально могу составить структурную схему политической
и военных разведок СССР в Турции. а также Разведуправления
НКГБ в Москве.

6. Одновременно могу написать подробный доклад о построении
органов военной контр-разведки в частях Красной Армии.
их компетенции и методах работы.

7- Кроме того, могу дать объяснения о проведенных НКГБ меро-
приятиях в отношение английской секретной службы в Москве.
/ ХИЛЛ. БАРКЛЕЙ/. также, как и источниках получения образцов английского дипломатического и военного шифров/в Москве/

   Условия. при которых может состояться передача
в Ваше распоряжение всех перечисленных выше материалов,- следующие:-

I- Сохранение в абсолютной тайне сделанных мной предложений.
Воздержание от передачи каких-либо депеш по настоящему
вопросу, с использованием радио или телеграфа.

2- Все согласования с Вашим руководством должны проходить

-3-

непосредственно и без участия каких-либо посредников.

3- Потеря мной должности и положения должна быть достой-
ным образом компенсирована, единовременным вручением
мне, по крайней мере- 50.000 фунтов стерлингов.

Я назваю эту цифру как минимальную, учитывая зна-
чимость передаваемых Вам материалов и последствия, с
которыми неизбежно столкнуться все мои родственники,
проживающие на территории СССР.

4- Предоставление мне убежища. также , как и гарантий
полной безопасности.

О любом Вашем решении / положительном или отри-
цательном/ прошу поставить меня в известность до 25-го сентября,
или в крайнем случае- до 1-го октября 1945 года.

Вызов меня для переговоров возможен по любому из
консульских телефонов, безусловно, с соблюдением требуемой осторо-
ности. / Лучше, если бы при таковой необходимости, вызов был бы
облечен в форму официального и персонального приглашения и обяза
тельно от имени консульства, что не вызовет подозрений/.

В заключение, заверяю Вас и в Вашем лице- Правитель-
ство Великобритании, что мой настоящий вклад и скромное участие
приблизят дату справедливого отмщения ради интересов могучего
содружества Британских народов, ради свободолюбивого и исстрадав-
гося человечества.

Ваш искренний друг

From a counter-intelligence perspective, Volkov's proposal boiled down to information relating to nine agents in London employed by the Foreign Office or British Intelligence, and one who currently 'fulfils the duties of the chief of an otdel (department) of the English counter-intelligence Directorate in London. Another works in the apparat of British consulate in Istanbul.'

When this document reached London it was examined by the Permanent Under-Secretary, Sir Alexander Cadogan, who instructed Tom Bromley on 19 September to pass it to the SIS where the Chief, Stewart Menzies, assigned Kim Philby to handle the matter. Philby, then head of SIS's Section IX, responsible for Soviet affairs, recommended that the offer be taken seriously. Naturally he tipped off his Soviet contact, Boris Krotenschield, alias Boris Krotov, codenamed BOB, and on 26 September began a journey to Turkey via Tunis, Malta and Cairo, arriving in Istanbul on 28 September, just inside the time limit set by Volkov, to learn that both Konstantin and Zoya had disappeared two days earlier, presumably withdrawn to Moscow, having been bundled aboard an unscheduled Soviet aircraft which had landed at Istanbul's Yesilkoy airfield without the permission of the Turkish authorities.

Liddell recorded this episode in his diary on 5 October 1945:

The case of the renegade Konstantin Volkov in the Soviet embassy in Istanbul has broken down. In accordance with instructions he was telephoned to at the Soviet consulate. The telephone was answered by the Russian Consul-General on the first occasion and on the second by a man speaking English claiming to be Volkov but clearly was not. Finally, contact was made with the Russian telephone operator who said that Volkov has left for Moscow. Subsequent enquiries showed that he and his wife left by plane for Russia on 26 September. Volkov had offered to give a very considerable amount of information but much of it appeared to be in Moscow. Volkov estimated at that there were nine agents in London, one of whom was said to be the 'head of a section of the British counter-intelligence service'. Volkov said he could produce a list of the known regular NKGB agents of the military and civil intelligence and of the sub-agents they employed. In the list are noted about 250 known or less well known agents of the above-mentioned services with details. Also available were copies of correspondence between London and General Hill of SOE in Moscow. Volkov maintains that the Soviet authorities have been able to read all cipher messages between our Foreign Office and embassy in Moscow and in addition to Hill's messages [XXXXXXXXXXXXX]. The Russian had, according to Volkov, two agents inside the Foreign Office and seven inside the British Intelligence Service.

Thus Liddell's version of the Volkov offer was inaccurate in two regards. Firstly, Volkov's figure of 250 had been in respect of British personnel known to the Soviets, not Soviet agents, whereas Liddell's rather ambiguous comment was open to misinterpretation. Secondly, Liddell had described two agents in the Foreign Office and seven in British Intelligence. Where had he acquired that breakdown? Volkov had simply talked of a total of nine spies on London, without detailing how many were in the Foreign Office. This error would reappear in subsequent versions, the details becoming very distorted, and this issue would dog the intelligence community, and outside observers, for many years.

The problem began with Kim Philby's *My Silent War* in 1968 when he recalled that Volkov had 'claimed to know the real names of three Soviet agents working in Britain.[3] Two of them were in in the Foreign Office; one was head of a counter-espionage organization in London.' This, of course, was not quite what Volkov had said, but Philby may have had his own motives for muddying the waters. He certainly did so in just one other respect, when he stated that 'three full days elapsed between the arrival of the Istanbul papers in Broadway and the take-off of my aeroplane bound for Cairo en route to Istanbul'. In reality, SIS had received Volkov's letter from the Foreign Office on 19 September, and Philby had departed a week later, on 26 September.

Then in 1989, a *Daily Telegraph* journalist, Gordon Brook-Shepherd, who had been granted privileged access to some SIS files by the then Foreign Secretary Douglas Hurd, published *The Storm Birds* in which he asserted that Volkov had 'offered to name 314 agents in Turkey and no fewer than 250 Soviet agents in Britain'.[4] Of the agents in Britain, two, he claimed, 'worked in the Foreign Office. Seven more were inside the British intelligence system'. Thus Brook-Shepherd, for whatever reason, had completely misrepresented the figure of 250 British officials known to the NKGB as 250 Soviet agents in Britain, and had redesignated the nine agents in the Foreign Office or British Intelligence as two in the Foreign Office and seven in British intelligence.

This distortion would probably not have mattered if it had not become the source for numerous subsequent authors who uncritically adopted the Brook-Shepherd version. Among this group was MI5's approved historian, Christopher Andrew, who opined that 'the most reliable account of Volkov's attempted defection is in Brook-Shepherd's *Storm Birds* which corrects a number of inventions and inaccuracies in Philby's version of events'. However, a close analysis of Philby's account does not reveal any significant variance with the known facts. He does refer to 'one August morning' as being the moment he was indoctrinated into the case by Menzies, whereas the true date was 19 September, and the suggestion that Volkov had only mentioned two spies in the Foreign Office, not nine. But if these were inventions, it is hard to discern their sinister purpose.

Professor Andrew had addressed the Volkov case first in *KGB: The Inside Story*, co-authored with Oleg Gordievsky, published in 1990, with an observation on the putative defector:

Among the most important wartime Soviet agents, he claimed, were two in the Foreign Office and seven 'inside the British intelligence system', one of whom was 'fulfilling the function of head of a section of British counter-espionage in London'.

This version, with the incorrect attribution of two spies in the Foreign Office, clearly had come from *The Storm Birds*, as the authors acknowledged in their source notes:

> The most reliable account of this episode, we believe, is Brook-Shepherd's *Storm Birds*, chapter 4, which corrects a number of inventions by Philby. The two agents within the Foreign Office referred to by Volkov were, in all probability, Burgess and Maclean. The seven in the intelligence services doubtless included Philby, Blunt, Cairncross, Long and Klugmann. Candidates for the other two war-time moles are Cedric Belfrage, who worked for two years during the Second World War for British Security Co-ordination in New York, and an SOE officer who cannot be publicly identified.

The problem with this assessment of Brook-Shepherd's reliability is that the account in *The Storm Birds* had been quite wrong, as Volkov's letter had never mentioned a pair of spies in the Foreign Office. Another aspect of the treatment given by Andrew and Gordievsky to the Volkov affair was a statement attributed to Gordievsky:

> According to the fictional version of Volkov's liquidation, later concocted by Philby and the KGB for Western consumption, Volkov was not spirited out of Istanbul until 'some weeks later'. In reality Volkov and his wife had left Istanbul aboard a Soviet aircraft sedated and on stretchers accompanied by the NKGB minders two days before Philby arrived.

This passage is worthy of comment only because of the faulty chronology presented by Andrew and Gordievsky. In their scenario Philby arrived in Istanbul on 26 September and the NKVD's hatchet men posing as diplomatic couriers 'had been issued Turkish visas in Moscow on 21 September', and had removed Volkov on 24 September, 'two days before Philby arrived.' However, SIS's records show that Philby did not reach Istanbul until 28 September, which rather undermines their version of events.

Professor Andrew returned to the exact same subject nine years later, in 1999 with his new co-author, another KGB defector, Vasili Mitrokhin, in *The Mitrokhin Archive*.[5] This time Volkov was described in rather familiar terms: 'Among the most highly rated Soviet agents he revealed, were two in the Foreign Office (doubtless Burgess and Maclean) and seven inside the British intelligence system.'

However, instead of directly crediting Brook-Shepherd as the source of this (false) information, the authors cited *KGB: The Inside Story*, but did add the comment that 'The most reliable account of this episode is in Brook-Shepherd *The Storm Birds*, Chapter 4, which corrects a number of inventions in Philby's version of events.'

On the matter of the precise date of Philby's arrival, the mistake made in *KGB: The Inside Story* was repeated, with the assertion that he 'did not arrive in Istanbul until 26 September'. But compounding this relatively trivial detail is an item attributed to Mitrokhin himself who is alleged to have had access to Volkov's confession in Moscow. Supposedly, Volkov 'confessed that he had planned to reveal the names of no fewer than 314 Soviet agents. Philby had had the narrowest of escapes.'

It will be recalled that in his letter Volkov's figure of 314 is defined as Soviet agents in Turkey, including 'active agents and also agents on ice. On some agents there are official descriptions.' This account, and the reference to 'official descriptions' might be interpreted as official covers, thereby suggesting that Volkov was offering to compromise not only active and dormant agents, but NKGB personnel operating under various official covers. Whatever his precise meaning, the list of 314 would hardly have included Philby, who did not fit into either category. Accordingly, Mitrokhin's mistaken version of the Volkov episode appears to lean heavily on the errors made earlier by his co-author. This, however, would not be the end of the matter, for eleven years later Andrew returned to it again in *The Defence of the Realm*, published in 2010:

> As an indication of the importance of the intelligence he had on offer, Volkov revealed that among the most highly rated British Soviet agents were two in the Foreign Office (no doubt Burgess and Maclean) and seven 'inside the British intelligence system', including one 'fulfilling the function of head of a section of British counter-espionage in London', which was almost certainly a reference to Philby himself.

Thus Andrew thrice repeated the spurious figure of seven Soviet agents inside British Intelligence, but apparently he had not looked at any original documents, nor gone beyond Brook-Shepherd.[6]

Much the same happened with Ben Macintyre's 2014 biography of Philby, *A Spy Among Friends*, in which he embroidered further with the statement that Volkov had offered to sell 'a complete list of Soviet agent networks in Britain and Turkey':

> He would furnish the names of 314 Soviet agents in Turkey, and a further 250 in Britain; copies of certain documents handed over by Soviet spies in Britain were now in a suitcase in an empty apartment in Moscow.

Curiously, Macintyre[7] sources his information to Christopher Andrew and Peter Wright's *SpyCatcher*, but neither refers to 250 Soviet spies in Great Britain, nor to a suitcase crammed with compromising secret documents. In fact the detail about a suitcase came from *Their Trade is Treachery* in which Chapman Pincher reported that Volkov had said that he had deposited documents in a suitcase in Moscow and would provide an address and the key if the United Kingdom could arrange for his safe defection and the odd figure of 27,000 pounds – probably a conversion of some round sum in rubles – in cash.

Pincher's version, the only one to mention a suitcase, had been given to him in conversation with Wright, his undeclared co-author, in 1980.[8] However, Wright's subsequent controversial memoirs, co-authored by Paul Greengrass, contained a patently incorrect extract from Volkov's letter:

Judging by their cryptonyms, there are seven such agents live in British Intelligence and two in the Foreign Office, I know, for instance, that one of these agents is fulfilling the duties of head of a department of British Counterintelligence.

Wright, of course, working in remote Tasmania in 1983, had not been able to refresh his memory by consulting the archives, so he was wholly reliant on his imperfect memory, and his principal area of interest was the allegation relating to the spy described as a person who currently 'fulfils the duties of the chief of an otdel (department) of the English counter-intelligence Directorate in London'. Concerned about the accuracy of John Reed's original translation, Wright asked GCHQ to review the text, and the result was a slightly different interpretation.[9] In the new version, the sentence read 'I know, for instance that one of these agents is fulfilling the duties of head of a section of the British Counterintelligence Directorate.'

The implication was that whereas the original seemed to point towards Philby, who had been head of Section V, SIS's counter-intelligence branch, and then head of Section IX, the anti-Soviet section, the new version appeared to describe an acting head of an MI5 section, thus prompting the molehunters to widen their search for suspects into an entirely different organization. Whilst the investigation would prove inconclusive, there remains no explanation of what text Wright had relied on when compiling his autobiography.

The mystery, and the misrepresentation, would recur with publication of the paperback of Keith Jeffery's authorized history of SIS in 2011, *MI6: The History of the Secret Intelligence Service 1909-1949*, the original hardback released the previous year having omitted all references to the Volkov incident.[10] However, in the paperback the author added a fifteen-page postscript to cover the episode but inexplicably reverted to patently incorrect statement that Volkov had said 'the NKGB was running two agents in the Foreign Office'. '"The Russians", said Volkov, "had two agents inside the Foreign Office in London and seven inside the British Intelligence Service; who were passing information of great importance".'

Professor Jeffery had the benefit of a trawl through the archives of both SIS and the Foreign Office which revealed the existence of a memorandum from John

Reed, signalled straight to London and dated 4 September, to alert his superiors to his report to be entrusted to the diplomatic bag, and a summary, entitled *The Case of Constantin Volkoff,* dated around October 1945. In his account of the incident, Jeffery declares that in the absence of any surviving SIS documents, he had relied on previously unpublished internal Foreign Office correspondence; the Cyrillic original and the translation of Volkov's letter; John Reed's memorandum of 4 September and, finally, the October summary which included a contribution from SIS.

> What makes Jeffery's treatment so remarkable is his claim that Volkov's letter had offered 'a list of the known regular NKGB agents of the military and civil Intelligence' in Great Britain comprising 'about 250 known and less well known agents'.

A comparison with the original demonstrates that Jeffery's quotations are not only incorrect but entirely misleading in the context of the scale of Soviet espionage that Volkov could expose. By conflating Volkov's reference to British personnel known to the NKVD with a list of actual agents, he has effectively exaggerated the entire issue. This would not be of any lasting historical significance except that the Volkov letter would become one of the key pieces of evidence to support the continuing molehunts of the 1970s. Was Volkov referring to a traitor in SIS, in which case Philby was the obvious candidate, as he had himself assumed so eloquently in his memoirs, or was the culprit really deep in MI5? This was the central conundrum that would drive Peter Wright and his colleagues to a state of near paranoia, prompt the veteran *Daily Express* journalist Chapman Pincher to write three books arguing that MI5 had suffered high-level hostile penetration, but had covered up the scandal.

Liddell himself was sceptical on the subject of Soviet penetration, and his employment and even affection for Anthony Blunt, whom he engaged as his assistant in 1940, suggests a degree of naiveté, though probably nothing more sinister. Liddell knew of Krivitsky's description of the British journalist from a good family who had travelled to Spain, and was also aware of the Eton–educated Scot who had entered the Foreign Office, but his diaries show he was thoroughly taken in by Blunt, Burgess and Philby until it was too late.

In later years Liddell himself would be accused of having been a co-conspirator. Both the historian John Costello[11] and the author David Mure[12] opined that the Cambridge Five simply could not have survived from 1934 to 1951 without collusion at the top, and they believed Liddell to have been the best candidate, although Pincher would opt for Roger Hollis as a traitor after lengthy briefings from his co-author in *Their Trade is Treachery,* Peter Wright.

The precise identification of Volkov's spies is still moot. So much would hang on the translation of the specific words, which seemed to have slightly different meanings, but with great implications. So much depended on the words 'counter-intelligence Directorate' that three defectors, Igor Gouzenko, Vladimir Petrov and Anatoli Golitsyn, were invited to offer their opinions, and all three, being familiar with the NKVD's use of idiom, agreed on the translation that seemed to suggest the culprit was in MI5, not SIS. When Golitsyn addressed the issue, he recalled having met in 1958 a KGB *Soviet Kolony* (the local Soviet expatriate community) department officer, Andrei Sloma, who had participated in the Volkov abduction, an event that was kept immensely secret even within the organization.

In January 1962, soon after his defection in Helsinki, Golitsyn had been interviewed by two FBI officers, Birch D. O'Neal and Jean Evans, about the unresolved British cases:

> Birch and Evans questioned me in particular about British cases and we talked about George Blake, also asking me about Guy Burgess, Donald Maclean, Kim Philby, John Cairncross, Anthony Blunt and Igor Gouzenko's ELLI. Evans asked me about Konstantin Volkov's letter and its reference to an agent in British counter-intelligence, but this was news to me. I realized that this was important, but I had not heard of Volkov before and therefore could not assess the case. When asked about the 'Ring of Five', I replied that I only knew the identity of one member of the original 'Ring of Five', namely Henri Smolka, who had the cryptonym ALI. The story of British penetration was long and complex, and all the pieces needed to be put together and studied as a whole.[13]

Golitsyn spent years working on an analysis of the British cases, and visited England briefly in the summer of 1963 with his wife and daughter as part of his research when Arthur Martin was authorized to give him access to MI5 files. Based at the Imperial Hotel in Torquay, and an MI5 office in the Edgware Road in north London, Golitsyn reviewed the various molehunts then underway, and eventually confounded his hosts by identifying Guy Liddell as having been a long-term Soviet spy.

When word of the defector's visit leaked to the *Evening News*, and then the *Daily Telegraph*, which published an article about 'Anatoli Dolnitsyn' on 15 July 1963, Golitsyn flew straight back to Washington, leaving behind MI5 in turmoil. According to Golitsyn, who worked on his thesis for several more years before concluding that Liddell had been a KGB agent, the best explanation for the Burgess, Maclean and Philby imbroglio was that all three had benefited from a high-level source inside MI5, and that the explanation for way that Philby had been so catastrophically compromised was that an elaborate deception had been perpetrated to protect another well-placed asset, Guy Liddell. Golitsyn's analysis seemed so far-fetched that it would be rejected in its entirely by MI5, thus leaving the problem of hostile penetration of the Security Service unresolved.

Chapter V

BARCLAY and CURZON

Liddell hardly knew Donald Maclean, for they had met only once, in Washington DC in July or August 1944 at a dinner party hosted by the diplomat (Sir) Michael Wright. At the time Liddell was on a month-long visit to the United States, and Wright, then Head of Chancery, had shared his house at 6 Kalorama Circle in north-west Washington with Liddell's friend Bartholomew ('Barty') Pleydell-Bouverie and Peter Solly-Flood, both of SOE, and Maclean. That encounter was his only connection with Maclean, then head of the Foreign Office's American Department who had been placed under surveillance in London in April 1951 as he had emerged during a lengthy molehunt as the most likely candidate for the spy codenamed GOMER who was known, through the VENONA decrypts, to have betrayed six classified documents from the British embassy in Washington to the NKVD in 1944 and 1945.

The first clue to the existence of a highly-placed Soviet spy in the British Foreign Office came with the decryption of the New York–Moscow traffic in August 1944 which showed that the Washington DC *resident*, Anatoli Gromov, had received consignments of classified data of a political nature from HOMER, a source in the British embassy. Eventually HOMER was to be linked to GOMER, GOMMER and simply 'G', and identified as Donald Maclean, who had been posted to the United States early in May 1944. However, the first relevant text was sent on 2/3 August from Stepan Apresyan, then the acting *resident* in New York, Vasili Zarubin having been transferred to Washington, about British alternatives for the Allied plan codenamed ANVIL, the invasion of France's Mediterranean coast:

[149 groups unrecoverable] PART I The army [37 groups unrecovered] CAMBELL. The Committee is [2 groups unrecovered] on political and economic questions for drawing up instructions to Eisenhower and Wilson [1 group unrecovered] treaties on civilian questions of the type already signed with Holland and Belgium and the treaty with [4 groups unrecovered] on the PO [4 groups unrecovered] Army of Liberation [20 groups unrecoverable] the Allies [1 group unrecovered] the European Advisory Commission in SIDON [London] will [8 groups unrecovered] in CARTHAGE [Washington DC] are taking part in the work of the Committee. Almost all the work is done by GOMER who is at present at all the sessions. In connection with this work GOMER obtains secret documents [6 groups unrecovered] The ISLANDERS [British] [13 groups unrecovered] The TRUST [Soviet

Embassy] in Carthage [12 groups unrecoverable] work including the personal telegraphic correspondence of the BOAR [Winston Churchill] with CAPTAIN [President Roosevelt] [64 groups unrecoverable]

2. The LEAGUE [US Government] decided to force the ISLANDERS to alter the allocation of occupation zones in Germany in accordance with the existing plan of the European Advisory Commission. 6 weeks ago CAPTAIN informed BOAR that the COUNTRY [USA] wishes to detach minimal occupation forces [34 groups unrecoverable] would [2 groups unrecovered] involved in the complex political problems of European countries. BOAR replied that the ISLAND's vital interests lie in the North sea Belgium and Holland and therefore he was not in agreement with the stationing of occupation forces a long way from these areas. CAPTAIN did not agree with this argument. At this stage the ISLANDERS continue to insist on their plan.

3. In April Richard Law passed to the ISLAND's Government a memorandum written by the War Office and the Foreign Office setting out the ISLAND's policy with respect to the use of the Army in south-west Europe. The document divides the aims to be pursued into 'inescapable' and 'desirable'. The inescapable aims include the occupation by the ISLAND of the Dodecanese to prevent a struggle for the possession of these islands among Turkey, Greece and Italy. The use in Greece of a large enough force of troops to organize relief, the despatch to Greece of military units to support the Greek Government, the basing in Trieste of adequate troops to control the Italo-Yugoslav frontier and maintain order there, [51 groups unrecoverable] … ed Bulgaria, the despatch of adequate troops to Hungary to take part in the occupation, the despatch of troops to Albania to restore its independence which the British guarantee/d [15 groups unrecovered] leading role [37 groups unrecoverable] weeks ago GOMER was entrusted with the decipherment of a confidential telegram from BOAR to CAPTAIN which said that WILSON and the other generals of the ISLAND were insisting strongly on a change in the plan to invade the South of France, suggesting instead an invasion through the Adriatic sea, TRIESTE and then north-eastwards. BOAR supported this plan. From the contents of the telegram it is clear that BOAR will not succeed in overcoming the strong objection of CAPTAIN and the COUNTRY's generals.

Yesterday GOMER learnt of a change in the plans [4 groups unrecovered] and ANVIL will be put into effect possibly in the middle of August. Commenting on this argument [15 groups unrecovered] the aims that are being pursued by each: the ISLAND – for strengthening of her influence in the Balkans; the COUNTRY – the desire for the minimum involvement in European politics. [7 groups unrecoverable] it is clear that the COUNTRY [72 groups unrecovered] [4 groups unrecovered] about him and STEPAN refused to pass the documents to him in view of [22 groups unrecovered]. Then he had convinced himself [39 groups unrecoverable]

In two weeks' time on the agreement [38 groups unrecovered] [41 groups unrecoverable] insufficient indication was given [31 groups unrecovered]

This was followed on 10 August by a brief telegram from Apresyan in New York, referring to another text relayed from the mole:

Your No. 3608. GOMER's information was transmitted not in our words and without comments. It was transmitted in a condensed form word for word without any personal conclusions.

The next despatch from New York was a very short one, dated 5 September 1944, revealing that the Prime Minister was to meet the President in Canada within the week. This text was the subject of sustained cryptographic attack in 1947 and 1948, but initially it was not connected with the later traffic from Washington attributed to a spy referred to simply as 'G', for GOMER, which is HOMER in Russian:

According to information from GOMER, CAPTAIN [Franklin Roosevelt] and BOAR [Winston Churchill] will meet about 9th September in Quebec to discuss matters connected with the impending occupation of Germany. A detailed account of GOMER's report will follow. [12 groups unrecoverable].

Two days later Apresyan sent a further report from Maclean regarding British policy on the post-war structure of Germany and on the current situation in the Eastern Mediterranean, but the opening sentence, mentioning GOMER, was not solved until much later, in 1951:

[3 groups unrecovered] GOMER's report of 2nd September (the verbatim quotations from the report are in inverted commas):

1. In connection with the Anglo–American economic talks GOMER points out that 'in the opinion of the majority of the members of the British Government the fate of England depends almost entirely on America. They consider that England can remain a strong and prosperous power if he maintains the volume of her imports which she can do in two ways:
   1. By getting supplies from America gratis by DECREE [Lend-Lease] or otherwise.
   2. By restoring her exports to the required volume.

The immediate aim of the British Government consists in [12 groups unrecovered] will be delayed until the end of the war with Japan and also receiving permission [17 groups unrecovered] NABOB [Henry Morgenthau] to admit HEN-HARRIER [Cordell Hull] and others who concentrate on internal political difficulties. In negotiations with the LEAGUE [US Government] the British will advance the following arguments: [16 groups unrecovered] England and eliminate her as an economic factor but this [39 groups unrecovered] England, [70 groups unrecovered]'.

2. 'The question as to whether the north-western and southern zones of Germany will be occupied respectively by the British of the Americans has not yet been decided and will be discussed by CAPTAIN and BOAR at their meeting which, as far as I know, will take place at Quebec about 9th September. Besides this no decision has been taken on two fundamental questions:

1. Is it desirable to attempt to maintain Germany on a moderately high level of economic stability and well-being or should the armies of occupation let her starve and go to pieces?

2. Is it desirable to help Germany to maintain a single administrative [2 groups unrecovered] or should the armies of occupation do all they can to split up Germany into separate states?

Citing the [Sir William] STRANG documents which you know of, HOMER emphasises that the plans of the British, in large measure, are based on the opinion of the British Foreign Office. A sub-committee of post-hostilities planning of the British Chiefs of Staff issued a paper on 19th August, the authors of which [1 group unrecovered] the consideration from a military point of view of all the facts for and against the division of Germany into at least three states corresponding to the boundaries of the three zones of occupation and it is recommended that the Anglo-American armies of occupation should, as a first priority, [32 groups unrecoverable] divided Germany [25 groups unrecovered] undivided Germany would more probably get into [43 groups unrecovered] and England [25 groups unrecoverable]

The Americans have created a special commission with the powers of a government department to examine policy relating to Germany. Among the questions which it is to discuss are

'1. Should Germany be helped (for instance by the American occupation forces) to maintain or restore order and economic stability?

2. Should Germany be split up into separate states?

3. How should Hitler, Himmler and the rest, be dealt with, if they should be caught?

4. Should the Ruhr be internationalised?'

NABOB strongly opposes the first point and proposes letting economic ruin and chaos in Germany develop without restriction in order to sow the Germans that wars are unprofitable. The assistant to the head of the ARSENAL [War Department], McCloy, points out that such a situation would be intolerable for the army of occupation, and that the responsibility for some minimum of order [4 groups unrecovered] and so forth – NABOB obtained CAPTAIN's consent to the sue of yellow-seal dollars by American troops instead of military marks as had been previously agreed with the British and the Russians. The purpose of this is to turn the American military occupation forces into the economic masters of Germany. McCloy, LAWYER [Harry Dexter White], high officials in NABOB's establishment as well as the British, are opposed to this. The British and McCloy are trying to get CAPTAIN to revoke the decision. McCloy [4 groups unrecoverable] division of Germany averring that this attempt is doomed to failure. His views have some significance since he has direct access to CAPTAIN.

3. Under the influence of BOAR and [Sir Rex] Leeper, the British intend to set up and keep in power in Greece a government well-disposed towards England and willing to help her and hostile to communism and Russian influence. Their tactics consist in supporting the King as much as possible but also in leaning on the so-called liberal elements which might take the King's place if the opposition to him becomes too strong. For military reasons the British were forced to support EAM and ELAS to a certain extent.

In order to achieve their political ends the British intend to land a British division from Italy in Greece to keep Papandreou in power. As you know, this plan will be realised very soon. The LEAGUE regard the British intrigues in Greece with some suspicion and GOMER hopes that we will take advantage of these circumstances to disrupt the plans of the British and all the more so since the HUT [OSS] still supports EAM and ELAS.

4. After Comrade Stalin had refused to allow American aircraft to land on our territory [9 groups unrecovered] personal message suggested to the CAPTAIN that he should agree to [30 groups unrecovered]

Thereafter the GOMER traffic appeared to consist of entire British Foreign Office despatches. The first batch of three, sent on 29 March 1945, was a copy of a signal, designated No. 714 and dated 8 March from the British ambassador in Moscow, Sir Archie Clark Kerr, addressed to London, which was repeated to his counterpart in Washington, Lord Halifax, about the future of Poland. This, chronologically, was the first to be attacked by the American cryptanalysts based at Arlington Hall:

To the 8th Department
Material of GOMER. [66 groups unrecoverable] His Majesty and the Government of the USSR, acting jointly or separately, – a document, a draft of which was sent in my telegram No. 698. If the Soviet Government has not yet reached some final decision in regard to the work of the Polish Commission (and I think they have not) there is some advantage in a written [7 groups unrecovered] meetings of the Commission [2 groups unrecovered] provide at least its full and careful consideration. I do not think that Molotov, despite his stubbornness, has said his last word. I feel that we can still succeed in getting invitations issued to all or most of our nominees from Poland, provided we are sufficiently firm [217 groups unrecoverable]

This was followed by signal 2535 of 16 March 1945, from the Foreign Secretary Anthony Eden to the Washington embassy, copied to Moscow:

To the 8th Department
Materials of GOMER. I am transmitting a telegram of the POOL [British Embassy in Washington] No. 2535 of 16 March this year to the POOL.
Sent to Washington under No. 2535 of 16 March and repeated to Moscow.
SECRET
Reference telegrams from Moscow Nos. 823 and 824.

1. These telegrams arrived simultaneously with the President's messages to the Prime Minister (No. 718). The message shows that the President is still not inclined to support us in putting to the Russians all these questions, on which we consider it important to reach an agreement with them at this stage. From the Prime Minister's answer, transmitted in telegram No. 912, you can see that he is urging the President to reconsider his position in the light of the proposals now submitted by Sir A. Clark Kerr, after consultation with Mr Harriman.
2. As soon as possible please see Mr Stettinius and after that, if you can, the President and show them [2 groups unrecovered] to Molotov, suggested by Sir A. Clark Kerr and supplemented by my telegram No. 2537. You should take part in the decision of these affairs. Use all arguments at your disposal to induce them to make a concerted effort with us on the basis of this draft. We are convinced that only on such a basis will it be possible to establish a foundation for the Commission's work. We believe that if we and the Americans together take a firm position, the Russians very likely will give way on some of the points.
3. If you do not succeed in persuading the President to accept Sir A. Clark Kerr's draft as it stands, in my opinion you can induce him to send Mr Harriman instructions covering at least the more important points put forth by us. (From the Prime Minister's message you will see that the

point on which we cannot give way is the question of a truce). If this were done, I should be ready to instruct Sir A. Clark Kerr immediately to concert with Mr Harriman in making a communication on similar lines. We fully realize the urgency of this question.

On 30 March Anatoli Gromov transmitted the Russian translation of the Foreign Office signal No. 1517, dated 7 March from Lord Halifax to the Foreign Office, repeated to Moscow:

PART I
To the 8th Department
Materials of GOMER. I am transmitting a telegram of the NOOK [British Foreign Office] No. 2212 of 8 March to the POOL [British Embassy in Washington].
Sent to Washington under No. 2212 of 8 March and repeated to Moscow, CASERTA and SAVING in Paris.
Supplementary to my telegram No. 1018 to Moscow.

1. The rapid deterioration in the situation in Romania has already led us to support the demands of the US Government concerning the invocation of the Three [150 groups unrecoverable] objectives, enumerated in 'a – d' in the fourth paragraph of the Declaration. [2 groups unrecovered] assume that the word 'measures' includes the establishment of an appropriate organization along the lines, for example of the Polish Commission.
4. The second and wider interpretation is that the words 'joint responsibilities' in the third from the last paragraph of the Declaration, should be taken to mean that no signatory government is permitted to take unilateral action as regards matters mentioned in the Declaration, in any liberated European State or in any former Axis Satellite in Europe.

PART II This interpretation is supported by reference to 'joint action' in the Preamble to [57 groups unrecoverable] require, which presumably presuppose general agreement before joint assistance.

5. The first interpretation, set forth above, would naturally mean that any one government, according to the Declaration, could veto any action if it so desired. This interpretation of the Declaration would greatly impair the possibility of its use in situations such as that in Romania.
6. The second alternative interpretation is the only one, which gives us the chance to use the Declaration to prevent arbitrary imposition of minority rule under Soviet encouragement in countries occupied by Russian troops.
7. Any [1 group unrecovered] arising from this interpretation can arouse serious objection. Insisting on such an interpretation we run the risk of a

head-on collision with the Russians who certainly will refuse to accept any such restriction of their freedom of action.

8. Since the US Government is the author of the Declaration about liberated Europe, I [1 group unrecovered], without preliminary consultation and agreement with them [4 groups unrecovered] any definite view about the proper interpretation [117 groups unrecoverable]

Later the same day a further text was transmitted by Gromov from Washington, and although not directly attributed to GOMER, and lacking the familiar introduction of 'To the 8th department. Materials of GOMER', was on a similar topic:

[75 groups unrecoverable] questions, though there are some major differences of tactics. This morning a member of my department discussed this question at some length in the State Department. Set forth below [46 groups unrecoverable] on this question and considers it essential to get a clear definition of the basis on which the Commission is to work. The relevant paragraph of the Crimea communiqué should be taken for the definition of the functions of the Commission. It is essential that all three parties to the Commission constantly [2 groups unrecovered] purpose for which it was set up, namely: 'to consult with members of the present provisional government and with other Polish democratic leaders from Poland and from abroad with a view to reorganizing the present government ... on a broader democratic basis, with inclusion of democratic leaders from Poland and from Poles abroad.'

3. Invitation to Poles. The Commission must itself agree on lists of Poles who are to be invited for consultation. One cannot allow any outside organization to influence the composition of this list.

4. It is unnecessary to achieve a moratorium on political persecution in Poland. All Poles should now act in such a way as to create an atmosphere of freedom and independence, since only under such circumstances can [2 groups unrecovered] a representative government or conduct free elections (In this connection the State Department feels that the text of the draft note to Molotov, set out in your telegram No. 2078, is too sharp and shows too great a distrust of Soviet intentions in Poland; they entirely agree with those objectives which you set, but feel that we will gain nothing if we are too harsh at this stage; they are considering now the possibility of issuing instructions to Harriman – to make a demarch on similar lines, but somewhat softened down in tone; at the present time, in their opinion, it is inadvisable to face Molotov with a combined note on this subject).

5. Observers. The State Department learned with gratification that you for the moment do not intend to go ahead with your idea of sending [12 groups unrecoverable] Sir A. Clark Kerr to press for full facilities for sending

to Poland a somewhat lower level technical commission. The aim of this commission will be to gather first-hand information about conditions now pertaining there in so far as they affect the question of appointing a government and the later elections.

On 31 March 1945 the Washington *rezidentura* sent a telegram addressed to the 8th Department described as 'Material from GOMER. I am transmitting telegram No. 2536 of 16th March from the NOOK [British Foreign Office] to the POOL [British embassy in Washington DC], classified SECRET', which was another copy of Lord Halifax's signal of 16 March.

In chronological terms, the very first VENONA[1] in the series which referred to GOMER was from Stepan Apresyan in New York on 28 June 1944, in which he described the logistics of Vladimir Pravdin's connection with the spy, inferring that the case had originated in London:

Your No. 2712. SERGEI's [Vladimir Pravdin] meeting with GOMER took place on 25 June. GOMER did not hand anything over. The next meeting will take place on 30 July in TYRE [New York]. It has been made possible for GOMER to summon SERGEI in case of need. SIDON's [London] original instructions have been altered [34 groups unrecoverable] travel to TYRE where his wife is living with her mother while awaiting confinement. From there [2 groups unrecovered] with STEPAN [Pavel Fedosimov] [11 groups unrecovered] on the question of the post-war relations of the ISLAND [England] with the COUNTRY [America], France and Spain [16 groups unrecovered] on the ISLAND and material [8 groups unrecovered] on several questions touching the ISLAND's interests [6 groups unrecovered] our proposals that [20 groups unrecovered] GOMER [36 groups unrecovered] there.

Although this decrypt was fragmented, the reference to a pregnant wife helped MI5 isolate the source to Donald Maclean, who had been First Secretary at the British embassy in Washington, and whose wife Melinda had stayed in New York at her mother's Park Avenue apartment until the birth of their son Fergus by Caesarean section on 22 September 1944, having miscarried an earlier baby.

Maclean had sought and received special permission to make regular weekend visits to visit her in Manhattan and at his mother-in-law's country home at South Egremont, Massachusetts. As for the other final VENONA texts, the final versions were circulated in July and October 1965, with a significant paragraph recovered in May 1960.

The main item, which could have been used to extract a confession from Maclean if he had not fled from his home in Kent hours before he was scheduled to be interrogated, in May 1951, concerned the government in Poland after the liberation:

To the 8th Department
Materials from GOMER. I am transmitting a cipher telegram, no. 95 of 8 March, from the ISLAND's [England] embassy in SMYRNA [Moscow] to the POOL [British Embassy in Washington]:
Sent to the Foreign Office under no. 714 and repeated to Washington.

1. The US Ambassador showed me a telegram of 7 March, containing his recommendations to the State Department about the Polish Commission.
2. As a first step Mr Harriman recommended one of the following two courses:
   a) He and I, on instructions, should insist on the Commission accepting the principle that each of its members should have the right to name a reasonable number of individuals for consultation. This list at first should be small, but later, after preliminary consultations, it could be expanded.
   b) He and I should insist on Molotov accepting in the first place two of our nominees from London and two from Poland. In return for this, we will allow Molotov to invite one from each area and again reserving the right to expand the first list later, after preliminary consultations. Mr Harriman wants to insist on inviting M. Mikolajczck and M. Grabski from London, Professor Kutrzeba and one of the strongest among our other candidates from Poland. He agrees that Mikolajczck is the most important figure. Mr Harriman, however, considers that a certain amount of pressure should be brought to bear upon Mikolajczck so that within the next 48 hours he will issue a statement accepting without reservation the Crimea decision, even though not necessarily approving of it.
5. Mr Harriman suggests that possibly both of the above courses should be tried. In the event of their failure he put forward as a compromise a third course, inviting the Polish Provisional Government representatives first and listening to what they have to say, on condition that Molotov agrees, in writing, that after hearing the Polish Provisional Government each member of the Commission shall have the right to invite any democratic leaders from Poland or abroad whom he considers useful for consultation. The names of the candidates would be submitted direct to the Commission who would discuss them but if after discussion and investigation the individual commissioner still wished to extend an invitation he would be free to do so.

   Mr Harriman concludes that without contemplating a breakdown now we should pursue no course on which we should not be willing to rest our case if Molotov remains adamant.

When this particular VENONA series started to emerge in 1948 the British interest was immediately obvious, so the FBI's Washington Field Office consulted the two local British intelligence liaison officers at the embassy, Peter Dwyer from SIS and Dick Thistlethwaite who represented MI5 as the embassy's SLO. Both undertook to initiate an investigation in London into precisely who at the embassy four years earlier had been privy to the Foreign Office despatches quoted in the texts, but the enquiry seemed to take an interminably long time, and the FBI suspected the British of deliberate foot-dragging. The task of identifying retrospectively who among the embassy's 6,000 staff had seen the six telegrams, which had been encrypted on a one-time pad system, was complicated by a further series of VENONA decrypts concerning British Security Co-ordination (BSC), William Stephenson's wartime intelligence agency based in New York. The NKVD had shown much interest in an SIS officer, Alexander Halpern, who had headed BSC's Minorities Section since 1941, and the texts seemed to prove that Cedric Belfrage had been a fully recruited spy.[2] In addition, there were suspicions against a lawyer, Samuel L. Barron, and an Anglo-Czech, Trudie Rient.[3]

Although Belfrage was later identified as a Soviet spy, the culmination of an investigation codenamed SPEED, he was found not to have been in the United States at the right time, so could not have passed on the GOMER telegrams. The case against the elderly Halpern, a White Russian who had been a member of the Duma before the Revolution and had served as secretary to the Kerensky cabinet of Social Democrats, had originated in the analysis of two VENONA decrypts, one of which had been sent by Pavel Klarin on 21 June 1943:

The organisation 'British Security Co-ordination' is not known to us. We have taken steps to find out what it is. We will report the result in the next few days. We know Aleksandr Halpern. We presume that is he who is meant. Halpern has been reported on repeatedly by MARS [Vasili Sukhomlin], CAVALRYMAN [Sergei Kurnakov], OSIPOV [Prince Nikolai Orlov], UCN/9, SERES [Dr Ivan Subasic], KOLO [Sava Kosanovic] and an agent [12 groups unrecovered] (see paragraph [4 groups unrecovered] 283 and 355 [53 groups unrecovered] Kerensky was [1 group unrecovered] Council of Ministers [1 group unrecovered] October Revolution fled to England [11 groups unrecovered] his wife Salome [23 groups unrecovered] Halpern is one of the heads of the British COMPETITORS [Intelligence] here who for cover [1 group unrecovered] have a number of official posts in the INSTITUTE [4 groups unrecovered] post of assistant to Stephenson head of the BAR and organiser of the British Consulate. He apparently has contacts with the Labour Party. He is described as an enemy of the USSR. He has been admitted [4 groups unrecovered] with the INSTITUTE in CARTHAGE [Washington DC] and TYRE [New York]. He is conducting active work among Russian and all European [1 group unrecovered] He maintains contact with [1 group unrecovered] ER, the Social-Revolutionary Victor Chernov and [5 groups unrecovered] DUBOIS, the Hungarian 'UCN/41'. OTTO HA.. [60 groups unrecoverable] [24 groups unrecovered] is described as a person hostile to us. Please sanction [24 groups unrecovered]

The text appeared to suggest that Halpern was known to Vasili Sukhomlin, a member of the Czech Information Service in New York codenamed MARS, and that BSC, codenamed BAR, was heavily penetrated. However, it hardly incriminated Halpern who routinely had legitimate, declared contact with Soviet diplomats. Despite his friendship with Guy Burgess, and the fact that his wife Salomea, a former *Vogue* model, had expressed pro-Communist sympathies, he would be eliminated from MI5's shortlist of suspects. Halpern, who had been the legal adviser to the British embassy in St Petersburg, and had lived in London from 1918, working as a barrister, died there in July 1956, aged 77.

The second suspect, Gertrude ('Trudie') Rient, had an unusual background, as MI5 learned from one of her friends, the British diplomat (Sir) John Russell, in August 1949. Born in Czechoslovakia, she had acquired British citizenship through her marriage a fellow student at London University, Mandakolathur Vishvanatha Gangadharan, a Hindu from Madras. They had married and, having been employed as an aircraft engineer by the RAF, in 1932 he accepted a job in Moscow but was arrested in November 1937 and subsequently disappeared. Trudie was later informed that he had been executed as a spy, and she had then found a job as secretary to the United Press International bureau chief, Henry Shapiro. Eventually she was able to leave Moscow through the intervention of the US ambassador Laurence Steinhardt and her friendship with Zoya Litvinova, whose adopted father (and rumoured lover) was appointed the Soviet ambassador in Washington in December 1941. When Trudie was in Washington she was employed by SIS as Halpern's secretary, and encouraged to maintain her contact with Zoya. Meanwhile, she had also become Belfrage's girlfriend, the journalist later to be confirmed as a Soviet source. In May 1945 she was employed by the US Office of Strategic Services as a translator, and in January 1947 married Walter R. Mansfield, a divorcee and partner in General Bill Donovan's law firm. The son of Boston's mayor and a Harvard graduate, Mansfield acted as an OSS liaison officer with Tito's Chetniks in Yugoslavia, and would become a federal judge, The FBI's investigation of his wife cleared her of any suspicion but, nevertheless, the possibility of a spy-ring centred on Belfrage, who might have involved his girlfriend Trudie, and was known to have strongly recommended Barron as his replacement when he left BSC in December 1943, was taken very seriously, even if Barron had been rejected by BSC's Herbert Sichel.

When Belfrage came to the FBI's attention in November 1945, following Elizabeth Bentley's allegations, he was placed under surveillance and this led to a file being opened on Trudie who, it was reported, obtained a British passport in the summer of 1941 which she used to travel to this country. While in Moscow Rient was employed by the office of the United States Military Attaché. She was finally discharged from this position, the exact background of which is not known. Her employment extended over the period from October 15, 1940 to August 12, 1941. From individuals who knew her while in Moscow it has been learned that there is a strong suspicion that she was then working with the NKVD. She apparently acted as an agent provocateur by entering into conversations in an attempt to secure sympathy because of the disappearance of her husband. By criticising the Soviet regime, she attempted to have other individuals join her in this criticism, details of which she reported to the NKVD. She always seemed to have sufficient funds without working and on one occasion was permitted by the Russians to take over an apartment previously occupied by an NKVD agent. Physical surveillance determined that Belfrage spent the evening of January 19, 1946 in the company of Mrs Truda Rient.

During May, 1946, it was ascertained that Belfrage was greatly enamoured with Mrs Truda Rient and had asked her to marry him. The offer of marriage was declined.

On 2 May 1949, Liddell referred to Trudie as a suspect after receiving a briefing from his SLO, although without actually mentioning her name:

Dick Thistlethwaite has arrived for discussions about the Washington case and the material on which it is based. The important point which emerges is that the individual at the back of the operations in the United States was Anatoli Gromov, who I think at the time was an attaché at the embassy. The whole position with regard to the material in the United States is extremely delicate, since Carter Clarke, who is in control of it, is prepared to take quite a wide view of what concerns this country. Should the Office of Naval Intelligence become aware of this, and in particular Admiral Inglis, considerable complications might result.

Robert Lamphere of the FBI is handling the material in the FBI and is extremely co-operative. It is still not clear how the actual leakage from the British embassy occurred, but there is at least a possibility that the documents were obtained through Alexander Halpern's secretary.

Another candidate who looked a likely prospect for the mole was James MacGibbon, a CPGB member who had served on the Joint Services Mission in Washington between July 1944 and 23 June 1945. Born in February 1912, MacGibbon was a London publisher and proprietor of MacGibbon & Kee who had been called up in December 1939 and had served in MI3(c), partly as an interpreter in a PoW camp, until his transfer to the United States, embarking on 1 July. He would be ruled out, not as a Soviet spy but as the person responsible for this particular leak, when father research demonstrated that GOMER had been active before MacGibbon's arrival in Washington.[4]

The molehunt was necessarily time-consuming, being constantly distracted by false leads, given the necessity to trace and vet dozens of locally-employed staff who had worked in the chancery or had been employed in the cipher section or registry. Nevertheless, the issue was taken very seriously by MI5, SIS and the Foreign Office, as is demonstrated by a meeting held in London in May 1949, attended by Valentine Vivian, Dick Thistlethwaite and Maurice Oldfield from SIS, and Dick White and Arthur Martin from MI5:

2 Recent cryptographic work on Russian signal traffic between New York and Moscow covering the period from the spring of 1944 to January 1945 showed that Soviet Intelligence was interested in Halpern who they seemed to know was in charge of the minorities section of British Security Co-ordination. This traffic also shewed that steps were being taken to transfer the control of Soviet agents from New York to Washington and that this was effected in the autumn of 1944. This latter point is only significant in that the fact that the British Embassy telegrams in the possession of the Russians in March 1945 were transmitted from Washington does not necessarily mean that the telegrams leaked direct from the Embassy or an ancillary office in Washington. There was ample time for these telegrams to have been acquired in New York and sent to Washington for transmission.

3 It was emphasised that the interest shown by Soviet Intelligence in Halpern in 1944 as evidenced in the Russian signal traffic has not as yet provided anything to show that somebody else in his section was responsible for the leakage. It was agreed, however, that since Halpern's section did contain both before and during this case certain known suspects, intensive investigation into it should continue.

4 With regard to the Embassy itself there was little to report since investigations had been held up while awaiting the security clearance of certain members of the staff who were in the Embassy in 1945 and were still there. One of these, Miss Doyle, had however been questioned and it was clear from her replies that there were a number of serious weaknesses in the security of the Embassy, not only in regard to physical security arrangements but that the reliability of certain of the then members of the staff, in view of what has been revealed, was open to question and required further investigation.

5 MI5 stated that all names so far submitted to them had now been cleared and that subject to further clearance by local security authorities in Washington, they could now be questioned as and when necessary.

6 The next steps to be taken were then discussed. It was agreed that every possible care should be taken to preserve the somewhat tenuous liaison that had been established with the FBI and with the American Sigint

authorities, both of whom were providing valuable information. It was also pointed out that it was clear that this leakage was probably not an isolated case of purely British interest but was more likely to be part of a large Soviet Intelligence network in America and elsewhere.

7 Mr Hater stated that the security of British State secrets was obviously of the highest importance, and that the Foreign Secretary was most anxious to be satisfied that all possible steps had been taken to ensure that these leakages were not still continuing. Therefore while the Regional Security Officer would of course co-operate in every possible way with the MI5 and MI6 representatives in Washington so as to preserve our liaison with the Americans, Sir R. Mackenzie must proceed in the discreetest manner possible with his investigations in the Embassy and associated Missions in Washington.

When Dwyer and Thistlethwaite were replaced the following year by Kim Philby and Geoffrey Patterson, little progress had been made. According to Philby's mischievous version of events, the official attitude was that any number of people could have had access to the telegrams, and that the task of tracing the clerical and cleaning staff, who were considered the most likely candidates, was unproductive.[5] However, on 19 November 1949 Philby made a very impressive contribution to the search and minuted to Bobby Mackenzie a record of a suggestion he had made earlier in the day:

1. During our conversation this morning on the leakage of Embassy telegrams in 1944-45 I expressed a doubt as to whether we were justified in concentrating too exclusively on members of the subordinate staff or on persons with known Communist affiliations.

2. Shortly before the outbreak of World War II, General Krivitsky, whose name is well-known to you, stated under interrogation in the UK that there was a Foreign Office source reporting regularly to the Russians. This Foreign Office source has never, to the best of my knowledge, been identified.

3. I am speaking without the book and therefore cannot give you an exact account of Krivitsky's description of this source. To the best of my recollection, it included the following points:

   (i) The source was of 'good family'.

   (ii) He was educated at Eton and Oxford. (I believe that under further questioning Krivitsky retracted this definite statement and explained that he had simply intended to convey the meaning that his education was first-class.)

   (iii) He was young. (The impression left in my mind – though I cannot remember what exactly gave me the impression – was that he must have joined the Foreign Service in the early or middle thirties).

(iv) He was a regular member of the Foreign Service.

(v) In the late thirties he was stationed in the FO in London.

(vi) His motives for working for the Soviets was purely ideological.

(vii) He was working for the GPU representative in the UK who told Krivitsky about him. This accounts for the vagueness of Krivitsky's data (Krivitsky, as you probably remember, was a Fourth Department man).

4. The description would, of course, fit a very large number of persons in the Foreign Service; and it is a far cry from Krivitsky's statements in London in 1939 to the leakage from the Embassy in Washington in 1945.

But in case this disquieting possibility is overlooked, I thought it advisable to draw it to your attention.

5. I am sending my Head Office a copy of this note in case you pass its contents on to Carey-Foster. Both MI5 and my Head Office have copies of the Krivitsky report.

This novel proposition, made to the 12th baronet, Sir Robert Mackenzie of Coul, who was himself an Etonian and graduate of Trinity College, Cambridge, and had succeeded to his title in April 1935, would have a profound and lasting impact on the investigation and, with the benefit of hindsight, seems an extraordinary intervention from Philby. Krivitsky, the defector who had been found shot dead in his locked hotel room in Washington in February 1941, had proved himself to be a veritable human encyclopaedia of accurate information about Soviet espionage. He had provided numerous leads, one of which was his claim to have seen an SIS document entitled *Soviet Foreign Policy during 1936*, dated 25 February 1937. The report had not been circulated widely, so SIS's Valentine Vivian had realized at that time that there was a serious leak in Whitehall, although the culprit had never been identified.

Philby's suggestion that the molehunter should revisit Krivitsky's material gained a positive reaction from MI5, with Patterson reporting to London on 29 November:

During a recent discussion here on the Embassy leakage Mr. Philby recalled that General Krivitsky stated under interrogation in the UK that there was a Foreign Office source reporting regularly to the Russians. As far as I know this source has never been identified. We have not got a full copy of Krivitsky's statement in this office and we therefore have to rely on our memories.

Mr. Philby remembers that the source was described as of 'good family' and expensively educated; that he was young; was a regular member of the Foreign Service.

It is possible that we have been concentrating too much on the subordinate staff and that we should perhaps look around among some of the permanent Foreign Office officials, any of whom may have been stationed in Washington during the period in which we are particularly interested.

Philby's idea was then endorsed by Arthur Martin on 8 December who corrected Philby on one point of detail:

> Philby is correct in saying that Krivitsky gave us information on the lines of the first paragraph of your letter and that the source he described (who incidentally was not definitely said to have been in the Foreign Office) has never been identified. This source could, of course, have been responsible for the 1944 Washington leakage and the possibility has been borne in mind from the outset of the enquiry. We are not clear however why you think it should have influenced the steps we have taken beyond, of course, underlining the need for the utmost discretion in making enquiries within the Foreign Service.
>
> Other defectors have mentioned various Russian agents in British Government circles, always with inadequate details. All these stories have been looked into individually as they arose but B2(b) now intend to re-examine them as well. We do not anticipate that this re-examination will provide any new information directly affecting your investigations but B2(b) will doubtless keep you informed.

The helpful suggestion that Krivitsky's mole might be relevant was then taken up by the Foreign Office, reducing the number of suspects to a handful of senior diplomats, as George Carey-Foster acknowledged on 9 December:

> Reference Kim Philby's minute to Sir R. Mackenzie of the 19th November.
>
> I think it right to say at this stage that there is absolutely no evidence to connect the Washington case with the 'Imperial Council' story contained in Krivitsky's interrogation report. On the other hand, I have looked up certain of the Washington staff shown in the March 1945 List of Permanent and Temporary Staff at Washington of which you, have a copy. From the description contained in Krivitsky's report the person concerned could only have been on the diplomatic side, and I have looked at the particulars of the following; Balfour, Makins, Hadow, Wright, Gore-Booth. Maclean, Pares, Middleton, King, Everson, Russell, Stevens. Of these the following may he considered

Balfour	FO Jan. '37 to Aug. '40
	Washington March f45 to Sept. '48.
	(Note: FO List states April '45).
	Attached to College of Imperial Defence for the whole of 1937.
Makins	FO Sept. '34 to Aug. '40.
	Washington Jan. '45 to Feb. '47.

Hadow	FO Oct. '37 to Oct. '39.
	Washington Jan. '44 to June '48.

Wright	FO Jan. '31 to Oct. '36.
	Washington Jan. '43 to Nov. '45.

Gore-Booth	FO Oct. '33 to Apr. '36
	Washington Nov. '42 to Oct. '45.

Maclean	FO Oct. '35 to Sept. '38.
	FO June '40 to May '44
	Washington May '44 to Jan. '49

2. The dates of service of the foregoing fit in with Krivitsky's knowledge of leakages from the Foreign Office in 1936 and 1937 and with the known leakages in Washington in 1945. There is, however, no other connexion at all.

3. I do not know whether the Foreign Office copies of the proceedings of the Committee of Imperial Defence in 1936 and 1937 have ever been examined. It is possible that these were filed and there may be some evidence of how they were handled in the Foreign Office. If this has not been done, perhaps you would like me to look them out and see if anything can be discovered.

4. On re-reading the paragraphs of Krivitsky's report concerning the 'Imperial Council' information, I agree that it seems pretty definite that the information emanated from the Foreign Office. On the other hand, you may feel that it is worth considering the point I made at our meeting the other day about the College of Imperial Defence. I think perhaps it would be useful just to examine the lists of the permanent staffs in 1935, 1936 and 1937. Presumably you would be able to obtain these. The Foreign Office members were respectively Houstoun-Boswall, Helm and Balfour.

This was the first time that the Foreign Office had considered a possible connection between Krivitsky's information, provided during his interviews in 1940, and the culprit responsible for the Washington leak. The fact that it was Philby who came up with this brainwave is quite remarkable, and perhaps all the more surprising given that in February 1950 Dick White would try to terminate the entire enquiry:

1. Following our discussion on 31st January, 1950, into the case of leakage of Foreign Office telegrams in the United States in March 1945 we have reviewed the enquiries so far made and considered what further action might profitably be taken. Before setting out our conclusions we propose briefly to summarise the evidence so far obtained.

2. Top Secret sources show that, copies of six cipher telegrams, originated by or addressed to the British Embassy Washington, reached the Soviet Consulate in New York between 16th March and 29th March 1945. They were telegraphed to MGB Headquarters in Moscow under the reference 'Material G'.

3. All the compromised telegrams received the same standard Embassy circulation known as Chancery (special). Copies were made on a duplicating machine in the Embassy Distribution Room. Twenty copies were circulated among thirteen British departments, not all of which were in the main Embassy building; at least two, and probably more, spare copies were retained in the Distribution Room.

4. Enquiries made by the Foreign Office Security Department into the system for handling such telegrams have covered all but three of the recipient departments and show that the telegrams would have passed through a great many hands legitimately and would have been available to a great many more.

5. The names of all known US-based staff at the Embassy and in associated departments during the period of the leakage, have been checked against Security Service records. [XXXXXXXXXXXXXXXXXXX] We have investigated Barron in collaboration with the FBI but have obtained no evidence which firmly connects him with the leakage, or indeed with espionage.

6. Two other persons, both in the Minorities Section [XXXXXXXXXX] have records which suggest they might have been susceptible to recruitment by the MGB. The first, Alexander Halpern, is known from top secret sources to have been a target for recruitment by the MGB in 1944 but we have no evidence that he was so recruited and strong evidence that, at September 1944, he had not been. The second – Mrs Walter B. Marsfield, formerly Mrs. Gertrude Gangadharen, @ [alias] Trudi Rient, has been investigated by the FBI with negative results.

7. In our view, the fact which emerges most strongly from the enquiries already made is that the field for further investigation is so wide that there is no possibility of reaching a solution unless more data becomes available. Nor can we see leads which, if followed, might be expected to provide such data. We have, for example, considered the advisability of completing enquiries into the system for handling telegrams 'by examining the methods and personnel in the three recipient departments shown on the circulation list as 'G/Capt Birley', 'Colonel W. A. Howkins (JSM)'' and 'Mr P Healey'.

8. We have, of course, already confirmed that our records contain no adverse trace of these three persons. We feel that more detailed enquiries could only serve to show that the known or potential circulation was even wider than we already know it to have been and that, even supposing.it were

found that we had adverse traces of one or more of the hidden recipients in these three departments, it would still be quite impossible to identify that person or persons with the source of the leakage.

9. There is a further aspect to the making of such enquiries. In view of our responsibilities to the owners of the source and the fact that the spy may still be in the Government Service, it is more than ever necessary that, before any new person is admitted to the enquiry, we should have very strong grounds for believing that relevant information of real value can be obtained thereby. We do not see how this can be the case with the three persons mentioned.

10. Although, as I have said, we feel that, for the moment at any rate, direct enquiries of the kind we have had to make to reach the present point should cease, we nevertheless see good grounds for hoping that farther evidence may become available in the future. We believe that the best chance of a solution lies in the unravelling of the KGB espionage network in the United States, of which this leakage probably formed only a small, part. Active investigation at present being made by the FBI may in due course throw light on the network, from which it may be possible to lead back to this particular source.

11. There is also the possibility that the top secret source may be extended in the future, and so either provide more direct information open up new leads. For example if the top secret source were to clear Halpern of all suspicion – and it has already, cleared him up to September 1944 – we would certainly consider a direct request for his assistance.

12. Finally, we would add that although we advise against further direct enquiries into the Embassy leakage case in isolation, the continuous research work going on here into all current security cases and items of evidence which have a bearing on Russian espionage and on leakages, from British Government Departments, may also at any time may provide fresh leads.

Thus White's suggestion was that MI5's investigation should be suspended until either the FBI's pursuit of the atomic espionage network in the United States bore fruit or VENONA came up with more names. Considering that Philby had recently helped reduce the list of suspects down to just six officials, White's approach seems inexplicable. Whatever his motives, his suggestion provoked a strong reaction from Carey-Foster on 9 March:

You will remember that you attended a meeting in Mr. White's office to consider the stage reached in the investigation of the leakages to the Russians from the British Embassy in Washington.

I have now received the MI5 summary of this case and their ideas on what further action should be taken.

They sum up the case in the opening paragraphs of their letter. I have the following comments to make.

In paragraph 5 they state that all the United Kingdom based staff at the Embassy and associated departments have been checked against Security Service records. There remains, of course, the very large number of locally engaged staff, British, Canadian and American. These are in the process of being checked with the FBI by the Regional Security Officer in the Embassy. So far as is known, all staff that were in the Embassy and associated Missions in 1945 and are still there have been checked.

I do not quite follow the argument in paragraphs 7 and 8 of Mr White's letter, that because the field is wide it is not worth while investigating certain individuals who actually received copies of the telegrams known to have leaked. You will remember I made this point at the meeting. The Security Service argument goes on to say that even if adverse traces were found to exist amongst the immediate staff of these recipients, they, MI5, would not be able to identify the person or persons concerned with the source of the leak. Surely this must depend on the adverse trace and where further investigation leads. I do not see why they should write off the three recipients of the telegrams who have not so far been investigated.

The argument set out in paragraph 9 has held good throughout all our enquiries and is the reason why it is taking so long. We have taken the greatest care to ensure that the source is not compromised. The possibility that the spy is still in Government service is exactly what we are afraid of and why I propose to recommend that we cannot leave the enquiry exactly as it stands.

In view of the statements in the remainder of Mr. White's letter, I cannot help feeling that the Security Service are taking the easy line and hoping that identification of the source of the leakage will result from further examination of Top Secret sources on the lines of the successes obtained in the case of the Australian leakages and the Fuchs case. This is all very well, but we happen to know that the material which led to the discovery of this particular leak is extremely limited and although the Americans are continuing to study this material the effort devoted to it is relatively small.

My recommendations, therefore, are

(a) that we should report progress to the Permanent Undersecretary and, if thought desirable, to the Secretary of State. Their latest information on this case is dated 2nd March, 1949.

(b) that the Regional Security Officer in Washington should continue with the investigations in the Embassy so that we can be satisfied, so far as is possible, that leakages of this sort are not continuing. The steps already taken to improve the security of the Embassy should be mentioned in the report to the Permanent Under-Secretary.

(c) that we should reply to the Security authorities telling them that we are not entirely satisfied with their arguments for letting the case rest without fully investigating the known recipients of the telegrams, and that we reserve our right to continue with the investigations inside the Embassy.

The three recipients of the telegrams not so far examined are mentioned in paragraph 8 of Mr White's letter. Whether or not the Security Authorities make any further enquiries about two of these people who were members of the Service Missions is a matter I suppose for them to decide. We have made sure as far as it is possible to do so that the British Joint Staff Mission is secure now and that there is a strict control of the copies of Foreign Office telegrams which they receive to-day.

The third recipient, Mr P. Healy, who has not so far been investigated, was a member of the Embassy staff and we must try to discover more about him and who else in his immediate circle handled the telegrams. I consider that the Regional Security Officer should do this in his further investigations in the Embassy.

Sir William Strang, the Permanent Under-Secretary at the Foreign Office, shared Carey-Foster's dismay, as he made clear on 30 March:

MI5, who have been assisting in these investigations, have summed up the case in the letter of the 16th February in which they say that, since the field is so wide, they do not think that any further enquiries can usefully be made until further data become available. They hope that new facts may emerge either from present FBI investigations into Soviet espionage in the USA or from new Sigint information.

While new leads may turn up eventually, it is nevertheless unsatisfactory from our point of view to leave the case like this. Mr Carey-Foster thinks, and I agree, that we must do all we can to satisfy ourselves that the spy is no longer in our employment and that the leakages are not continuing. We can hardly say that we have done everything possible, so long as we have not at least found out all we can about all the people who are known to have received copies of the telegrams in question.

Of the 20 people to whom the telegram was officially circulated, three still have not yet been investigated. Two of these were in the Service Missions, and one, Mr F. Healey, was employed in the Embassy. He is no longer employed under the Foreign Office, and at present we know nothing about him except that MI5 have no unfavourable information about him, nor do we know who were the people employed under him and who are likely to have seen his copy of the telegram. We cannot therefore yet be certain that no one who worked under him is still employed by us.

While it is presumably for MI5 to decide whether they pursue the investigation of the other two outstanding recipients I think we ought at least to complete our own investigation by going as thoroughly as we can into Mr Healey and those who worked with or under him. It is true that the odds are against this leading to anything useful, but we should certainly look rather foolish if it subsequently came out that the individual responsible for these leakages was still employed under the Foreign Office, and that we had failed to investigate every one of the known recipients of the telegrams who was employed under the Foreign Office at the relevant time.

I do not think that there is anything in the arguments used in paragraphs 7–9 of Mr White's letter of the 16th February which should preclude us from completing our own investigation, so far as we still can. We have of course always exercised the utmost care in our enquiries to safeguard the source, and we shall continue to do so.

I would therefore propose, if you agree, to inform Mr. White that we propose to instruct the Regional Security Officer at Washington (Sir R. Mackenzie) to find out what he can about Mr Healey and any members of the latter's staff who are likely to have seen the telegrams in question.

* * *

When Geoffrey Sudbury joined the Eastcote BRIDE team in early 1950, his first priority was GOMER having been told by Wilfred Bodsworth in strict confidence that Klaus Fuchs had been identified by a decrypt, and this target was just as important. It was only when enough of Apresyan's message of 28 June 1944 succumbed to Bodsworth's prolonged cryptographic attack, on 30 March 1951, that it was transformed into a smoking gun with Donald Maclean the obvious suspect, and the urgent news was transmitted to MI5. Impressed by what Bodsworth had achieved, his American counterparts sent a congratulatory telegram 'dazzled by your brilliance'.

While the investigation in London was handled by MI5 there were three people at the embassy who conducted the investigation in Washington. They were the embassy security officer, Sir Robert Mackenzie, the MI5 SLO Geoffrey Patterson, and Philby. Their objective was to narrow down a field of suspects to one individual, and Philby played a central role in the molehunt, as is clear from the minutes of a meeting held at the Foreign Office on 11 September for which he flew back to London to attend:

(a) It is by no means certain that 'G' was the source of all 'the information in the Russian telegram; the telegram may be a summary of information from many sources.

(b) The statement that Roosevelt's telegrams to Churchill were routed through Foreign Office channels is almost certainly inaccurate. Mr

Carey-Foster said that he believed Churchill–Roosevelt telegrams passed by US Naval charnels in both directions. The Security Service undertook to check this point in records at 10 Downing Street.

It was agreed that, since the evidence so far obtained indicated that the source might equally well be American or British, the FBI should be informed of the findings set out in the memorandum. The SIS and Security Service representatives in Washington were asked to inform the FBI on their return to Washington. The Security Service undertook to provide them with a suitable brief.

It was pointed out that since the Head of the Cipher Room in the British Embassy, Washington, in 1944, would normally have been responsible for deciphering Churchill/Roosevelt telegrams the phrase 'was entrusted with' could scarcely be applied to him and that therefore he might safely be questioned. While there was general agreement that this step would be desirable in due course, it was felt that more information should first be obtained about the identity of the compromised documents. Accordingly it was agreed that:

(a) The Security Service should continue the search for papers concerning the apportionment of occupation zones in Germany.
(b) The Security Service should keep in close touch with GCHQ in order to identify the telegram concerning General Wilson and a change of plan.
(c) The Security Service should discover to whom, besides the Foreign Office, information copies of Churchill/Roosevelt telegrams were sent.
(d) The Foreign Office should discover the circulation given to the memorandum on 'British interests in SE Europe' (FO reference U/2769/491/ dated 17th April 1944) within the British Embassy, Washington.
(e) The Foreign Office should continue their efforts to compile a staff list of the Cipher Room in the British Embassy, Washington, in August 1944.

This top-level gathering included Valentine Vivian from SIS, Dick White, Geoffrey Patterson and Arthur Martin from MI5, and Mackenzie and Carey-Foster from the Foreign Office, but showed that by this date, September 1950, the field was still wide open, with no favoured suspects and a daunting challenge represented in part by the need to name, trace and vet the nearly fifty staff who had worked in the embassy's cipher room. Indeed, the problem of matching precisely which telegrams appeared in the VENONA decrypts had not even been solved. At this stage, when Philby had been *en poste* for almost a year, this huge but necessarily secret investigation was a major preoccupation for the trio based in Washington but a few months later, in an extraordinary, counter-intuitive contribution to the enquiry, perhaps as part of a double-bluff, Philby made these suggestions to his Chief on 2 April 1951:

2. You cannot fail to have been struck by the similarity in style and content of the telegrams sent from New York to Moscow on August 2/3, 1944 (Nos. 1105-1110) and on September 7, 1944 (Nos. 1271-1274). The August telegrams were based, in part or in whole, on information from G; the September telegrams were a summary of information from GOMER. It is difficult to resist the conclusion that G is the same agent as GOMER, and that the two sets of telegrams are parts of a single intelligence operation.

3. There is one small point, the significance of which may have escaped you: Telegram 915 of June 28 from New York to Moscow shows that GOMER kept a rendezvous on June 25, and that another rendezvous was arranged in New York for July 30. Both June 25 and July 30, 1944 were Sundays, Telegrams 1263 of September 5 and 1271 of September 7 show that GOMER wrote a resume dated September 2, which was in Russian hands by September 3. September 3, 1944 was a Sunday.

4. It is also worth noting that telegrams 1105-1110 were despatched three to four days after the meeting arranged for GOMER on July 30, and that telegrams 1271 and 1274 were despatched four days after September 3.

5. A further coincidence is that June 25, July 30 and September 3 are separated by five-weekly intervals.

6. While our information is still fragmentary, and while the above line of thought involves certain if's and but's, a picture beginning to, emerge of an operation involving regular though well-spaced meetings in New York. These meetings took place at weekends. The inference is that; the agent could only make contact in New York at weekends, an inference which strengthens the already strong reasons (content of the messages, etc) for supposing the agent was normally stationed in Washington.

7. We are considering the possibilities of obtaining information about movements of Embassy personnel for the period under review (e.g. rail and air fares were normally booked through the Movements Officer). It may also be significant that GOMER handed over nothing on June 25. This might indicate that he was absent from his post during the immediately preceding period. Alternatively, it might be that this was his first contact in America.

8. Material G, which reached the Russians in March 1945, deserves some consideration in connection with the above. While G and GOMER delivered summaries of information based on their own knowledge, material G represented straight-forward filching of Embassy documents. A possible explanation of this difficulty may rest in the fact that Anatoli Gromov arrived in Washington on September 19, 1944, and we know from telegram 1389 on October 1 from New York to Moscow that certain duties were passed by New York to Gromov. It is possible that GOMER was also passed over to Gromov, and that GOMER was therefore able to

transmit to Gromov locally originals of documents that he would have hesitated to take to New York. With a contact in Washington, he could have delivered the documents at night and received them back early the following morning.

9. It is also of some interest to note that Gromov was attached to the Russian Embassy in London from November 1936 to January 1944. It is conceivable that one of the reasons for his move from London to Washington via Moscow, was the transfer of GOMER from, say, the Foreign Office in London to the Embassy in Washington. The date of Gromov's move might therefore give some clue as to the date of GOMER's.

10. Please forgive me one more flight of fancy before I conclude. To the best of my recollection, the 'Foreign Office source' mentioned by Krivitsky was run by Paul Hardt of the GPU. Hardt left London in June 1937. Gromov we know to have been in 1944 an officer of the MGB, the lineal descendent of the GPU. Therefore, would it not be plausible to suppose that Hardt spent the seven months between the arrival of Gromov and his own departure in handing over to Gromov his contacts, including the 'Foreign Office source'?

11. I have discussed the contents of this letter fully with SLO and the Embassy Security Officer. If you consider it worthwhile you will presumably show it to MI5 and the Foreign Office Security Officer.

Whilst it might have been expected that Philby would have taken the opportunity to muddy the waters, or resort to outright sabotage, to protect Maclean, he appears to have done the exact opposite. Indeed, in this thoughtful analysis he made several points which would prove crucial to the identification of Maclean. Firstly, Philby linked the Russian source 'G' to GOMER. Secondly, he connected G to regular weekend travel between Washington and New York, drawing attention to three specific Sundays, and thirdly he suggested a connection between the spy mentioned by Krivitsky during his debriefings in 1940, Paul Hardt, the alias adopted by the illegal *rezident* Theodore Maly, and Gromov's maybe not-so-coincidental transfer from London to Washington. These were all clues that turned out to be entirely accurate, and would help finger Maclean.

It may be that Philby had already decided that Maclean was doomed, so he might as well cover himself by demonstrably playing an active part in his exposure. Maclean, of course, had been posted to Washington in May 1944 and returned to London in September 1948. If that was Philby's plan, it seems to have worked to some extent, as SIS would later cite his assistance as evidence of his loyalty.

Philby's apparent speculation about Gromov's involvement was probably well informed, but definitely risky. In fact Gromov's real name was Gorsky, and he had served as acting *rezident* in London between 1938 and February 1940, and then as *rezident* from December 1940 to 1943 when he had been recalled to Moscow for his new assignment to follow Donald Maclean to the United States, where he had arrived on 18 September 1943. He was to remain in Washington DC as *resident*, replacing Vasili Zubilin, until January 1946, and he next turned up in Tokyo as head of the local Soviet Trade Delegation.

As the field of suspects narrowed, the SLO became increasingly excited, and noticed what appeared to him to be a close match to the Krivitsky profile, as he reported to London on 3 April:

> At the risk of boring you with what is really speculation at this stage, I thought I might contrive to keep you up to date on how our minds are working at this end.
>
> Since writing to you yesterday we have been pursuing the train of thought outlined in paragraphs two and three of my last letter. Who would fit in with the following movements and requirements?
>
> (a) be Eton and Oxford.
> (b) be 'young' at the time Krivitsky made his statement.
> (c) be in London in the latter thirties.
> (d) be in Washington in 1944–45.
> (e) be of such a calibre that the Soviets would accept his opinion.
> (f) be worried (probably) and (again probably) have wife with him in Washington.
> (g) be in such a position in the Embassy as to have an overall picture of the political and economic situation, particularly as applied to Germany and Europe.
> (h) be able to have access to, and perhaps have something to do with deciphered telegrams.
>
> A name which fits in with all the above is that of Paul Henry Gore Booth, now Director General of British Information Services in this country and a Counsellor at this Embassy. Mackenzie tells me that Gore Booth joined the Foreign Office in 1933 and I believe he served there until going to the Far East in the late thirties or early forties.
>
> He was here in 1944 and 1945.
>
> As far as I know we do not know that the Soviets followed any particular pattern in allotting cover names. They are liable to be misleading as well as, on occasions, helpful. However, one cannot overlook the fact that a spy master might possibly find it easy to give the name GOMER to somebody called Gore. In following this tack I might add that Gore Booth is a classical scholar – I believe he was head boy at Eton – and for all I know he may be an expert on HOMER!
>
> Mackenzie and Philby are putting this theory to their respective bosses and, even if it is wild speculation, I thought you should know this. I do not

wish to cause you too much consternation, but you will remember that Gore Booth attended Carey-Foster's initial meeting, in February 1949, at which this case was discussed and, I believe, at which the source was blown. DB was also present.

Other persons who might fit the requirements mentioned in paragraph three above would be Michael Wright, Head of Chancery in 1944-45, and possibly Donald Maclean.

It is interesting to note that in Michael Wright's absence from the Embassy Gore Booth acted as Head of Chancery and would then have the duty of deciding how DEYOUS were to be deciphered

I believe Gore Booth is leaving in the near future for a period of leave and duty in the UK. The FO will no doubt give you details.

I do hope that our speculations neither confuse you – nor the issue!

Patterson's enthusiasm for Gore-Booth as a Soviet mole may have been influenced by his suspect's relative unpopularity among the embassy staff who regarded the teetotal non-smoker as a somewhat austere, aloof Christian Scientist. This telegram received short shrift from James Robertson at Leconfield House who replied four days later:

We think this is genuinely helpful but at this stage consider enquiries … should not be confirmed to preconceived theories but cover all Chancery, cipher and registry staff. Feel sure you will agree and exercise moderating influence on premature speculations.

However, at the Foreign Office there was a rather more encouraging reaction from Carey-Foster, who was obviously rather shocked by what he had read:

Thank you very much for your most interesting and useful letter of the 3rd April. I had just heard about this new material and we are considerably disturbed that this should have been in existence all this time without our knowledge. We wonder how much more is lying about in Washington.

2. On the receipt of your letter of the 29th November, 1949, I had made a similar analysis to that which you have now made, based on periods of service in the Foreign Office and Washington. I decided that on the basis of the Foreign Office list, which is not always precisely accurate, the following names should be considered: Balfour, Makins, Hadow, Wright, Gore-Booth, Maclean.

If we eliminate certain of these on the grounds of the more detailed information supplied by Krivitsky it boils down to Balfour, possibly Makins, and Gore-Booth. Again on the basis of Krivitsky, one would have thought we could eliminate Balfour and Makins on account of age. This therefore leaves Gore-Booth.

The foregoing analysis, which agrees with yours, simply indicates the most likely suspect on the assumption that the Krivitsky agent is identical with agent G. we have, however, no, repeat no, evidence that this is so.

3. A quite separate analysis recently made here by MI5 and prior to the receipt of the new material, based entirely on evidence collected as a result of our joint investigations of the Washington case only, suggests that the culprit is to be found among the junior members of Chancery plus George Payne. The further material now available strengthens the MI5 case. This does not of course mean that we should ignore the analysis based on the Krivitsky material. On the contrary, it gives a strong indication of where the process of elimination should start.

4. I enclose for your information an extract from the Record of Information obtained from General Krivitsky during his visit to this country, January-February 1940. I think you will note that there are some further points of interest, in the index to the Record of Information there is the further point against the name 'Percy' in the list of Soviet secret agents mentioned by General Krivitsky. It is stated that Krivitsky 'cannot disassociate the name of Percy with the source of leakage of the CID material'.

5. I have discussed this with MI5. We consider that you might take further action on these lines: we agree that you should draw the travel files as you suggest, but it would be as well if you could arrange for these to be drawn by Jones so that you do not show a direct interest in them. If you get hold of them, I presume it is your intention to try to find out which members of the staff, particularly of Chancery, made frequent journeys to New York. Do you think you could also draw some of the relevant Chancery files in order to identify more precisely the work on which each member of Chancery was engaged? This should cover all the junior members of Chancery below Michael Wright.

6. We are endeavouring to identify at this end some of the documents which must be concealed with the information contained in the new material. We do not wish you to be bothered with that aspect. You might, however, care to see if you can identify the special commission with the powers of a Government department which was created by the Americans and which is referred to in the third part of telegram No. 705.

Meanwhile, Arthur Martin had reached some conclusions about Maclean: and on 12 April sent a signal to Patterson:

Carey-Foster has written Mackenzie asking priority to be given to searching Maclean's travel records.

2. Maclean now considered top suspect. Besides BRIDE evidence, mental breakdown in May 1950 reflects severe nervous strain cause of which he seemed anxious to conceal.
3. He also fits Krivitsky data in all important respects.
4. Please do not repeat not inform FB I yet of these suspicions.
5. Reference para 1. While giving priority to Maclean, travel records still required for other suspects.
6. Telegraph estimated time required for reporting on Maclean.

This was a turning-point in the investigation and the first time that Maclean had been mentioned anywhere as MI5's top suspect. However, Patterson still regarded Gore-Booth as the best candidate, and when he went to see the FBI's Bob Lamphere the following day, he was conscious that Hoover might want to intervene, as he reported to London:

When I visited Lamphere today he asked me casually whether we had ever given the FBI a copy of Krivitsky's statement about the source in the Foreign Office. I told him I did not know and that there was no copy in my office. He then said that he would make enquiries within the Bureau to see what they had.

Lamphere also mentioned Paul Hardt. I think we can assume that Lamphere's mind is running along parallel lines to our own and that it will not be long before he asks us which members of the Embassy fit in with Krivitsky's description. By a process of elimination he will probably end up with the same conclusions as we have. I should add that neither Philby nor myself has mentioned to the FBI our latest suspicions (the subject of my letter of April 3rd), for the obvious reason that the body is still physically here and I do not want the FBI to jump to premature conclusions and begin to get excited.

I thought I should warn you of this latest development because the situation may become rather delicate vis a vis our American friends. Unfortunately, my information that our favoured candidate was returning home in the near future appears to be incorrect. I had hoped that he might be at home before Lamphere pin-points him.

The competing suspicions crystallizing around Maclean and Gore-Booth were dealt with at a meeting in the Foreign Office on 17 April attended by Arthur Martin, Dick White and James Robertson from MI5, and Carey-Foster and Pat Reilly, at which it was agreed that:

1. Enquiries should be pursued at the discretion of the Security Service concerning the political sympathies of both Gore-Booth and Maclean

before they joined the Foreign Service, It was suggested that relevant papers would be available to the Civil Service Commissioners.

2. Enquiries should be pursued concerning the movements and habits in the United States of both Gore-Booth and Maclean. It was agreed that in the first instance these enquiries should be confined to an interview with Michael Wright to be undertaken by the Foreign Office. The Foreign Office asked, and the Security Service agreed, that until Wright had been interviewed no information and no request for assistance should be passed to the FBI.

3. Investigation should be made by the Security Service, the extent of which should be left to their discretion, into the current activities of Maclean.

4. It was agreed that if at a later stage it should become necessary to interview the source of the report that Maclean had admitted to being a member of the Communist Party, there would be no objection to this course of action. The Foreign Office will arrange the interview.

It was at this stage that MI5 adopted the codename CURZON for Maclean, and he became the focus of attention. According to Maclean's PF, Ronnie Reed imposed a telecheck, numbered 1214, on the telephone at Beaconshaw, Tatsfield 352, on 18 April and Reed noted that 'I am not for the moment applying for a letter check, as I would like to see what extent the telephone check is productive before doing so.'

Physical surveillance by the Watchers, led by David Storrier, commenced on 27 April but could not be extended beyond London. Maclean usually travelled by train from Victoria either to Oxted, Woldingham or Upper Woldingham on the Sevenoaks line, but sometimes took the Greenline bus from Eccleston Bridge. Meanwhile, MI5 was wrestling with the problem of what to impart to the FBI, as Patterson explained to headquarters on 1 May:

I saw Lamphere yesterday and again today and he tells me that they are now giving priority to this case. Now that Fuchs, Rosenberg, Gold and others have been disposed of the man we are now seeking to identify would seem to be the most important spy, as revealed by the source, who is as yet unidentified. Therefore, to use Lamphere's words, 'the Bureau want action'.

I understand that this 'action' will take the form of a review of all available information plus enquiries at the State Department. The Bureau will, I think, try to draw all State Department files which might contain the information on which the messages were based. They also hope to discover which members of this Embassy were present at certain meetings, or perhaps served on committees, with members of the State Department. They may start with Western Europe, Greece, the dismemberment of Germany, etc., in the hope that they may find copies of letters or minutes which may be more or less identical with the information available to us. I should add that I know this unofficially.

This research at the State Department may take some time, but it is possible that the Bureau will come up with a few names of people, for instance, Gore-Booth and Donald Maclean, who were at that time in constant touch with their American opposite numbers on matters which we know were of interest to the MGB. The Bureau are, in fact, doing what we are doing and hope to find out who had access to the relevant information.

Lamphere agrees with me that the culprit, or one of them, could he an American official, but he is still looking towards the British Embassy as the home for this spy. He asked me yesterday if I could definitely rule out Alexander Halpern, and I told him that although I could not be as conclusive as that it seemed unlikely, on available evidence, that he could have been the culprit. Halpern could of course have been shown some of the signals during his frequent visits to the Embassy and he may have known Pravdin. But the rest of it does not fit in.

I am keeping in close touch with Lamphere and thus hope to know in advance of official notice how their investigations are proceeding.

MI5's dilemma was what to tell the FBI, and when, but the indecision placed Patterson in a difficult position. On 5 May Carey-Foster expressed his anxiety to Mackenzie:

Ml5 have not yet heard from Geoffrey Patterson and I wonder if it is possible for you to let me have your own views on the risks of the Americans uncovering the agent, assuming the latter to be British.

3. We have reached the point here when a decision has got to be made whether we should tell the Americans of the position we have reached in our investigations and, if so, when should we tell them. Eastcote have been working hard on the source material and have unravelled a further piece of information which appears to refer to the agent. They cannot get any further without getting collateral from the Americans but do not wish to pass the results of their work to Arlington Hill for fear that they would immediately go to the FBI and result in intensive enquiries on the latter's part. On the other hand, they cannot hold up indefinitely passing the results of their work to the Americans.

4. MI5 do not themselves wish for any assistance from the FBI in regard to their enquiries, but are chiefly concerned that any enquiries that the Americans have already instituted may have led them to the same conclusions that we have reached, with the possibility that the Americans might forestall us by indicating to us a short list of suspects. MI5 are therefore in favour of Eastcote giving Arlington Hall the results of their work, and that simultaneously the FBI should be told the results of our investigations to date, with a request that they should take no action and should certainly not tell the State Department. As you can see, there

is some danger here since one of the principal suspects is head of the American Department in London, and if this is clear to the FBI it would probably be difficult to restrain them from bringing the case to a head.

5. There is still a further possibility and that is that MI5 should interrogate Maclean, as soon as they can prepare their case. The earliest that would be is something like two weeks. There are certain obvious risks and disadvantages in this course, particularly if it is completely unsuccessful. On the other hand, if it is successful the advantage of it would be that the United Kingdom authorities would have a much better control of the subsequent situation vis-a-vis the Americans, even though the latter might make some difficulties since the offences took place in America and involved some American information.

6. The only other course possible is to do nothing and hope that something will turn up as a result of our investigations, but this is where I want your opinion as to what the Americans are doing and the likelihood of their forestalling us. As I have told you, Roger Makins will have reached Washington by the time you get this letter. I had a brief discussion with him before he went and told him that we were reaching a point where we would have to decide whether or at to bring in the Americans. Naturally he did not have time to give much consideration to it, but he was of the opinion that we should adopt the course referred to in paragraph 5 above.

I should be grateful if you would discuss this matter with him in view of your own knowledge of the position in America, and let me have your joint views as soon as possible, as we are about to put the case up for decision to William Strang.

Carey-Foster's position was supported by Patterson who reported on the same day that he was scheduled to jointly brief Roger Makins with Philby on the following day:

It is clear that a decision will soon have to be made as to when, and how much, we should tell the Americans of the progress we have made on the case. Carey-Foster gives your views in paragraph 4 of his letter to Mackenzie. Mackenzie and I hope to meet Sir Roger Makins tomorrow to discuss the matter thoroughly; Philby may also be present. The decision that will have to be made is clearly of the greatest importance because the repercussions of the Americans, should we be able to prove that the culprit is your chief suspect, will surely be violent and embarrassing politically.

From the point of view of MI5-FBI relations I feel that it is important that we should not give Mr. Hoover cause to think at any stage that we are deliberately withholding information from him.

If he is personally convinced that co-operation between the British authorities and the FBI has been complete he can at least say this when the politicians begin to blast HMG. But if he suspects that it has not, he can add his considerable weight to the arguments against us and this would react unfavourably on our own relationship.

It would seem to me to be a matter of (a) timing and (b) in what form we present the information to the Bureau.

As regards (a) I hope the information contained in my Wash/35 of May 7th was of some use. Lamphere told me (off the record) that he was experiencing some delay in obtaining the files he wanted because the State Department were in the process of moving their records. I cannot discover how long the delay may be. He is also still thinking in terms of Halpern and Robert Fisher. As your chief candidate was never suspect here (as far as I know) and has never been mentioned by me there is no obvious reason why Lamphere should pin-point him unless he receives further information either from Arlington or from us. A study of the State Department files may cause Lamphere to place our man among the list of suspects, but he should not be in a position to do this immediately.

Lamphere continually asks me what progress we have made with our study of local files and if London has yet been able to come to any conclusions. I have implied that locally we are under some limitation and cannot, for obvious security reasons, draw all the files we want from the Embassy Registry. I have also implied that a great deal of research will have to be done on available Foreign Office records in London before we will be allowed to peruse the matter here. Although I think he may be beginning to think we (and, in particular, your Washington representative) may not be conducting the investigation with the utmost vigour, at least I do not think that he yet suspects that we have, in fact, done a lot of beavering and have narrowed down the field to I such a degree that we are reasonably sure who the culprit may have been.

I do not have the full facts that are available to you in London, and I have not yet seen Makins and am thus unaware of the Foreign Office views and wishes, but I thought you might like to know the position as I see it, I am inclined to think that GCHQ should pass to Arlington the results of their latest work. This could perhaps wait until your case is near completion – if this can be within two weeks. You can then instruct me to tell the FBI the results of your investigations. I do not think we can count on the FBI not telling the State Department (and possibly AEC and others) although we can ask them to keep the information to themselves at the moment. I may be wrong, but I think a lot depends on how we present the news to the Bureau. Rather than a formal telegram or memorandum (at this stage) to Mr. Hoover I think there is a better chance of keeping it quiet if I tell Lamphere during our daily talks and also Mr. Ladd. They will then feel that we are keeping them in touch on a day to day basis and the shock will therefore be less when (and if) an interrogation should prove successful. The Bureau, once they have the name, will inevitably make enquiries and initiate an enquiry here. A difficult situation would certainly arise should our investigations (and possible interrogation) prove unsuccessful because of the position which the suspect holds in the Foreign Office, but if we are willing to gamble on success it is better to take this risk than to have the FBI up in arms against us.

I personally feel that the FO ought to tell the Ambassador something about the case at the time we tell the Bureau just in case the news should get to the State Department. His Excellency also should be briefed to face an outburst should an interrogation prove successful and the news becomes public.

On 9 May Patterson reported on his meeting with Makins:

I told Makins what progress the FBI were making and that at present they were thinking in terms of Halpern and Fisher. I also said that unless they unearth new information we may be able to stall for another week or two without causing them to suspect that we have a very hot suspect.

A point made at our meeting, and a good one, was that if we tell the FBI that we have narrowed down the field and give them a list of possible suspects in which we would have to include Maclean and Gore-Booth it is almost certain that the Bureau would initiate an investigation into both of them. As Gore-Booth is here the results would be embarrassing. Also, on reflection, I feel fairly certain that Mr. Hoover would find it necessary to tell the Attorney General and possibly others because one man is D-G of BIS, and the other is in the North American section of the Foreign Office. Both are in positions of great importance to the Americans, and I fear that political considerations might outweigh the desire for discretion and delicate handling.

As a matter of principle I think we ought to hand over the latest material to Arlington, but of course I do not know exactly what information it contains and it is thus difficult to advise. If it will provide the FBI with a valuable clue there should not be a lengthy delay between its delivery to Arlington and some sort of approach by us to the FBI. If it should facilitate the FBI investigation to such an extent that they can pick out Maclean it is clear that we would lose control of the case and the Americans could claim that they solved it for us. We want to avoid this and also any charges of non-co-operation.

In order to avoid a premature leak we could wait (assuming that it will be soon) until you interrogate, or are about to interrogate, Maclean. I would then tell the FBI that a study of all available information had picked him out as a probable candidate and that the latest GCHQ material had added weight to your conclusions. You then decided to interview him without delay. We may have to think up a good reason for this sudden decision because they will think it odd that we did not consult them before, particularly as Mrs Maclean is American born and the FBI may possibly have some record of the family.

It will be as necessary for you to convince Cimperman as it will be for me to convince his colleagues here.

From the strictly MI5 point of view I would like to be frank with the FBI now, but I quite see that the Foreign Office have very good reasons for not taking any chances on a leakage in Washington, and I suppose we must defer to their wishes.

If Maclean does talk we will of course have the usual demands from the Americans for copies of statements, the right to interrogate etc., etc,. However, they may have learned something from the Fuchs case and I also hope that by keeping Cimperman well in the picture you may be able to keep the Bureau on the right lines.

I look forward with the greatest interest to further news from you on this matter. It is clear that Washington is going to be very hot this summer.

Naturally the SLO was anxious not to mislead the FBI, and was justifiably in fear of offending J. Edgar Hoover. Apparently the FBI had focused its attention on Alex Halpern, a figure well known to MI5 and SIS, and another potential suspect, 'Robert Fisher', a cover-name for Cedric Belfrage.

Born in London, and a graduate of Corpus Christi College, Cambridge, Belfrage had been employed as a film critic in Hollywood by the *Daily Express*. A former CPGB member, he was first identified as a Soviet spy by Elizabeth Bentley in November 1945 who claimed that he had given Jacob Golos a Scotland Yard handbook on surveillance 'and also information regarding British policy concerning the Middle East and Russia and made certain contributions of bits of information which he apparently secured from his contact with high-raking British officials in the United States'. This denunciation would be corroborated by a dozen VENONA texts dated between April and September 1943. At that time, on 20 November 1945, Liddell mentioned receiving a memo from BSC about Bentley's disclosures:

This woman has been working for some years with World Tourist Inc. New York, a travel agency operated by Jacob Golos until his death in 1943. During the war Golos organised a US Service and Shipping Corporation which sent food parcels to Russia. Both these firms were used as a cover for an espionage organisation which, after the death of Golos, came directly under Soviet control. It previously worked under the Communist Party and had always retained strong Party connections. Bentley acted as a courier between various agents and sub-agents. The network follows the usual pattern of Soviet Intelligence and extensive penetration of American government services has been brought to light. There is reason to believe that the espionage ring was controlled by the NKVD. About thirty agents have been identified but the ramifications have not yet been fully explored. Reference has been made to

Cedric Belfrage. This man is said to have handed over a long report on the training of agents by Scotland Yard.

Interviewed by the FBI at his home in upstate New York on 2 and 3 June 1947, Belfrage typed out a four-page statement in which admitted having held clandestine meetings with Soviet contacts, and passed them classified material. Although he claimed his purpose had been 'with a view to finding out what I could about Communist and Russian politics', he acknowledged that he had not informed BSC about any of this, and was therefore liable to prosecution by the British authorities. In his statement to Special Agents Lawrence Spillane and Michael O'Rourke he described having 'met Jerome on eight or nine occasions, usually for lunch':

During these eight or nine meetings with Jerome be asked me a number of questions mainly relative to the policies toward Russia and the prospect of a second front. I was not in a position to tell him anything about this but I suggested that I might be able to supply some information on other subjects. My thought was to tell him certain things of a really trifling nature from the point of view of British and American interests, hoping in this way to get from him some more valuable information from the Communist side. I supplied him with information about Scotland Yard surveillances and also with some documents relative to the Vichy Government in France, which were of a highly confidential nature with respect to their origin but which contained information of no value whatever. In the course of our conversations Jerome took notes on the information concerning the above-mentioned items.

Somewhere about the middle of the period during which I was meeting Jerome, Claude Williams came into New York and I learned that he was going to see Earl Browder. I was interested to meet Browder and suggested that I should go along I went to an apartment in Greenwich Village where two (possibly three) others were present in addition to Browder, none of whom I knew. There was a discussion going on when we entered and the introductions were very perfunctory, and I paid little attention to the others. Browder spoke almost continuously during the hour or so I was there, analysing the world situation as he saw it. I recall that one of the others present was a man whom I remember as a little man. I cannot clearly remember his fact but I have been shown two photos of him which I would say may well be the man present on that occasion. The photograph shown to me is that of Jacob Golos, according to Messrs O'Rourke and Spillane.

Belfrage's confession linked him to Golos, Jerome and Browder, all of whom had been part of the espionage network betrayed by Bentley. Beyond his statement, Belfrage went into further details during the interview which stretched over two days.

Befrage further stated that on his first contact with V.J. Jerome in New York during 1942. He was quite sure that Jerome contacted him because he was employed by BSC. Belfrage stated that he realized Jerome's main interest in him was to obtain information from the files of BSC.

In regard to the highly confidential document relative to the Vichy government in France, Belfrage stated that he recalled giving V.J. Jerome several telegrams which had been sent from Laval's Vichy government in France to the Vichy Embassy in Washington, DC. He indicated that the British government obtained these documents and inasmuch as they had been sent through the diplomatic pouch Belfrage did not want to have the full details of such a transaction in a signed statement. He stated that a violation of this kind on his part would subject him to a fine of 10,000 pounds and 5 years in jail inasmuch as he violated his oath under the British Secrets Act which he took prior to his employment with the BSC. Belfrage stated that he would testify under oath that he furnished such highly confidential documents to V.J. Jerome. He said that he would be willing to state that these telegrams which he obtained from the confidential files of the BSC were given to V.J. Jerome.

With this background, and aware that the relevant Washington telegrams had been circulated to BSC in New York, BSC was perfectly entitled to regard Belfrage as a suspect for the Washington leak, and on 24 February 1949 Liddell mentioned that Belfrage was a suspect:

I had a word with George Carey-Foster after the meeting about the Washington case. He has called in several Foreign Office officials of counsellor rank to try and obtain from them some information about the general set-up at the Washington embassy at the time of the leakage. He says that at the moment it is difficult to see how we can make much progress, since there is apparently no comprehensive list either here or in Washington of the people employed. I gather that the papers which are known to have been leaked were circulated, amongst others, to British Security Co-ordination. This makes Belfrage another starter.

However, almost as soon as Belfrage was investigated by MI5 it became clear that, whatever else he may have passed the Soviets in 1942 and 1943, he could not have been responsible for the leaks in 1944 because by then he had been transferred to SHAEF, and in August that year was working in Paris. However, the news that MI5 had eliminated Belfrage did not reach the FBI until May 1951, leaving him as their chief suspect, in the guise of 'Robert Fisher'.

* * *

On 10 May Patterson revealed a disagreement with Philby, and also raised the danger of Maclean fleeing the country, as had happened when the nuclear physicist Bruno Pontecorvo had defected to the Soviet Union at the end of August 1950:

Mackenzie, Philby and I have had some difficulty in agreeing on the timing of an announcement to the FBI. We, of course, realise that it is a decision for London and not for us, but we felt that it was up to us to make a recommendation. Whether it is decided to tell the Bureau before, during or after the interrogation is clearly dependent on a number of important factors and our natural desire to be frank with the Bureau may be overruled. What I have done with Sir Roger Makins and Mackenzie is to stress the point that Mr. Hoover must have a full brief on his desk before anything about Maclean appears in the press.

If he does not, heads will fall and our position will become precarious.

We seem to agree that, too much notice to the FBI might cause a leakage here, but we are not in agreement as to whether we should wait until after the initial interrogation before saying anything or to tip off the Bureau a day or so ahead.

When the final plan of action is agreed I hope you will be in a position to keep Cimperman in close touch with your progress. I naturally want to avoid accusations by the FBI that I personally have had access to information on this case which I have not passed on and I therefore think that I must appear to be as surprised as they will be when we hear that you have interrogated Maclean successfully and that you are about to arrest him. As I have pointed out in earlier letters I have had to imply, in order to avoid embarrassing questions, that research was being done on Foreign Office files and that enquiries were being made, but that I personally was not au courant with the situation in London. They readily accept this answer because the FBI Headquarters operates on a 'need-to-know' basis viz a viz their own Field Offices. I am thus inclined to think that from the point of view of tactics it would be better to make Cimperman the main channel of information from London to Mr. Hoover. With the Fuchs case so clearly imprinted on our memories I would much prefer the 'heat' to be transmitted via FBI channels between London and Washington rather than become actively involved with Mr. Hoover. If I am, however, kept fully informed of the position I can put in a lot of spade work with Ladd and my other friends in the Bureau.

We have briefed Mackenzie as fully as possible and I feel sure that he is now fully acquainted with my views. While talking over the matter we agreed that a plausible excuse for sudden action by you, without an opportunity of warning the US authorities, would be that you discovered during your investigations that the suspect was planning to leave on a motoring holiday on the Continent and urgent action was necessary in case he attempted to join Pontecorvo.

Although the impression began to form that all the accumulated evidence, including the very latest cryptographic breaks made by GCHQ at Eastcote, pointed to Maclean, Arthur Martin was not quite so confident, and urged caution on Patterson. In retrospect, Patterson's fear about a surprise defection proved to be prescient.

According to SIS's subsequent investigation, the likely catalyst for the actual escape plan was Philby's sight, and misinterpretation, of a telegram received by the SLO from Martin on 16 May. The pace of the investigation was quickening, and Philby was five hours behind London, so he may have been panicked by Martin's instruction to Patterson that he should conclude a particular line of enquiry, an interview with the former head of the Washington embassy's cipher room, by 23 May. This very firm directive may, SIS thought, have led Philby to think that action against Maclean would happen faster than he had anticipated, and there would be an interrogation or arrest soon after the 23rd. Whatever the precise cause, which would be the subject of debate for some years, this was the day that Philby intervened and initiated the defections. In fact, the previous day Martin had prepared a preliminary schedule for confronting Maclean soon after 7 June, but evidently Philby had not seen that particular document which proposed four stages:

May 15th to May 28th	Investigation to be continued in UK; SLO Washington to interview Thomas in New York; but no information to be passed – either by GCHQ or Security Service – to Americans.
May 28th	GCHQ to inform Arlington Hall of the crypt recovery through their representative in Washington who would be warned not to draw special attention to it.
June 4th	SLO Washington to inform desk officer in FBI that as result of new recovery Donald Maclean was under strong suspicion; simultaneously Cimperman to be similarly informed.
June 7th approx.	FBI to be informed through SLO Washington that Maclean to be interrogated on following day; Cimperman to be similarly informed.

Note: GCHQ have agreed that irrespective of whether they succeed in confirming the present tentative passage they will not inform Arlington Hall until May 26th. If in the meantime they do not succeed in confirming this passage they would be prepared to consider withholding the information from Arlington Hall for a further period after May 28th.

Thus MI5 had choreographed a scheme to prevent the Americans from learning that Maclean had become the chief suspect until the investigators were ready to confront him. Part of the delay was the need to eliminate any wartime embassy coderoom staff who might have been accompanied by a wife in New York. The best source was a cipher clerk, W.L. Thomas, then working at the consulate-general in New York, but when he was interviewed by Patterson on 18 May it was clear that only Maclean fitted the profile. With this final loose end tied up, MI5 was almost ready to swoop and drafted a review on 18 May to inform the Foreign Office and SIS of the investigation's current status, and to explain the potential impact on the Anglo-American signals intelligence community:

> Donald Duart Maclean, head of the American Department of the Foreign Office, is suspected of having engaged in espionage on behalf of the Russians in 1944/45 while serving in the British Embassy, Washington. His activities have been under investigation by the Security Service since 20th April, 1951.
>
> In view of the political implications of this case it is now considered essential that the precise form and timing of the future conduct of the investigation should be agreed between the Foreign Office end the Security Service. The interests of one other British department – GCHQ – have to be taken into consideration; GCHQ is responsible for the Signals Intelligence source from which the evidence of espionage is derived.
>
> The relevant factors in deciding upon a suitable programme are:-
>
> Practical Requirements for the Investigation, Interrogation of the Suspect.
> 1. Investigation by the Security Service may provide evidence that Maclean is engaged in espionage; it can never prove that he is not so engaged. If, therefore, the results of the investigation are negative it must be followed by interrogation. Interrogation will result in either a) a confession which may or may not provide admissible evidence for court proceedings but which still certainly justify Maclean's dismissal from the Foreign Service, b) a statement by which Maclean will establish his innocence or c) a statement of professed innocence which will not be accepted.
>
>   The Security Service would wish for a period of two to three months in which to conduct their investigation and at the same time accumulate the necessary background information for interrogation. They consider that only if given this period could they feel satisfied that they had taken all possible steps to discover Maclean in an act of espionage. They admit, however, that even if Maclean were still spying their investigation could not be guaranteed to lead to its discovery; and that, for the purposes of interrogation, the necessary background information could be collected within a considerably shorter period.
>
>   If after investigation and interrogation no proof of espionage was obtained yet suspicion remains, means must be found to remove Maclean

from the Foreign Service. It would clearly be advantageous if this could be done under the existing machinery of the 'Civil Service purge'. The investigation into Maclean's current activities has already produced evidence of one communist associate and the Security Service would expect that further investigation would reveal any other such associations should they exist. They maintain, therefore, that for this additional reason there are grounds for prolonging the period of investigation up to a maximum of two to three months.

GCHQ is continuing its research into the signals intelligence source from which it hopes, though cannot guarantee, to derive further evidence relating to the period 1944/45.

The longer they can be given to conduct their research the better must be their chances of success.

Considerations arising from Anglo–American Collaboration.
2. Under the BRUSA [Britain–United States Signals Intelligence Agreement] agreement, GCHQ and the American ASA [Army Security Agency] (who are jointly responsible for the signals intelligence source from which the evidence of espionage is derived) are pledged to exchange all intelligence which either produces. The Americans have supplied GCHQ with most of the firm evidence which is so far available from the signals intelligence source. GCHQ have themselves produced additional evidence, of great significance to the identification, which as yet can only be graded as 'possible'; under joint instructions from the Foreign Office and the Security Service they have withheld their evidence from the Americans.

   For its part, the Security Service collaborates closely with the American FBI on all security matters. It places high value on the maintenance of mutual confidence between the two services that each will exchange intelligence fully and frankly with the other and indeed the Director-General of the Security Service has personally given his promise to the head of the FBI that his service will always do so. In the conduct of this particular case there has been full collaboration between the two services since the receipt of the first information in January 1949 and it is known to the Security Service that the FBI is conducting its own parallel enquiries. The Security Service has so far withheld from the FBI its suspicions of Maclean. There are therefore strong grounds, based on existing agreements, for continuing to collaborate with the Americans in this case. GCHQ would normally have passed their contribution to the American signals intelligence authorities when they first made their discovery some fortnight ago. The technical aid which the American ASA might be able to give could well result in the confirmation and, perhaps, expansion of the GCHQ evidence. If the evidence from GCHQ were passed to the

Americans it might, in the view of the Security Service, provide the FBI with the means of arriving independently at the tentative identification of Maclean. The Security Service would necessarily have informed the FBI of its suspicions of Maclean immediately they were formed although it does not require any assistance from the FBI in its investigation. The Security Service's over-riding reason for wishing to inform the FBI is its belief that failure to do so is bound to become known to the FBI, and to result in a complete breakdown of the mutual confidence between the two services with its attendant public recriminations in the wider field of Anglo–American relations. The Security Service contend that, irrespective of whether its investigation or interrogation of Maclean is successful, the FBI has the means of arriving independently at a strong suspicion of Maclean; that moreover the FBI may at any time through the American signals intelligence agency receive positive proof of Maclean's guilt and that in any case, having embarked on its own investigation, the FBI will continue to press the Security Service for further information.

There is yet one more reason why the Security Service feels bound to inform the FBI at least before interrogation takes place. The interrogation of Maclean must be based upon the signals intelligence evidence and therefore must jeopardise to some extent the security of that source. Since the security of that source is a joint Anglo–American responsibility the Security Service reels that it would be a serious breach of faith to act independently.

Despite these strong grounds for informing the Americans, both through GCHQ and the Security Service, there are perhaps equally serious objections to doing so. Experience has shown that the FBI is abnormally subject to political pressure and that confidential information passed to it cannot be regarded as secure. In a case of this international political importance it is possible, at worst, that there would be wilful disclosure of the intelligence to persons outside the FBI through whom the information might be made public. At best the FBI might well feel that since Maclean is head of the American Department of the Foreign Office and has in the past been intimately connected with American Atomic Energy policy, it could hardly refrain from passing due warning to the State Department and the Atomic Energy Commission.

If this were to happen, not only would there be the risk of a public disclosure, but these American departments could hardly be sympathetic to any prolongation of Maclean's present employment; nor probably would they willingly leave the investigation, interrogation and subsequent disposal of Maclean entirely in British hands.

The dilemma lies therefore in reconciling the need for further time in which to complete the investigation with the obligation to inform the

Americans and so to court political pressure and, at worst, premature public disclosure.

The following programme has been drawn up in an attempt to achieve a compromise between these conflicting considerations.

May 15th to May 28th	Security Service investigation and GCHQ research to be continued but no information to be passed, either by GCHQ or Security Service, to the Americans.
May 28th	GCHQ to inform American signals intelligence agency of their new information but without drawing any special attention to it.
June 4th	Security Service to inform the FBI that, as result of new GCHQ evidence, Maclean was under strong suspicion. This could be done through the Security Service's permanent representative in Washington or at a personal interview in Washington between the Director-General of the Security Service and Mr Hoover and simultaneously in London through the FBI liaison officer.
June 7th approx.	Security Service to inform FBI through its representative in Washington that Maclean to be interrogated on the following day; Cimperman to be similarly informed.

This programme has the following advantages:

(a) it allows the Security Service a further three weeks in which, short though the period is – it can prepare for interrogation and attempt to obtain evidence suitable for 'purge procedure' should the latter prove necessary.

(b) it allows GCHQ to fulfil its obligations towards the American signals intelligence agency; nor need the latter become aware that information that been temporarily withheld.

(c) it allows the Security service to appear to have collaborated fully with the FBI which should at least lessen the recriminations which must inevitable come if the case becomes public knowledge.

(d) it reduces to a reasonable minimum the possibility that the FBI might independently identify Maclean.

(e) it leaves the conduct of the investigation and interrogation free from American departmental pressure and reduces the possibility of premature public disclosure in America to a reasonable minimum.

(f)   should interrogation fail or court proceedings deemed inadvisable it places the Security Service in a strong position to explain the situation to the FBI.

Although the Security Service would have wished for more time in which to complete its investigation it is satisfied that it can carry out this programme. It must however emphasise:

(a)   that it is unlikely to obtain positive proof of Maclean's guilt before interrogation.
(b)   that the most probable outcome of the interrogation is that Maclean will profess innocence but not beyond doubt.
(c)   that the case for purging Maclean, if it can be submitted to the advisers at all, will probably not be accepted by them and that the Secretary of State would therefore have to over-ride their decision, should he consider this to be the most suitable means of removing Maclean from the Foreign Service.

On the following day, 19 May, MI5 produced a summary of the case against Maclean:

The only source of information concerning the spy who in 1944/45 passed British classified material to a Russian official in the United States is Signals Intelligence; the information comes from the deciphered texts of ten diplomatic telegrams, all fragmentary and none containing a real name. The analysis of the ten telegrams has enabled certain probable, but not proven, deductions to be drawn from which a comparatively narrow field of suspects can be listed. Within this narrow field D.D. Maclean appears best to fit the available data.

It is first deduced that all ten telegrams refer to the operations of a single spy. The evidence for this is reasonably strong and, if accepted, places the spy in the British Embassy. It is then deduced that, since the spy was already connected with the deciphering of at least one telegram from Mr Churchill to President Roosevelt, he or she was either a member of the cipher room of the Chancery. Finally it is agreed that since the spy certainly had access to non-cipher documents, was well-informed on political affairs (in particular post-hostilities planning) and moreover expressed personal views which were apparently valued by the Russians, he or she was more probably a member of Chancery than of the cipher room.

At this point in the argument the Signals Intelligence evidence ceases to be firm though it could fairly he rated as 'probable'; the conclusion drawn from it however is open to no doubt whatsoever.

It shows that the spy's wife was, in June 1944, living in New York. Only Maclean, among members of Chancery, could fit this description.

Moreover, among the members of the cipher room – the less likely section of the field of suspects – it has been possible to check the whereabouts of all wives but one. None that could be checked were in New York at the relevant time.

Turning from this purely circumstantial evidence, a study has been made of Maclean's personal history in order to discover whether it contains any clue which could suggest a motive for espionage. These facts have been established:

(a) While at Trinity Hall, Cambridge between 1932 and 1934 Maclean held strong political views which were well to the left.
(b) In January 1951, while under the influence of alcohol, Maclean, in response to remarks unflattering to the Communist Party, said 'of course, you know that I am a Party member – and have been for years'.
(c) In May 1951 Maclean met on friendly terms an undercover member of the British Communist Party who is himself a Civil Servant.

There is in addition considerable evidence to show that Maclean's personality is far from balanced. Medical testimony to this effect is available on his Foreign Office personal file. In particular one episode in his career reflects serious instability of character. In 1950, while holding the rank of Counsellor in the British Embassy, Cairo, Maclean, after a period of prolonged heavy drinking, suffered a temporary nervous collapse. Despite this realisation of his dangerous state of health and of the effect it might have on his career, he consistently refused to take the medical treatment offered to him, preferring to attend a lay psychiatrist of his own choosing. It could be speculated that there might be significance in the fact that Maclean's nervous state in 1950 dated approximately from the publicity given to the trial of Dr Fuchs; and that his refusal to accept official medical treatment could have been from fear of his capacity to conceal events in his past life.

Finally it must be recorded that Maclean – admittedly in common with other members of the Foreign Service – does fit in all important particulars the description given by Walter Krivitsky of the spy who operated in London on behalf of the Russians in 1936/37.

That is the sum of the case against Maclean. Before reaching a final assessment note must be taken of specific objections which to be made to the case and of one counter-solution:

(a) An isolated passage in the signals intelligence evidence reads: 'G (i.e. the spy) is systematically setting up an agency so that ... (remainder unavailable)'. This could be interpreted as meaning that the spy himself was himself setting up a network of sub-sources of information, a description which could hardly fit a man of Maclean's standing who was himself a most valuable source and would require to be protected by the Russians from all possibility of compromise. In answering this objection it must first be made clear that the technical probability of the accuracy of this passage is considered by GCHQ to be extremely low; it rates for example far lower in terms of technical probability that the vital passage relating to the spy's wife in New York.

Secondly it must be realised that the Russian word AGENTURA (which has been translated as 'agency') is in all probability a term of art, the precise translation of which is still in doubt.

(b) One passage in the Signals Intelligence evidence reads 'the State Department regard the British intrigue in Greece with some suspicion and HOMER (i.e. the spy) hopes that to disrupt the plans of the British we will avail ourselves of this circumstance ...'. It can be argued that the holding of this anti-British view might indicate that the spy was not himself British. In the view of the Security Service the sentence indicates no more than that the spy was a communist; a British communist's opinion of British policy towards Greece in 1944 would have been as antagonistic as that of a communist of any other nationality.

(c) It has been suggested that the spy could have been an American cipher clerk with an unconscious sub-source in the British Embassy or the BJSM. It is submitted that strictly on the facts available, this theory cannot be ruled out. It presupposes that the American cipher clerk would be of the caliber to express opinions acceptable to the Russians on scraps of information received casually from his British sub-source; that he himself must have had access to at least one non-cipher State Department document; and that he moved in circles which would include a British official or diplomat of some standing.

Whatever weight may be attached to these objections they show that the case is not conclusively proved, Nevertheless the identification of Maclean is the logical conclusion from a series of strong probabilities, strengthened by indications of motive and evidence of instability of character. Indeed it is felt that the evidence could only be dismissed if Maclean were able to prove conclusively that he was not in New York on the three specific dates when the acts of espionage are known to have taken place.

Although MI5 presented GCHQ's decrypt of Stepan Apresyan's message dated 28 June 1944 as proof that the mole had a wife in New York, the actual text, which was fragmented and surrounded by unrecoverable cipher groups, was far from proof that the pregnant wife referred to was HOMER's. In reality it was because

Melinda was pregnant at that time which drew attention to him. This was a subtle difference, but had gone unmentioned by Martin.

This document was MI5's far-from-conclusive assessment which tactfully omitted details of the physical and technical surveillance in London that had failed to spot anything more sinister that Maclean's contacts with known CPGB members such as Peter Floud, at the Victoria & Albert Museum, and Philip Toynbee, the *Observer* journalist who had been his confederate when he had raided the Cairo flat of an American embassy secretary in May 1950, the incident politely glossed over as his alcohol-fuelled breakdown.

As Martin's paper was distributed to a very limited circle of top officials, Philby had already set in motion Maclean's escape plan.

* * *

Maclean would flee the country on the evening of Friday, 25 May 1951, and Liddell would note in his diary for the following Tuesday that the Watchers had failed to spot him on his arrival by train from his home in Tatsfield. The Watchers had last seen him at Victoria Station on Friday evening, catching the 6.10 to Sevenoaks.

It was on the same morning that Liddell noted a call from David Footman at SIS who declared that Guy Burgess had disappeared, and this aspect of what would become one of the major political scandals of the era would have a profound impact on all who had known him. Not only had Liddell known him for rather more than a decade, he had also employed him and had regarded him as a colleague, albeit a rather unsavoury one.

Liddell mentions Burgess for the first time on 24 September 1940 when he dined with him and Anthony Blunt at the Reform Club. By then Blunt had joined MI5's B Division as Liddell's assistant, and then on 11 April 1941 Liddell refers to the possibility that Burgess might play a role, subordinate to Footman, in a joint MI5/SIS study of European social movements. That subject is not raised again, and one of these present, Jack Curry, would later veto a proposal that Burgess, then employed by the BBC, should actually join MI5.

The next reference to Burgess occurs five months later on 15 September 1941, when Burgess visited Liddell to discuss the behaviour of his Foreign Office colleague Peter Hutton, who had been indiscreet to a Swiss journalist, Eric Kessler. Hutton, of the News Department, had disclosed details of some exchanges between Churchill and Stalin, and this information had reached Freddie Kuh, the London correspondent of the *Chicago Sun*. These events had been reported to Burgess by Kessler, whom he had recruited as a source for MI5 codenamed ORANGE. Having been co-opted as the press attaché at the Swiss embassy, the homosexual Kessler had become a valued asset for MI5 where Blunt acted as the intermediary between St James's Street and Burgess.

The issue of Hutton's unauthorized disclosures was exacerbated by MI5's suspicion that Kuh was a Soviet agent. Born in Chicago, Kuh had begun his career as a reporter on the *Chicago Evening Post* but in 1919 had been hired by the *Daily Herald* as the newspaper's Balkan correspondent before joining United Press as chief of its bureau in Moscow where it was suspected he had been recruited by the NKVD. Thus it would appear that Burgess incriminated Hutton and Kuh, but by doing so protected Kessler and perhaps enhanced his own status with MI5. Whatever his motive, MI5 could not take any formal action against Hutton because to do so would compromise Kessler. Accordingly, the matter was quietly dropped and he returned to the United States in January 1951.

What is very curious about this episode is the risk Burgess ran by denouncing Hutton, an act that he must have realized would draw attention to Kuh, a Soviet agent who, as an American in England, was extremely vulnerable. Years earlier Kuh had been implicated in a major Soviet espionage network operating in London and Paris under journalistic cover by William ('Trilby') Ewer, codenamed B-1 and HERMAN by the Soviets. His organization, the Federated Press of America (FPA), posed as a legitimate, independent news agency. A well-known CPGB member and *Daily Herald* journalist, William Ewer had been a major spy between 1919 and 1929, and was reputed to have run sources in the India Office, Home Office and Scotland Yard. Educated at Merchant Taylors', Ewer had graduated from Trinity College, Cambridge, where in 1907 he had been a friend and contemporary of Kim's father St John Philby and had recruited another *Daily Herald* veteran, George Slocombe, alias Kenneth Milton, to be his Paris representative. In November 1924 MI5's intensive surveillance had identified Ewer and his lover Rosa Edwards, née Cohen, as running the news agency and had spotted three former Special Branch detectives, Hubert Ginhoven, Charles Jane and Walter Dail, mounting a counter-surveillance operation for Ewer.

The FPA was raided in April 1929, but no action was taken against Ewer because there was never any evidence that he had gained access to classified information. MI5's inside knowledge of the FPA came from one of the staff, former police Sergeant Arthur Lakey, who had been dismissed from the Metropolitan Police during the second 1919 police strike, and then joined Ewer, only to act later as an informer. After the raid Ewer travelled to Poland but returned to England in September 1929 and was left alone by MI5 because of his political connections. However, in May 1949 Ann Glass suggested revisiting the case because of Ewer's unidentified sources in Whitehall. Liddell recorded on 15 May 1949:

> Ann Glass came to talk to me about the old case of William Norman Ewer, of the Federated Press of America.
>
> There was no doubt that Ewer had been a Soviet spy and that George Slocomb, now on the *Evening Standard*, had assisted him. Freddie Kuh's part in the conspiracy was a little doubtful. Ewer had been in touch with someone in the Foreign Office, and it is now suggested that he should be interrogated in order to ascertain the identity of this individual, I wondered a little whether if this were done, after a lapse of twenty years, it might not invite criticism

as to why it had not been done before. Apart from this, I did not see that there was any special inducement for Ewer to tell us the answer. The case will need very careful consideration. After the arrest of Detective Inspectors Hubert Ginhoven and Jane, the two Special Branch officers implicated in the case, Ewer must have concluded that we knew about his activities. No action appears to have been taken at the time of the arrests, as they coincided more or less with the General Election it was felt generally that another Zinoviev Letter incident should be avoided.

Liddell had always been cautious about pursuing Ewer, mainly because of the *Daily Herald*'s strong influence over the Labour Party, but the problem of current Soviet penetration of the Foreign Office was becoming increasingly pressing for those few indoctrinated into the GOMER leak from Washington, and the issue was raised again six weeks later, on 17 June:

> I discussed with Dick White and John Marriott the case of William Ewer. Dick and I felt, and I think John agreed, that as it would be necessary to consult members of the Labour Party before taking any action, the matter was of very considerable delicacy and our action might be misunderstood.
>
> Apart from this, it seemed extremely unlikely that Ewer either could or would enlighten us about his alleged agents in the Foreign Office, Colonial Office and CRO. These so-called agents may well be little more than contacts; in any case, Ewer would represent them as such if he were prepared to talk at all. Unfortunately, there is very little on record here to show the political implications of the case and the reasons why no action was taken at the time.
>
> The general belief is that it was thought to be bad politics to have a show-down which might lead to the cry: 'Another Zinoviev letter.' I thought we might perhaps try and get a bit clearer on this point by talking to Jane Archer, who handled the matter. There is nobody else here who knows anything about it.

By 21 September 1949 Ann Glass had acquired support for her proposal for an approach to Ewer, although Liddell remained sceptical and was still concerned about the political implications, as he made clear:

> Dick White told me that Kenneth Morton Evans is anxious to reopen the cane of William Ewer.
>
> He feels that this is warranted by our success in spotting an active agent through a revision of the Jacob Moness case.[6] I said that I thought that before taking any steps, we should try and get hold of somebody who knew Ewer personally; we could then get a better idea of to how to make our approach. Dick suggested Malcolm Muggeridge, or possibly Philip Jordan.
>
> Our next step will be to decide whether we should say anything in high quarters and whether we should enlist the support of any minister in speaking

to Ewer before we tackle him. My own view is that while we might have to say something to the Prime Minister about our intentions, it would be better to approach Ewer on our own level. It would certainly be less embarrassing and he might in consequence be more co-operative.

Morton Evans, formerly of the Radio Security Service, had advocated an attempt to enlist Ewer's help by citing the example of Jacob Moness, a spy in the United States whose name had come up during the ARCOS raid in May 1927. A later review of the material seized during the operation, which had been planned by Liddell, had revealed that Moness and his daughter Paulene were active spies in New York. The details had been passed to the FBI with impressive results, exposing an entire espionage organization.

Evidently the idea of using Malcolm Muggeridge, who had worked in SIS during the war, or the *News Chronicle* war correspondent Philip Jordan as intermediaries was dropped, and on 7 November, Liddell noted that a plan, for Max Knight to pitch Ewer, had received Sillitoe's approval:

> Malcolm Cumming and Max Knight came to talk to me about a proposal that the latter should interview William Ewer about his former espionage activities, and in particular his connections with individuals in the Foreign Office. Max, who knew Ewer, thought that he could quite easily ask him out to dinner and endeavour to obtain his co-operation. I have told the D-G about this, who approves.

Ewer was finally interviewed by Max Knight in 1950, beginning with a long lunch at the Connaught Hotel in January.[7] At the outset, the MI5 officer explained his purpose:

> I said that from time to time we made a habit of going over what might be termed 'classic cases' in the light of new information or the general trend of international politics, as by so doing we frequently not only re-educated ourselves, but also obtained new information and clearer interpretations of matters which were originally obscure. Ewer listened very attentively to all this and merely nodded his agreement. I then said that two or three cases in the last decade had seemed to indicate that there might still be persons in high Government position who would not be above giving information to the Russians and that this, naturally had been the occasion for one of revisions. Ewer then said he would do his best to help though he might wish to have some reservations in regard to certain individuals.

Knight was especially interested in any of Ewer's alleged sources in Whitehall, and in Freddie Kuh:[8]

At a suitable point in my conversation I referred back to Ewer's statement that he did not think any of the original sources were likely to be working now, and I asked him point blank what he thought about Freddie Kuh. This seemed to disturb Ewer slightly, and he gave me the impression that he had harboured a faint hope that Kuh was not going to come up for discussion. However, he eventually became resigned to this, and he told me that, while he had no definite information or evidence with regard to Kuh's present activities, he thought that he was a man who would work for anybody if it suited his purpose; that he had, of course, worked with the FPA, and had had a number of Russian contacts. Ewer thought him to be overwhelmingly ambitions as a journalist, and quite unscrupulous. He said he had probably the best contacts of anybody in Fleet Street, and that he had caused Ewer some considerable difficulty and embarrassment not so very long ago. This was because, during the war, he had succeeded in obtaining as his mistress a girl named Pauline who had been Admiral Thompson's secretary, and who, when she left the Admiral, went to work at Downing Street for Francis Williams. To quote Ewer with regard to the latter appointment, 'we had the devil of a job to straighten that out.'

This was quite a revelation for MI5, bearing in mind that Admiral George Thompson had been the wartime Chief Censor, and that the former editor of the *Daily Herald* Francis Williams, who had served in the Ministry of Information during the war, had been appointed Attlee's press secretary in 1945.

During the first interview Ewer explained that he had been motivated to co-operate with Knight because of his disenchantment with the Soviets and the CPGB over the fate of his lover:

With regard to Rose Cohen, Ewer said that she was at one time a girl friend of his, and that she represented a very painful chapter in his life. He intimated that her eventual fate had done more than anything else to disillusion him about the Russians and Communism. He told me that he supposed I knew that she had gone to Russia, had been framed by the Russians as a British spy, sent to Siberia for 10 years, and if not actually dead, was virtually dead. He added that what he would never forgive the British Party for was that none of the Party leaders here, who knew what good work she had done for the Cause, made any attempt to intervene on her behalf.

On 27 January, Liddell referred to Knight's recent breakthrough:

Max Knight has had a discussion with William Ewer, who was apparently quite friendly and ready to disclose his past when he was working under cover of the Federated Press for the Russians. I have not seen Max's report yet, but I understand that quite gratuitously Ewer issued a warning about Freddie

Kuh, who certainly had worked for the Russians in the past and might well be doing so still. Ewer, of course, knows more about Freddie Kuh than anybody else. We know of his contact with the Russians, Czechs, and the Poles, but such is the nature of his work that it is impossible to say, by the ordinary means available to us, when Kuh's work passed from high-grade journalism to espionage.

At his second interview, in April 1950, Ewer asked to say more about Kuh:

In the course of subsequent conversation, I pressed Ewer over Freddie Kuh. He did not add very much to what he told me before, but he did admit that he thought Kuh was 'up to something'. He said that it was not the result of any knowledge, but a sort of combination of a good many years' contact with Kuh and a personal hunch. He said that he thought that if Kuh was doing anything for the Russians, it would be mostly political intelligence, though, of course, it was possible that, in the course of his ordinary professional work, he might come across (a) persons who might be useful to the Russians, and (b) some sort of information about military matters. If he did do so, Ewer was certain that Kuh would not scruple to pass the information on.

The FPA case had been especially painful for Liddell and his colleague Hugh Miller because the proof that Jane, Ginhoven and Dail had effectively switched sides to work for the Soviets meant that Special Branch had been penetrated at a high level over a long period. This realization had been the catalyst for both men, then employed at Scotland Yard as civilian analysts, to join MI5 in 1931 and remain distrustful of most Special Branch detectives.

* * *

ORANGE would be the subject of Liddell's next two encounters with Burgess. The first, on 8 March 1944, concerned information that Kessler had received about General Marian Kukeil, and Burgess had been accompanied by an MI5 officer, Kemball Johnston, who had been his contemporary at Trinity College:

Kemball Johnston and Guy Burgess came to see me about ORANGE. Burgess has ascertained that ORANGE got his information about General Marian Kukeil from the Swiss military attaché who got it from the Polish military attaché.

The nature of the information about Kukeil which appears to have caused a problem is unknown, but at the time the general, who formerly had been the deputy Minister of War in the Polish government-in-exile in London, then had commanded the 1st Polish Corps, based at Coatbridge in Scotland, and in 1943 had been appointed Minister of War.

Then, on 13 October 1944, Blunt and Burgess visited Liddell to discuss Kessler's return to Switzerland where, it was thought, he would be of continuing value as an agent. The final reference to ORANGE was on 2 November 1945 when Liddell attended a meeting at which it was agreed that

> Graham Mitchell shall run him in future in conjunction with Burgess since a good deal of his information relates to Fascist activities abroad, and Mitchell is the kind of person who is likely to get on with Burgess.

On 24 October 1945 Burgess is mentioned as the source of information about Count Constantine Benckendorff who, he had alleged, was associated with Moura Budberg.[9] In fact Benckendorff, also a member of the Travellers Club, was a White Russian who had been in the Tsar's Imperial Navy, had served in naval intelligence and in 1908 had spent a year in London as an assistant naval attaché at the Russian embassy. He had been decorated with the DSO by Lord Curzon for his role in the delivery to the Admiralty in October 1914 of copy 151 of the *Signalbuch der Kaiserlichenmarine*, the German naval codebook which had been recovered from the wreck of the cruiser *Magdeburg*, and carried to Scapa Flow from Alexandrov by Benckendorff aboard HMS *Theseus*. Benckendorff, whose father had been the Russian ambassador in London at the time of the Bolshevik revolution, had been one of Budberg's many lovers. He published his autobiography, *Half a Life*, in 1954, and died in London in September 1959, aged 79.

On 1 February 1947 Liddell recorded that in the evening he met Burgess accompanied by a Foreign Office colleague, Richard Scott, C.P. Scott's grandson, and remarked of his new appointment as the Minister of State's private secretary, 'not, I venture to think, a very suitable appointment'. During this period, when Burgess was so close to Hector McNeil, he was still in contact with Liddell, as is mentioned on 19 January 1948 when he saw Anthony Blunt and was told a story, retailed by Margery Rees who had heard it from Burgess, about a bungled attempt by Jim Skardon to approach a company that was thought to be contracted to supply components for a penicillin-manufacturing plant to the Soviets.

A month later, on 20 February 1948, Burgess lunched with Liddell, apparently to denounce Andrew Revai. Once again, this seems to be an example of Burgess seeking to ingratiate himself with Liddell by taking the very dangerous step of incriminating a Soviet agent. A Hungarian journalist, and one of Burgess's former lovers, Revai had been the London correspondent of *Pester Loyd*, Budapest's German-language daily, and employed occasionally from 1942 as 'Canidus', to broadcast on the BBC's Hungarian Service. When Hungary had joined the Axis Revai had founded the National Federation of Hungarians, and became its president in 1943, giving him unrivalled access to émigré Hungarians. After the war Revai had opening a picture gallery and art publishing business, the Pallas

Gallery on the second floor of a grand house in Mayfair's Albermarle Street with a partner, Robin Chancellor.

Burgess was in contact with Liddell again three months later when he telephoned to pass on some information about a pair of Danes he had met. One, he thought, might be able to provide information about Jewish terrorism. Liddell was non-committal.

On 16 July 1949 Burgess was in touch with Liddell by telephone, to seek his advice concerning the New China News Agency (NCNA). By now Burgess had been transferred to the Foreign Office's Far East Department and was attempting to establish himself as an expert on China, and his request concerned the legal grounds on which the NCNA bureau in Hong Kong could be closed down. At the time the NCNA was regarded as a Communist front, but the civil war was still raging on the mainland. Liddell's opinion was that the bureau could not be shut unless there was evidence of its involvement in acts of incitement to violence.

In January 1950, two months after the notorious episode of Burgess's drunken antics while on holiday in Gibraltar and Tangiers, he was again seeking Liddell's help, his Foreign Office career apparently in jeopardy and the threat of an Official Secrets Act prosecution hanging over him. He actually came in to see Liddell on the morning of 16 February, and the following day Liddell spoke to Ken Mills, MI5's Defence Security Officer in Gibraltar, who gave his scathing version of Burgess's appalling conduct. There the matter rested, to be decided by the Foreign Office's Personnel Department, until a few days later, on 21 January, when Burgess telephoned to ask for Liddell's support, and was given a polite brush-off. As far as his diary is any guide, Liddell spoke to Burgess for the last time on 1 July when they met, apparently casually, and discussed Britain's recognition of the Communist government in China.

The sum total of Liddell's references to Burgess between 1940 and 1950 suggests a rather one-sided relationship, with Burgess only tolerated because of his value as someone capable of recruiting and running quality assets such as Kessler and Revai. He seems to have tried to boost his usefulness by offering new sources, such as his unnamed Danish friend, who was his house-guest in May 1948, and passing on gossip. The lasting impression is that Liddell had severe doubts about Burgess's suitability as Hector McNeil's private secretary, and could not have been anything but dismayed by his conduct in Gibraltar, but drew a distinction between misbehaviour and deliberate disloyalty. As it turned out, Liddell could not have been more wrong.

Burgess's lengthy connection with MI5 made his defection in 1951 particularly embarrassing. His brother Nigel had been an MI5 officer until June 1946, and he had remained in close contact with the organization. These two complications, compounded by Burgess's friendships with Anthony Blunt and David Footman, made the issue of MI5's handling of the aftermath especially sensitive, and meant that the Security Service was always on the defensive.

While it had been relatively easy to reconstruct Maclean's movements in the days before his escape because he had been kept under observation by the Watcher Service while in London, Burgess was much more of a challenge as he had never been a suspect. He had been spotted meeting Maclean several times in Pall Mall by the Watchers, but MI5 was obliged to rely on Burgess's circle for an account of his activities. Statements were taken from Burgess' coterie of friends and lovers, Peter Pollock, Jack Hewit and Bernard Miller, and from Andrew Revai, Anthony Blunt and Goronwy Rees.[10] As MI5 tried to reconstruct Burgess' movements over the previous week, the embarrassment factor grew. On Saturday, 19 May Burgess had driven up to Cambridge for an Apostles dinner, but had dropped in on the former wartime MI5 officer Kemball Johnston at his home in Henham, Essex on the way. On Sunday and Monday he had stayed with Peter Pollock at Sharlowes Farm, his Elizabethan manor house in Flaunden, Hertfordshire. On Monday Burgess had returned to London to entertain his new acquaintance, the American medical student Bernard Miller, whom he had met on his recent transatlantic voyage aboard the *Queen Mary*, at the Reform Club and the Gargoyle. On Tuesday he visited Hilda and Tommy Harris (also a wartime MI5 officer), met Maclean for a drink at the Grosvenor Hotel for just ten minutes, before visiting the Shakespeare pub and dining at the Reform; on Wednesday he met Maclean for lunch at the Queen's Hotel in Sloane Square and, after a visit to the Duke of Wellington pub in Eaton Terrace, dined at home with Hewit; on Thursday he lunched with Maclean at the Reform Club and then visited Eton and his old home in Ascot. He then returned to London and dined at the Hungarian Czardas in Soho with Pollock, Revai and Miller.

On the day of his departure Burgess received a telephone call from David Footman and arranged to dine with him on 1 June. He also made calls to Stephen Spender (to speak to Wystan Auden) and to Goronwy Rees' wife. He also met Blunt at the Courtauld Institute and, having rented a car which was delivered to him at the Reform Club and that evening drove down to Maclean's home at Tatsfield. According to MI5's reconstructed chronology, Burgess arrived at Beaconshaw at 7.30pm, dined at 8.45 and then left for Southampton at 10.00, driving cross-country.

Thus, according to MI5's Watchers, Burgess had been seen to meet Maclean for lunch at the Royal Automobile Club on 15 May, for a brief drink on 22 May, and then lunch in Chelsea on 23 May and then lunch again at the Reform on Thursday, 24 May.

At the time, no great significance had been attached to the encounters between Burgess and Maclean because it was not unnatural that the two diplomats, one the head of the American Department, the other just returned from the United States under a cloud, might have legitimate business to discuss. MacLean, of course, had been under surveillance since 18 April, and by 5 May had been a candidate for interrogation. On that date Martin, Robertson and White had gathered at the

Foreign Office to meet Reilly and Carey-Foster and decide on what should be said to the Americans, and how soon Maclean could be called in for an interview.

Discussion centred upon whether or not it would be advisable to inform American agencies of the progress made in the investigation. Three courses of action seemed possible:

a).   GCHQ should advise Arlington Hall of its latest tentative recovery of the message of 28 June 1944; the Security Service should inform the FBI that their suspicions were centred on Maclean⁻, that he is currently under investigation and that, in order that their investigation should not be prejudiced, the FBI should give no circulation to the information; the Security Service should continue their investigation of Maclean along the lines already agreed.

b).   Neither GCHQ nor the Security Service should pass any information whatsoever to American agencies but should continue their own lines of investigation, accepting the risk that either Arlington Hall or the FBI might independently obtain information which would direct their own suspicions towards Maclean,

c).   The Security Service should interrogate Maclean with the least possible delay (a fortnight at the most) and inform the FB I of the result of the interrogation immediately it was completed.

The Foreign Office undertook to reach a decision on which of these three courses should be followed by Tuesday, 8th May.

MI5's overlapping chronology for Maclean had been easier to assemble because his daily routine involved his daily commute in from Surrey, lunch in Pall Mall and his return home via Victoria. The purpose of the surveillance was to spot any suspicious contacts and provide early warning if he had plans to flee the jurisdiction, but the Watchers made several unexpected discoveries. Firstly Maclean, who appeared to be entirely composed (unlike Burgess who was seen to be drinking quite extraordinary quantities of neat gin), appeared to be having an affair with Isabel Lambert, a woman he was seen to meet on 15 May at the flat in Whitehorse Street belonging to the philosopher and former SOE officer Professor A.J. Ayer. An hour later he emerged with her and spent another hour drinking in the Grapes in Shepherd's Market. Then they lurched out, hailed a cab and were driven to another pub, the York & Albany in Regent's Park, with her sitting on Maclean's lap, in an embrace. A beautiful model, Isabel Lambert had been married to the *Daily Express* correspondent Tom Sefton Delmer, was herself a well-known artist and at the time of her affair with Maclean was married to the composer Constant Lambert.

Among the others Maclean was seen to meet were the *Observer* journalist Philip Toynbee, an open CPGB member, whom he was seen to visit at his home in Sussex Gardens on 9 May; and Peter Floud, a director of the Victoria & Albert Museum, and a suspected member, like his brother the MP Bernard Floud, of a CPGB underground cell, whom he met on the following day. Curiously, Peter Floud, whose home telephone in Hampstead has been tapped for some weeks, was monitored when he called Lady Maclean on 17 April, trying to find Donald, apparently unaware that he had bought a home in the country.

Liddell refers to Maclean's meeting with Floud as an interesting development because Floud was known to be a member of the Berger Group, a CPGB cell composed mainly of lawyers and headed by Harry Berger, an activist who had been court-martialled in 1943 for leaking classified documents, and subsequently had been employed by John Platts-Mills MP.

On Friday, 25 May, his 38th birthday, Maclean turned up at his office as usual, and then joined two old friends, Robin Campbell DSO and his wife Lady Mary Campbell, for lunch at Schmidt's in Charlotte Street. Robin was the one-legged war hero son of Sir Ronald Campbell, a diplomat who had served before the war at the embassies in Belgrade and had been Maclean's ambassador in Paris in 1940. Lady Mary, née St Clair Erskine, was the daughter of the Earl of Rosslyn. After lunch Maclean made a visit of a few minutes to the Travellers Club and returned to the Foreign Office where he remained until he caught the 6.10 from Victoria.

What makes the detail of these last few days of the defectors so intriguing is that that there followed two completely different versions of what happened once the two men had left London. According to the official version, pieced together from MI5's files and Liddell's diaries, the Watchers reported Maclean's failure to show up at either Victoria Station or his office on Monday morning. Allegedly, the telephone intercepts at Tatsfield and on his mother' third-floor flat at 87 Iverna Court 'gave the impression that Donald Maclean was at home' on Saturday, 28 May, and on Sunday 'No calls were made or received at Tatsfield and the telecheck on Lady Maclean still gave the impression that Maclean was at home.' However, on Monday, 28 May Maclean's PF reveals that 'It was learned from the telechecks on Tatsfield and Lady Maclean that Donald Maclean had in fact been away at the weekend and was not yet back.'

This last assertion is quite at odds with what Liddell recorded in his diary, for he says nothing relating to either Maclean or Burgess on the Monday, but on 29 May he states;

The Watchers failed to pick up Donald Maclean since his departure for the country on Friday, and we now learn from the Foreign Office that he was given a day's leave on Saturday. He has not apparently been seen since and TCs [telechecks] indicate considerable anxiety in the family.

Thus, according to a summary of events in Maclean's PF dated 14 October 1952, the first MI5 knew of Maclean's disappearance was at 10.58 on Tuesday morning when Melinda telephoned the Foreign Office to declare her husband's absence. However, the previous day Liddell had confided to his diary: 'In view of the past association between Burgess and Maclean observed by Watchers, it seems pretty clear that the pair of them have gone off.'

This sequence raises several questions, dating back to the arrival of Burgess at Beaconshaw on the Friday evening when, according to Melinda, who was interviewed by Jim Skardon at Beaconshaw on 7 June, he had been introduced to her as 'Roger Styles'. Maclean had then informed his heavily pregnant wife, who was also looking after their two boys, both recovering from measles, that he was going away for the night, and she had packed him an overnight bag, then served dinner. Having said goodbye to his two sons, Donald and Fergus, who were in bed, he had disappeared into the night. The first question which might have been asked by MI5, which had monitored the conversations in the house through a device known as 'Special Facilities' which converted the telephone into a permanently live microphone connected directly to MI5's headquarters in London. As Melinda already knew Burgess, and had even worked at the BBC at the same time as him, she had participated in the charade, presumably because she either knew, or believed, that the house had been bugged. As Liddell's diary confirms, SF had been in place for the past three weeks, according to his entry for 1 May: 'We are trying to get [XXXXX] on Donald Maclean, but meanwhile we are entirely dependent upon Watchers, who in any case are an essential ingredient in an enquiry of this kind.'

The logic behind the deployment of SF at Tatsfield was MI5's inability to maintain physical surveillance on Maclean at his home or on his train journey because of the likelihood of compromise in a country environment. This had been a major challenge during the Klaus Fuchs case when the Watchers experienced great difficulties in monitoring their target's movements near Harwell. The introduction of SF, then regarded as an extremely secret technique, solved the problem of keeping an eye on Maclean when he was not in London. The SF equipment was usually installed by GPO engineers who had 'faulted' the line and called at the address to make the repair. In Maclean's case, Arthur Martin had enquired on 8 May about the possibility of assigning the diplomat a telephone scrambler, which would provide a pretext to install a suitably-adapted model. However, Martin's proposal failed when it was explained that only two of the most senior Foreign Office staff merited such equipment, so Maclean certainly did not qualify for it and would be bound to be suspicious if it appeared. Internally, there was further discussion about 'sources of investigation' regarding CURZON, but the actual documents relating to B4, B Division's technical section headed by Malcolm Cumming and Hugh Winterborn, on 8 and 9 May have been removed from Maclean's PF and the index entry crossed out. That SF was available during the investigation is undoubted, as Maclean's PF mentions that WEStern 2992 was 'faulted' by B4 pm 31 May. The subscriber for this telephone was Lady Maclean.

The SF system linked a target's telephone to Mrs Grist's staff on the sixth floor of Leconfield House, known as 'the Gristery' where operators monitored and recorded the conversations. Just such an arrangement was in place on 11 May at Tatsfield when Ronnie Reed prepared for the surveillance cover during the upcoming Whitsun weekend and minuted 'During the Whitsun holidays Mrs Grist's section will be monitoring CURZON's home telephone'. At the height of the panic following the defections, MI5's B4(b) section placed four potential co-conspirators, Peter Pollock, Andrew Revai, Philip Toynbee and Peter Floud under what was termed 'special watch', another euphemism for SF.

There is a further contradiction between Liddell's contemporaneous diary entry for Tuesday 19 May and Maclean's PF which asserts that

> Captain Liddell is thought to have gone to the Foreign Office where he would have had confirmation of Maclean's continued absence. From this point onwards it was presumed that Burgess and Maclean had disappeared together.

However, this is not what happened. In fact, as Liddell records, he and Dick White went to see Len Burt at Scotland Yard after lunch, and called at the Home Office to confer with the Deputy Under-Secretary of State William Murrie who, in the absence of the Home Secretary, David Maxwell Fyfe, was unable to authorize a directive to seize the missing diplomats' passports. Liddell and White had then returned to Leconfield House to receive a telephone call confirming the Home Secretary's agreement, followed later the same evening by a telephone call from Anthony Blunt who had reported that he had been told of Burgess's unexpected absence by Jack Hewit on Saturday. Actually, Liddell did not visit the Foreign Office until 31 May.

Perhaps the most controversial aspect to Liddell's diary is the continuation for that Tuesday evening, after his conversation with Blunt:

> Later we received a message from Immigration to say that Maclean and Burgess had left Southampton on Friday night for St. Malo, which they should have reached at about 10 o'clock on Saturday morning. They had apparently disembarked there contrary to the excursion terms on which they were being carried. The facts had been reported by the captain of the ship *Falaise* on its return to Southampton.
>
> We decided that the best thing was for Dick to leave on the first plane for Paris, in order to stimulate the activities of the Sureté, who had already been alerted through [XXXXXX].
>
> Dick spent the night with me until 1 a.m. and left at 5.30 a.m. with an outdated passport.

Thus, on Liddell's evidence, the master of the *Falaise* had reported to the immigration authorities, after his return from the Channel cruise, that Burgess and Maclean had disembarked in St Malo without authorization. This news allegedly had prompted the decision to send White to Paris to offer encouragement to the French police.

This slightly improbable scenario was disputed by Arthur Martin and the Night Duty Officer at Leconfield House on the evening of 25 May who claimed that Maclean's departure at Southampton had been reported to MI5 at midnight, news that had led Dick White to try and fly that same night to France to intercept Maclean in St Malo. The plan had failed when White had rushed to the airport, only to discover that his passport was out of date.

If true, this version sheds an entirely different light on Liddell's diaries and, indeed, on the strange contradictions contained in MI5's files. It follows that, if MI5 had been informed of Maclean's departure on Friday evening, the events of the following three days are open to a rather different interpretation.

In any event, Liddell went into high gear on 30 May and saw both Tommy Harris and Anthony Blunt in his office, together. This was the occasion that Blunt acknowledged that he had known Maclean at university, and had regarded him as a Communist. It was also said that Maclean was a homosexual, although his wife was unaware of it. His record of the conversation went into Maclean's PF:

On 30.5.51 Anthony Blunt and Tommy Harris came to see me. I told them that the matter was a serious one; that Burgess had left the country for France in the company of another Foreign Office official, and that Burgess had booked a ticket in his own name and another ticket in the name of Miller, which had subsequently been used by his companion. Blunt asked whether the Foreign Office official was Maclean. I said that he was and asked him what he knew about Maclean. He said that of course he had known Maclean in his University days, but had not seen much of him since.

He did, however, know him as a friend of Guy Burgess, and as one who had been closely allied with him as a fellow member of a Communist group at Cambridge, in which were included people like John Cornford and Maurice Cornforth.

Blunt had been astonished, on returning to Cambridge in 1934, to find that these intellectuals had drifted right into the Communist camp. Guy Burgess was a member of the group, but in 1935, for some reason or another, became embittered. He had wanted to blossom out as a Marxian historian, but evidently thought better of it and drifted away from the group. He had, however, always remained Marxian and had within recent years become bitterly anti-American.

Burgess told Blunt, and also an American friend called Bernard Miller, that he had to help a friend over the weekend who was in some sex trouble and was being blackmailed. Both Blunt and Tommy Harris tried to speculate who this friend might be and Maclean had been one of the suggestions, since it was known that Maclean was a homosexual. It was not thought that his wife was aware of this.

The American friend, Miller, whom Burgess had met aboard the *Queen Mary*, had left the ship at Cherbourg but had subsequently visited this country, where he intended to study as a medical student. He is going back to the United States and will return here in July. He cannot throw any more light on the disappearance of Burgess.

I asked Blunt and Harris whether they believed the story of Maclean being blackmailed, or whether they thought it was a story put over by Maclean to deceive Burgess, or by Burgess to deceive his friends. They said that quite frankly any of the above reasons were possible. Tommy Harris then mentioned that he and Blunt had discussed the possibility of Burgess having been blackmailed in America and forced to disclose information. What I think had given rise to this in their minds was the knowledge that Jack Hewitt, when he unpacked Burgess' suitcase on the latter's arrival from America, had found a large quantity of pound notes. Did these imply that Burgess was now working for the Russians, or was it just a common Black Market offence? I think they both thought it was unlikely that Burgess would have sold himself to the Russians but they felt that he was such an unstable character that almost anything was possible.

We then discussed the anxiety of Mrs Burgess about her son. She had been anxious to go to the Police, but had been dissuaded from doing so. She had been told that the matter was already being dealt with by the Police on a high level and that she could rest assured that everything possible was being done. I told Harris and Blunt that she could be told that her son had been traced abroad. This would probably satisfy her.

Both Harris and Blunt assured me that they would on no account disclose to anybody that Burgess had been accompanied.

Later that same evening he stayed up late into the night with Harris, who described Burgess' behaviour when he had called the previous Wednesday, presumably just before, or just after, his lunch with Maclean in Sloane Square. However, it was on 1 June that Liddell made a breakthrough when he interviewed Goronwy Rees, the Welsh academic and bursar of All Souls whom Burgess had telephoned at their home in Sonning, Berkshire, on the morning of his departure, but instead spoke to his wife Margery for an hour. Rees said that she had found the conversation 'sinister' and promised to return to make a statement. This he did, but it was made to Dick White in the presence of Anthony Blunt, and was not seen by Liddell until 12 June because he had been away from his office for ten days, on a visit to Wales,

What Rees now had to say amounted to a bombshell. Burgess, he said, had been a Communist up at Cambridge in 1932–3 but had publicly abandoned the Party in 1935. In around 1937 he had confided that this move had been directed by the

Comintern, and he mentioned an economist, Rolf Katz, and Edouard Pfeiffer, described as head of Daladier's personal secretariat, as his contacts. He said that he passed confidential political information to a Russian whom he met in small cafes, whose name was unknown to him. Rees concluded by asserting that the conversation with his wife had taken place on Thursday, 24 May, and had ended with the remark that 'he was leaving England and would not be back for a long time'.

> I first knew Guy Burgess when he was an undergraduate at Cambridge and I was at Oxford. At this time he was an active Communist. This would be about 1932 to 1933. He later (query) 1935 left the Party with considerable publicity. This gave considerable offence to many of his friends including myself though I was not a member of the Party. I did not then see him for some time but heard that his political views had totally altered, that he had become in effect a fascist, and was active in promoting associations between this country and the German National Socialists. I did on one occasion meet him by chance and reproach him for his change of views and his new right wing associates one of whom was Captain Jack Macnamara to whom I believe Burgess was then Secretary. We parted on bad terms and again I did not see him for some time. In I believe 1937 or perhaps earlier we did meet again and once again became close friends. A little later I wrote an article in the *Spectator* by which Burgess professed to be very deeply impressed. He said to me that he was working on behalf of an anti-Fascist organisation and that his task was to collect confidential political information and later he said that this organisation was in fact the Comintern or rather a secret branch of it. He also said that this was the reason why he had left the Communist Party because he had done so under direction. Be had obeyed his orders only because of the depth of his political convictions and in spite of the great personal pain it had caused him in breaking with his friends. He said that he wished me to help him in carrying out his work and said that one of his other sources of information was Anthony Blunt.
>
> He at no time mentioned any other names as being direct sources of his but I always assumed because of his frequent contacts with them that among them were
>
> (a) Rolf Katz, an economist and financial adviser to whom I don't know. I think I am right in remembering that Burgess once said or hinted that he had been in Moscow and had been some form of economic assistant to some organisation of the Comintern.
> (b) Edouard Pfeiffer, a Frenchman who was described as head of Daladier's personal secretariat. Pfeiffer was a politician of some importance in France and he also held some official post in the Boy Scout Movement. As I understood it Burgess was acting as an intermediary between Pfeiffer

representing Daladier and Mr Chamberlain and state of his personal associates among them being a Sir Joseph Ball. These negotiations were too secret for normal methods of communications. I should add here that Burgess never asked me to obtain or provide any information for him though in the normal course of conversation we naturally discussed whatever I knew. I should also add that owing to Burgess's strange personality I was never quite certain whether he was what he professed to be or whether indeed I was myself what I was supposed to be in this strange combination. I did once ask him to whom he gave his information and he replied that he had a contact with a Russian whose name he did not know and whom he met in small cafes. The only verifiable fact that did lead me to think that Burgess was telling the truth was that on one occasion he took some notes from a large bundle which was lying in a cupboard.

We now arrive at the time of the German-Soviet Pact when Burgess was away in France with Blunt.

On his return I told him that the Soviets had ruined any chance of preventing war and that I wished to have no more to do with his organisation if indeed such a thing existed. He did not agree with my views but was extremely distressed. His said that Blunt also had expressed the same views and that under the circumstances we had better give up the whole affair but that for obvious reasons it was best if we never mentioned the subject again even to each other. After the war I did once or twice refer to the subject but on each occasion he became extremely agitated and refused to discuss the matter. I once in a moment of anger told him untruthfully that lest he should have any doubts on the subject I had deposited a factual account of our association with my bank. At this he was very surprised and alarmed and asked me to describe the document. I should add that from the time of the German Soviet Pact I had no doubt that Burgess had in fact given up his previous association. After the war we remained on very intimate terms and I still had no reason to doubt this view. In recent months when Burgess was in America I have received several letters from him in which he has expressed very strongly his disapproval of American foreign policy and his belief that the Americans were deliberately provoking a third World War which was now imminent. On his return from America and indeed on the same day that he arrived he came to see me in the country. He was in a highly exalted but excited state of mind. He repeated the views he had formed of American foreign policy severely criticised our Embassy for failure to represent the true state if affairs and showed me two draft despatches of his which the embassy had refused to send. He said that he intended to show these despatches to the Foreign Office and also that he intended to press his views upon several influential persons the most important of whom in his eyes was Mr Kenneth

Younger whom he believed to sympathise with his options. I formed the opinion that he thought his efforts would have a genuine effect upon the course of policy here. This was the last time I saw him but on Friday 25th May he had a long end strange conversation with my wife of which I have given a full report elsewhere.

Rees would later allege that, alarmed by his wife's account of her conversation with Burgess, he had telephoned David Footman on 25 May and asked to be put in touch with Liddell. When he had heard nothing by Sunday afternoon he had called Blunt who had come down to Sonning the following day to spend several hours persuading Rees to remain silent. Eventually Rees would make his charges known, and he accused Robin Zaehner, Stuart Hampshire, Blunt and even Liddell himself of having been Burgess's co-conspirators, horrifying MI5. When the time came for Rees's statement to be sent to the FBI as a demonstration of co-operation, Liddell saved some embarrassment by editing it, as he acknowledged on 27 June:

Dick White has agreed a memorandum with SIS on the subject of Kim Philby, which is to go to the FBI. I have made various amendments, and in particular the exclusion of a reference in Goronwy Rees' statement to the effect that Burgess thought that Kenneth Younger would be sympathetic to his views about China.

For his part, Liddell found it hard to suspect Blunt, commenting on 12 June that 'I feel certain that Anthony was never a conscious collaborator with Burgess in any activities that he may have conducted on behalf of the Comintern.'

Philby was also under the spotlight, and on 4 June he submitted his highly tendentious observations in which he sought to distance himself from Maclean by deliberately mis-spelling his surname:

1. During the last few days, careful reflection on this distressing affair has led me to modify sensibly reactions to the disappearance of Burgess,
2. In my telegram, I stated that Burgess was undisciplined and irresponsible to a degree that makes it scarcely conceivable that he could have been involved in any clandestine activity. While it is still most difficult for me to believe that a man of his character could have been employed as a Soviet agent, a few isolated facts about his behaviour in Washington, which I have been piecing together in my memory, suggest that the possibility cannot be excluded. Each fact is perfectly explicable in itself, but Burgess's disappearance with MacLean and his continued, failure to reappear, give them a possibly sinister significance.
3. The facts are as follows:
   (a) Burgess possessed a sun-lamp, which, he used seldom, if ever, for its normal purpose. I do not know how or where he acquired it, and of

course do not propose to institute enquiries at this stage. He probably brought it from England.

(b) On one occasion, Burgess mentioned to me that he possessed a camera. He described as his 'only piece of war-loot', whatever that may mean. I did not pursue the matter. I cannot say definitely that he had it with him in Washington. He did however say that he knew nothing about photography and therefore could not use it.

(c) Very occasionally Burgess was in the habit of working at home after office hours. I can only remember definitely one occasion on which he did so, but it may well have happened more often.

(d) Burgess travelled fairly frequently to New York. Here again, I cannot remember exactly how often he travelled but at a guess I should say about six times in the course of his eight months' stay here, During these visits, he saw Jebb and his, staff, and doubtless sought an outlet for energies normally repressed in the polite atmosphere of Washington.

(e) Finally, Burgess left behind three books, one of which was Stalin's 'Marxism and the National Colonial Question'. As Burgess was an omnivorous reader, this probably has little or no significance, but I mention it for what it is worth.

4. As stated above, all these facts are susceptible of wholly innocent interpretations, and are taken out of the context of a vigorous and eccentric life. Nevertheless, I feel that their possible combined significance is such that I could not fail to report them. There is, I am afraid, very little doubt that Burgess had available the essential requirements of an espionage agent.

5. I note from the FO list that MacLean entered the FO in the autumn of 1935. His term at Cambridge, assuming that he went through the normal three years, was presumably 1932-35. Burgess was an undergraduate, so far as I can remember, from 1930-33 and he remained on as a tutor for a year or two longer. It seems quite possible therefore, that there may have been a very early connection between him and MacLean. It is even conceivable, that one recruited the other. In which case, if either had succeeded in getting wind of the investigation, it would be natural for them to concert a joint get-away.

PS. Since the above was typed, I have remembered that the sun-lamp was given to Burgess by Eric Kessler, former Swiss Chargé d'Affaires, in Washington, on the occasion of his transfer to Romania in December.

MI5's investigation was intended to establish precisely how Maclean had escaped, the identities of both his immediate co-conspirators and his past contacts or sources, conscious or unconscious. What is particularly striking about the event is the timing, for it was on the day before, 24 May, that a high-level conference had been held at the Foreign Office to decide the exact timetable for Maclean's interrogation. The meeting had consisted of Sir William Strang, Sir Roger Makins, George Cary-Foster and the SIS Foreign Office Adviser Pat Reilly. Attending from MI5 were Sir Percy Sillitoe and Dick White. The final memorandum minuted the decisions taken, and provided a step-by-step route to what was intended to be a confrontation that would extract a confession from Maclean and conclude the molehunt that had been initiated by Krivitsky back in January 1940.

2. In general discussion the following points were made:-
   (a) Current MI5 investigations had not resulted in the collection of any further evidence.
   (b) The possibility of using the 'purge' procedure for removing Maclean from the Foreign Service on present facts would be difficult but it could possibly be arranged.
   (c) The only positive facts in our possession were that certain secret British information had been passed to the Russians in 1944 and 1945 and that the agent concerned appeared to have a wife resident in New York in 1944.

3. Sir Percy Sillitoe emphasised that extreme care was necessary in such cases where the positive evidence was so small. The danger of attaching too much importance to coincidences was very real. Nevertheless it was true that the investigations suggested that Mr Maclean was the most likely suspect and there were no legal reasons why a suspect should not be interviewed. Without interviewing the principal suspects it would be impossible to clear up any investigation. He therefore considered that an interview must take place.

4. It was therefore agreed by the meeting that Mr Maclean should be interviewed.

5. Sir Roger Makins then outlined the position as he saw it from the political point of view. He considered that this was the worst possible moment for anything to occur which would aggravate anti-British feeling in America. If the results of this case became public he considered that it would cause a sensation in the USA. It must be remembered that Mr Maclean had worked in Washington for four years on a number of secret matters and that he was at present head of the American Department in the Foreign office. Sir Roger Makins's opinion was that the Americans would be bound to leak if they were told the results of our investigations.

6. Sir Percy Sillitoe considered that he had considerable influence with Mr Hoover and that it should not be forgotten that the latter had not altogether ruled out that the agent might be an American, in which case Mr. Hoover would probably not give away any information given to him by Sir Percy Sillitoe about a British agent in case it turned out to be wrong. Sir Percy Sillitoe emphasised the three reasons, apart from

the fact that the Americans were also making investigations, why it was necessary to approach the Americans before we took any positive action such as interviewing the principal suspect. These were:-

(a) The BRUSA Agreement in regard to Signal intelligence material, which bound Eastcote to pass the results of their work to their opposite numbers in Washington.

(b) The fact that the basic evidence in this case was derived from a source available jointly to the Americans and the United Kingdom and any use that was made of it which might lead to its compromise, without the approval of the other partner, would be a breach of faith.

(c) The personal arrangements he had made with Mr Hoover whereby they had agreed to keep each other informed of any major case which might seriously affect their own or Anglo-American relations.

7. Sir Percy Sillitoe considered that all these obligations should be honoured and it was therefore necessary to go ahead with the plan which was now under consideration. The first move in this plan which would set the ball rolling was the passing by Eastcote to their opposite numbers in America of the additional fragment concerning the wife living in New York. From then on there would be no stopping developments. Sir Percy Sillitoe considered that if he consulted Mr Hoover as soon as possible after the operation had been set in motion it would be the best way of influencing Mr Hoover and preventing a leakage. He could also not rule out the possibility that some help might be obtained from the FBI which would provide further evidence. He was therefore prepared to undertake the task of informing Mr Hoover personally as the best way of reducing to a minimum the damage which the case might do.

8. During his discussions with Mr Hoover Sir Percy Sillitoe would do his best to scotch any suggestions by Mr Hoover that he should send over an officer as an observer in any interrogations which were to take place in the United Kingdom.

9. The meeting agreed that the course suggested by Sir Percy Sillitoe offered the best hope of avoiding disaster.

10. The programme which was therefore agreed by the meeting is as follows:

May 28. Eastcote would pass results of their work to Arlington Hall.

May 29. The MI5 liaison officer would tell the FBI that the information contained in the Eastcote fragment had helped to narrow the field and intensive investigations were taking place in the United Kingdom.

June 9. Personal telegram through MI5 channels from Sir Percy Sillitoe to Mr Hoover stating that because of important developments he considered it necessary to come over to discuss the matter personally.

June 12/13. Sir Percy Sillitoe, after further discussion with Mr Steel, would inform Mr Hoover of the principal suspect's name and of the action it was proposed to take. He would ask the FBI to undertake such enquiries as might seem profitable in the United States.

Between 18 & 25 June Interrogation would take place. Sir Percy Sillitoe would remain in Washington until the interrogation had taken place in order to give the results to Mr Hoover and to try to co-ordinate future action.

11. The foregoing programme has been influenced by the fact that Mr Maclean's wife is due to have a baby on or about the 17th June. Until Mrs Maclean has gone to a nursing home it would not be possible to interrogate Mr. Maclean since it might be necessary to make a search of his house.

12. The meeting agreed that just before the MI5 liaison officer informs the FBI on May 29th he should outline the whole case, including the possible consequences of informing the FBI to Sir Oliver Franks and Mr Steel.

13 It was agreed by the meeting that Sir Percy Sillitoe should inform the Prime Minister of the facts tomorrow, 25th May, and that the Secretary of State should be so informed.

14. It was agreed that Mr Reilly should take up with C the question of whether or not the chairman of the American Sigint Board should be approached in regard to obtaining approval to use the source material for interrogation.

15. Sir William Strang enquired whether any action had been or could be taken to restrict the secret information passed to Mr Maclean. Sir Roger Makins explained that when he had been in a position to do so he had in fact refrained from passing to Mr Maclean certain papers which he would normally have marked for him.

    It was generally agreed, however, that nothing further could be done about this without arousing suspicion.

16. Some discussion took place in regard to the arrangements and form of the interrogation but it was decided that further discussion would be required on this point. It was considered that it would probably be necessary to send Mr Maclean on leave immediately after the interrogation.

Once this schedule had been agreed, Sillitoe and White returned to Leconfield House and briefed the lead investigators, James Robertson and Arthur Martin. Coincidentally, they had just acquired a new piece of potentially incriminating information. A former Foreign Office secretary, Patience Maitland-Addison, who had also worked for MI5, and had subsequently married the assistant military attaché in Paris, Colonel Pain, reported in January 1950 that she had recently attended a party hosted by a CPGB member, Hugh Slater. In the early hours a very drunk Maclean allegedly had boasted that he was 'the British Alger Hiss' and had been a Communist for years. Although the incident had been reported to the Foreign Office, no action had been taken, but it was added to an MI5 file which already listed Maclean as an associate of the *Observer* journalist Philip Toynbee, a known CPGB member and former leader of the Party's branch at Oxford.

MI5, of course, was dismayed by this news, as a link between Slater and Maclean was potentially significant. Born in South Africa, Slater was a veteran CPGB activist and had been a reporter on the Comintern's English-language newspaper *Imprecor*. A graduate of the Slade School of Art, he had served as a political commissar with the International Brigade during the Spanish Civil War and was later appointed director of operations.

On 30 May Jim Skardon, operating under his usual alias of 'Seddon', had his first opportunity to interview Melinda Maclean, (codenamed Mrs CURZON) at Lady Maclean's flat in Iverna Court in Kensington:

In accordance with arrangements made by Mr Carey-Foster I went to 8 Carlton House Terrace and met Mr Willan of the Establishments and Personnel Department, Foreign Office, at 2.15 p.m. on 30th May, expecting to go with him to Beacon Shaw, Tatsfield, to see Mrs. CURZON.

She however was in London to meet her mother, the plane was delayed, and she had telephoned Mr Willan shortly before 2.15 to say that she could be seen at Lady CURZON's address before 3 pm Willan suggested that it would save time if we went and saw her there.

We were met at the flat by the mother-in-law who ushered us into a bedroom to avoid other people in the flat, and there Willan and I interviewed Mrs. CURZON.

I was introduced as SEDDON and Willan did not, in my presence, refer to me as from Scotland Yard though I am pretty sure that it was assumed that I came from there.

I found Mrs. CURZON to be very self-contained. She was obviously worried about the departure of her husband but she was rather more annoyed than disturbed. She explained in fact that this was not the first time it had happened. In the most natural way it was possible to question her about domestic and official matters, and as a result the following picture of her married life was obtained.

They met in Paris and were married there. They remained together until after the Battle of Britain when she went off to New York to have her first baby. They were separated then for six months. Otherwise she has travelled with him and been with him at his various stations until April or May 1950, when he left Cairo hurriedly following a nervous breakdown. They had taken a house at Alexandria for the summer but when she heard from him that he was not returning she went off to Spain where she stayed with her mother, and later to Paris until sometime in September or October 1950 when CURZON bought Beacon Shaw, Tatsfield, and they came together again. These were the only separations of which she seemed to have any immediate recollection, and I did not press her for information as to events in the United States in 1944 at this stage. She was aware that her husband had been treated by Dr. Rosenbaum, and she said that his condition was such that if he took just one drink he became pretty drunk. They have been very happy throughout the winter though ten days ago he did stay in London over night after a cocktail party at which she believes he became rather drunk.

She was unable to explain his conduct either in Cairo or in the immediate present, except to say that when under the influence of drink he did the most extraordinary things.

On Friday 25th May he telephoned her to say that he was bringing a friend home for dinner. It was his birthday and the man turned out to be somebody he introduced as Roger Stiles. She had never met him before. She described him as about 35, 5' 9', thin face, black hair and medium build, and although she gained no positive impression as to his means of livelihood, from his talk which was mainly about books she gathered that he was engaged in the publishing line. They announced that after dinner they would be going off to see somebody, and might be away the night.

CURZON packed a bag with sufficient clothes merely for a weekend visit. Mrs. CURZON was pretty incensed at this conduct, for apart from expecting the baby within a fortnight and having two children down with measles, CURZON's sister and brother-in-law were visiting them on the Saturday. She thought his conduct was pretty outrageous. The two men left at about 10 p.m. in the motor car driven by Roger Stiles, which Mrs. CURZON could say no more than it was a new-looking tan-coloured saloon car.

She had heard nothing to suggest that he might be undertaking any sort of excursion until the announcement was made at dinner time, and when she was told by Willan that it was known that CURZON had left this country and had arrived in France, she was completely at a loss to explain the matter.

She was a little puzzled at the suddenness of this escapade, for whereas CURZON had been extremely unsettled and unhappy in Cairo, he had thoroughly enjoyed his work and apparently his home during the last few months.

Asking Mrs. CURZON to maintain the utmost discretion in this matter and advising her not to initiate any new enquiries and to allow old ones merely to peter out, we promised to keep her fully informed of such developments as occurred.

I asked Mrs CURZON whether she had looked through her husband's papers and letters to see whether there was any reason to be found amongst these to account for his journey, and she said that in fact he kept no papers at home but carried out all his private and business correspondence from Foreign Office. In this connection she asked that her own letters should be readdressed from Foreign Office and offered, if it would serve any useful purpose, to go through such private papers as might be in his desk at the office to assist the enquiry.

She also said that should it be required she could produce a photograph which was a fairly good likeness of CURZON.

Before leaving the flat we saw Lady CURZON for a few moments and broke similar news to her of CURZON's departure from this country.

She then said that she was not very surprised as it had crossed her mind more than once that he might make a journey over the Channel. She was unable to give any coherent reason for this suggestion. We promised her that we would be thorough in our enquiries and begged her to maintain complete discretion and promised that we would keep her au fait with developments. She and Mrs CURZON both seemed to be very grateful for the trouble and kindness shown by Foreign Office.

MI5's last opportunity to question Melinda took place a week later, on 7 June, when Donald's brother Alan, also a diplomat, accompanied Skardon to Beaconshaw, immediately following the arrival of a telegram at Iverna Court which had been sent, in her son's name, to Lady Maclean from Paris.

At about 11 a.m. on 7.6.51 I met Alan Maclean at Iverna Gardens and his mother was with him. Lady Maclean was quite sure that the telegram which she had received from Paris that morning was prepared by Donald, since the signature was that of a family nickname given to Donald, and she thought the text was typical of him.

Alan went with me to Tatsfield where at Beacon Shaw we saw Mrs Maclean. She had not by that time received the confirmatory telegram from the Post Office, but repeated to me briefly its contents as telephoned to her. For the first time Mrs Maclean seemed to be somewhat upset, for whereas she was formerly annoyed rather than worried she now seemed to have some anxiety. According to her the telegram was clearly phrased by her husband.

The arrival of the telegram to some extent made quite pointless any enquiries relating to Donald's friends which might have produced information as to his present whereabouts. However I pointed out to Mrs. Maclean that lest the telegram was a fake and since in a few days I should not be able I to talk to her at all, I did propose to take the opportunity of making the few enquiries of her then and there as a contingency against the future. We then dealt with the whole of her married life and the following particulars were obtained from her.

She was a student at the Sorbonne when she met Donald Maclean in Paris. At that time she was living at 11 rue de Belohasse on the Left Bank. They were married on the last day before the British left Paris on June 10th, 1940, and they went off to St. Jean de Lus. At this time it was the intention that Linda should go home to America, but in the event she came to London with her husband and they settled in a furnished flat rented from some people named Hutchinson in Mecklenburg Square. They were bombed out of this flat, and in September 1940 she went home to the USA to have her first baby, Fergus. She returned to England in April 1941 when they had a flat at Rossmore Court where they lived until April 1944 whilst Donald was stationed at Foreign Office.

When he was transferred to Washington, owing to the housing situation Donald lived for a time with Michael Wright in Washington and until two days before Christmas Mrs Maclean was living with her mother. Before the birth of her baby she was living with her mother at 277 Park Avenue, New York, and after it at an address to which her mother moved at 3 East 69th Street. For a month during the period May till December (she is unable to place it before or after the birth of the baby) Mrs. Maclean was with her mother at a house which she had at Merriebrook, South Egremont, Mass. Whilst in Washington her husband cultivated no friendships outside the Embassy circle. His particular friends were the Hendersons. For three years from December 1944 Donald and she lived at 2710 35th Place, Washington, and for the last period of their stay at an address in Pea Street.

During the period of their separation Donald quite frequently visited New York to see Mrs Maclean, and when I suggested that it was possibly every week-end she replied that it was more likely about once a month.

In 1948 the family moved to London for six weeks before going on in November to Cairo. For the first part of their stay in Cairo they were living at 10 Saleh Ayoub and later at 19 Ibzanki. This brought them up to the period March 1950 when Donald had his breakdown. His best friends there included Bill Morris who is still there, and she remembered particularly of their visitors Philip Toynbee of the *Observer* who stayed with them for a few weeks immediately before Donald went amok. From May until November 1950, they were separated once more, and she believes that during this time her husband, cultivated a friendship with one Robert Kee. He became very fond of this man who was employed by *Picture Post*. She believes that Robert Kee is at present in the South of France. On her return to England after visiting Spain and France with her mother, they lived for a time in a hotel whilst they found the house at Beacon Shaw, Tatsfield.

I questioned Mrs Maclean about the events leading to Donald's disappearance, and upon reflection she told me that she thinks that it was on Thursday, 24th May, that Donald told her that he would be bringing a friend to dinner on Friday night. To the best of her recollection he mentioned the name of 'Roger Stiles' himself when suggesting the party. On the 25th May Donald caught the 6.10 train and arrived home at about 7 pm. Half an hour later the friend 'Roger Stiles' arrived. They wandered about in the garden for a bit and had dinner possibly between 8 and 8.45 p.m., and although her first view was that they left the house together at about 10 p.m., she thought that it might have been half an hour earlier that they did in fact depart. She has no yardstick upon which to base her recollections. They did not seem to be particularly anxious or hurried.

When I completed my questioning of Mrs Maclean, Mrs. Dunbar came into the sitting-room and introduced herself to me. She is a spritely American natron, and professed herself to be overjoyed to meet a member of Scotland Yard. After some desultory conversation touching upon Donald's financial affairs and a family consultation as to the desirability of closing down the house and cutting their losses, a suggestion made by Mrs Dunbar, Alan and Mrs. Maclean by chance left me alone in the company of Mrs Dunbar. She immediately said, 'Mr. Seddon, I want you to understand that I'm just one hundred per cent behind this family – by that I mean the whole Maclean family. But if there's any way in which I can help you with your enquiries in relation to this man Donald I shall be only too pleased. Here I am – you know where to find me.' There was no doubt that in this American woman we have at least one ally, undesirable though she may seem to be. It was not convenient, since the whole family foregathered quickly once more, for me to press home the advantage, but Mrs Dunbar does remain a possible source of positive information who will not object to direct questioning. (It may be well to exploit this source after Linda has gone into hospital).

Alan Maclean left the house with me at about 1.20 p.m.

I advised both branches of the family to refer any press enquiries to Foreign Office.

Alan Maclean discussed with me my visit to Rosie, and said that the name William Bath should be Henry Bath who is more a friend of Alan's than of Donald's. He mentioned other mutual friends, namely the David Tennants who run the Gargoyle Club, as being friendly also with Donald.

Alan is still clearly worried and his anxiety was not relieved by the arrival of the telegram which started, 'Had to clear out suddenly', but he assured me, though he expressed the view that his opinion was probably worthless, that his brother Donald whom he knows as well as anybody is not and has not been for years a Communist Party or a sympathiser with its ideals. He said this quite diffidently, with the expressed knowledge that probably those who should know people best probably know least about them. I do not believe that Alan has any positive information which would be of assistance to this enquiry. I have however enlisted his sympathetic help I feel sure.

On 6 June 1951 Anthony Blunt made a statement:

A year or two before the war Guy Burgess told me that he was working for an organisation which I later believed to be the Secret Intelligence Service and that he was engaged in organising anti-Fascist propaganda. This was connected with a body called the Joint Broadcasting Committee (?). For this work which was carried on in a highly cloak and dagger style he told me that he was in contact with a large number of people including his old Communist friends. The only people that I can remember either meeting or hearing him mention in this context are as follows:

(1) Rolf Katz of Central European origin who during part of the period in question lived in London and part in Paris. I believe he later went to South America.

(2) (?) Edouard Pfeiffer a close political friend and associate of Daladier. He was a fairly prominent French politician.

Burgess was also connected with an organisation called the Anglo-German Fellowship of which the most important members were Captain Jack Macnamara who was then Member of Parliament and was, I believe, killed during the war, and the then Archdeacon of South Eastern Europe whose name I do not know, remember also that Burgess told me a story of carrying communications to Pfeiffer for Daladier on behalf of Chamberlain, the impression being given that this was arranged by the organisation for which he was working.

I further remember that I was with Burgess in France just before the war, and that when we reached the South of France we decided that we must come back because war was imminent, and that he would be needed by his organisation. On the way we heard the news of the German-Soviet pact. This was clearly a very considerable shock to Burgess and I recollect that he talked about the latter, producing a series of alternative and contradictory explanations and hypotheses.

Blunt's carefully-crafted statement mirrored, almost word for word, what Goronwy Rees had submitted to Liddell, and there are some important common denominators. For example, both identified Katz and Pfeiffer as Burgess's Comintern contacts, and touched on Burgess's employment by SIS, a potential source of embarrassment. In effect, both Rees and Blunt offered as an alibi their belief that Burgess had been entitled, by virtue of his SIS role, to ask his acquaintances for sensitive information.

Pfeiffer, who died in 1966 without ever having been questioned, was a homosexual lawyer who had headed the private office of the French Minister of War, Edouard Daladier. As for Rolf Katz, he was a well-known Comintern propagandist who had indeed been in London, until he was arrested in 1936 by Special Branch and deported. He had accumulated a large MI5 PF because of his political activities in London as a writer, having been published by Victor Gollancz's Left Book Club. During the war he had released *J'Accuse* under the pen-name André Simon but in 1946 had returned to his native Czechoslovakia, as Blunt probably knew. In May 1951 he was back in Prague, having been based briefly in Paris as a correspondent for *Rude Pravo*, but the following year he would be arrested, tried and hanged on trumped-up espionage charges during a Moscow-inspired purge of the Party.

For Blunt, the unresolved question of his complicity would recur with annoying frequency, but Courtenay Young and Ronnie Reed thought they had achieved something of a breakthrough when they interviewed him for over two hours during the afternoon of 15 May 1956, as was reflected in their subsequent report:

At no time during the interview did Blunt admit or begin to admit that he had ever been a conscious agent. However, some interesting points and some conflict of testimony between Blunt and Rees did emerge.

We first of all took Blunt over the few days before and after the flight of Burgess and Maclean. Blunt said that the last time he had seen Burgess was on the morning of Friday, 25 May when he came in for a cup of coffee with Blunt at the Courtauld. He said that Burgess was in a much better state that day than when he had seen him earlier in the week after his return from a weekend with Peter Pollock. Then he had been worse than he, Blunt, had ever known him. He thought it was a combination of drink and drugs and there was also a story that Burgess had taken a bolus intended for a horse (Peter Pollock's sister is a vet). Thinking back afterwards Blunt had said that perhaps Burgess had come round to make some sort of veiled farewell but had changed his mind. Nothing new regarding this chronology emerged.

The most interesting point concerned Blunt's visit to Rees at Sonning. Blunt said that he and Harris had been talking over Burgess's past actions and on the assumption that he had flown because he had been guilty of espionage were wondering how far back the trail led. This in turn led Blunt to go and see Rees to compare notes with him. Blunt said that he and Rees agreed to go together to see Captain Liddell as a result of their talk. We put to him Rees's version of the story, namely that he felt he ought to unbosom himself about the Comintern story and that Blunt had felt that this was not necessary and had put pressure on Rees not to go. This version Blunt completely denied and said was 'absolutely untrue'. We asked him why he though Rees would have invented it and he said that he could not imagine.

As regards the conversation in the Park, Blunt said that he had no recollection whatever of it. It might have taken place but if it had absolutely no recollection of it. We gave him Rees's version, namely that he had said 'you know what Guy is really up to', and Blunt had replied tersely 'yes'. Blunt agreed that this conversation might well have taken place but said that the question was ambiguous. Rees may well have meant Burgess's Comintern activities. Blunt, on the other hand, knowing nothing of these, would have taken it to refer to 'twenty things', i.e. it might have followed on some particular discussion about Burgess getting a job, wanting to join a club or some aspect of his sex life.

Blunt did not seem at all upset at this conflict of testimony. The only moment in the whole interview when he did seem slightly upset was when I was rather pressing him that by the time he was well installed in this Office if he ever thought about Guy's pre-war activities he must have realised that they could not have been for Section D and the dates did not fit. Blunt maintained that he knew Burgess was working for Sir John Ball and whatever one might think of the Conservative Party and Sir Horace Wilson it was still working for the British. He had always thought that Burgess's activities were for the British up to the time of the flight.

I then informed Blunt of the Volkov episode and the catalogue he provided. I mentioned the 'visit of the British greens' and pointed out that in all probability referred to Captain Liddell's visit to Canada which indicated a leakage from either MI5 or MI6. I suggested that if we equated Burgess with the source, this was the kind of information he could easily have picked up through gossip from Blunt, Harris, Captain Liddell himself, or even myself. Blunt took rather a high line at first and said he thought that that particular thing was one which would not have been gossiped about. I then mentioned the theft of documents from the Military Attaché's office and attempts to photograph his office. Blunt said that he knew of no such attempts and we agreed that that idea did not take us very much further. On the membership of a high level Intelligence Committee Blunt said that as far as he knew there were none except the JIC. I suggested the XX Committee and mentioned 'that curious thing you and I sat on'. Blunt supplied the name himself (TWIST) but thought it was not very high level. I suggested again that that might derive from Bentinck Street gossip and Blunt in effect tacitly admitted that such gossip existed.

I then produced [XXXXXXXXXXX] and pointed out that that knocked out Bentinck Street gossip. I also pointed out that it knocked out MI6 because they did not have PFs and said that it pretty well narrowed the field to Hugh Shillito, Kemball Johnston and ourselves. Kemball Johnston was really out; I let myself out, which left Hugh Shillito and Blunt. His reply was 'I think this certainly is a really tougher one'. He went on to say that one of the things that had worried him for a very long time was having taken files back to read in the evening at Bentinck Street. He admitted Burgess had come quite frequently to the Office and thought it quite possible that he had been left alone in the room. He could offer no solution as to how Burgess could have obtained these documents, if he did, unless he had stolen them from the Office and later replaced them or done the same thing at Bentinck Street. He did point out, however, that it was unlikely that he would take Russian dossiers home as those were not the kind of files on which action was needed by our section so he would not need to study them. At the conclusion of this phase of the interview Blunt said 'I think this is extremely obscure and I am sorry I cannot offer any help.'

Blunt went on to say that Burgess during his career as a spy could have built himself up, where necessary by inventing. This was exactly the same technique as he employed in his private life. By way of illustration of Burgess's character he gave us the story that Burgess had gone to Captain Liddell and told him that he suspected that Revai was a Communist agent. He later went to Revai and told him that somebody had put in a report to the authorities that he, Revai, was a Communist agent but that he need not worry about it because he, Burgess, had put it straight. We agreed that it was impossible to work out Burgess's motives for this episode but Blunt said that he was glad he had told us he knew that Revai was under suspicion (date unstated) because Revai had been told by someone who had heard it indirectly from someone in the Security Service that Revai's telephone was being tapped. After hearty laughter on all sides this subject was dropped.

As regards Rees's statement that Blunt and Burgess used frequently to go down and eat in a Chinese restaurant in the East End close to a shop where Burgess used to buy dungarees, etc. Blunt said that he never ate Chinese food because it gave him indigestion (that he has made this statement per this part I can confirm from personal experience); Burgess never wore dungarees and in any case he, Blunt, had never been either to the shop or to the restaurant. The only time he and Burgess had been together in the East End was when they occasionally used to go on what Blunt described as a 'mild church crawl' when Blunt would go and look at churches and old houses.

The interview was cordial throughout. At first Blunt appeared slightly nervous but later was completely composed and natural.

Though not taking us any further in our endeavours to solve any mystery, the interview was not unprofitable. There is a clear conflict of testimony between Blunt and Rees and one which I do not see can be resolved. Blunt denies having attempted to dissuade Rees from coming to see Captain Liddell. He denies Rees's statement that he and Burgess used to visit Commercial Road and he says he has no recollection of the conversation in the Park and says that if it did take place the question had no sinister implications for him.

The FBI investigation of Maclean's contacts in the United States turned up a curious connection with an Austrian-born art historian. The FBI's New York Field Office had taken a close interest in Gustav Glück who, in 1946, had been employed by UNRRA in London. Glück's FBI file recorded that he had been the lover of Martha Dodd, an espionage suspect who had been identified as a spy codenamed LIZA, and was also associated with Vasili Zarubin, the NKVD *resident* in Washington. A surreptitious search of Glück's address book had revealed Maclean's name and embassy telephone number. Martha Dodd, the daughter of the pre-war US ambassador in Berlin, had been named to the FBI as a Soviet spy by another agent, Jack Soble. At the time Dodd had been married to the millionaire CPUSA supporter Alfred Stern.

The American dimension to the Burgess and Maclean scandal would become a major preoccupation for Liddell who knew the value of continued transatlantic co-operation in both the counter-intelligence and signals intelligence fields. Initially

Percy Sillitoe, accompanied by Arthur Martin, had flown to Washington to brief J. Edgar Hoover, but their mission was a delicate one. On the afternoon of 14 June, while the pair was still away, Dick White called in Philby, as Liddell reported:

Dick had a long interview with Kim Philby and Jack Easton. Kim had submitted a note on all that he knew about Burgess. He denies emphatically that he had ever discussed Maclean with Burgess or that Esther Whitfield, his secretary, who was extremely discreet, would have been likely to do so either. He did agree, however, that if Burgess had been intent on finding out something, he might have gathered certain straws in the wind through a possible knowledge of meetings between Geoffrey Patterson, Bobby Mackenzie and himself.

Dick then questioned him about his first wife. He said that he had married her in Vienna in about 1934, knowing that she was a Communist, but that he had subsequently converted her, His marriage had broken up in 1936 and, so far as he knew, she was no more than a left-winger. He himself had never been a Communist, but his sympathies with the left had been strong when he married his first wife in 1934. Dick intends to question him further about his own position.

Meanwhile a telegram has come in from the D–G, saying that the CIA are already conducting enquiries about Philby, whom they regard as *persona non grata*, and that the FBI may take up the running before long. He thinks, therefore, that we should disclose to the FBI now that Kim s first wife was a Communist. I felt a little doubtful about volunteering this information at the present moment, when we had not even been asked. We have, therefore, left the decision with the D–G, emphasising that if he feels it necessary to communicate this information now, he should make it clear that no proper assessment of Philby's position has so far been possible, and that they should not prejudge the issue on the information about his former wife. This is to be subject to C's approval, which we cannot get until tomorrow.

Philby, of course, had just flown in from Washington, and protocol dictated that his interview at Leconfield House should be attended by a senior SIS officer, hence Easton's presence. The encounter was not intended as a hostile interrogation, but a preliminary interview, the first opportunity to place on record his position on certain issues, such as the possibility of a leak through Esther Whitfield, and the details of his relationship with Lizzie. White himself was on delicate ground here, as he must have been acutely aware, as his own wife, Kate, had also been a CPGB member. On the following day, Liddell returned to the subject:

We got C's clearance for the telegram to Washington. Meanwhile we have been dealing with rather difficult Parliamentary Questions about the screening of Burgess. We have replied that there is nothing in Burgess's record to indicate that he was a Communist or associated in such a way as to cause reasonable doubts about his reliability. In fact he had already been in the Foreign Office for several years before his name was referred to us in January, 1950. We gave an NRA on the strictly security side, but drew attention to discussions with the Foreign Office security branch with regard to Burgess's conduct in Gibraltar and Tangier, in which we had stated that we regarded him as thoroughly untrustworthy and unreliable.

On Saturday, 16 June Liddell had further news from Washington:

The D-G telegraphed to say that he has had a very satisfactory interview with Walter Bedell-Smith, who has suggested that in future we should carry the liaison instead of SIS. This is, of course, not a very practical idea; we cannot do SIS's work any more than they can do ours. On the other hand it is arguable that SIS might be able to do without a representative in Washington. Certainly with the FBI we could easily carry the burden.

On Monday, 18 June Sillitoe and Martin were back in London, apparently satisfied that Hoover had been placated.

The D-G returned about midday. He seems to have been successful in keeping Hoover quiet. The only grievance seems to be that we did not tell the FBI about our shortlist, but I think we shall be able to weather that one. Our stock at the moment seems to be good both with the FBI and with CIA. The only complication is that the FBI know about BRIDE whereas the CIA do not.

With the famously irascible FBI Director temporarily neutralized, and Philby placed on leave while his future was contemplated, the CIA declared that Philby would not be welcome to return to Washington. If Hoover seemed content, for his own reasons, to allow MI5 to investigate the debacle, Bedell Smith was quite emphatic that Philby was *persona non grata*. SIS immediately replaced him with Machlachlan Silverwood-Cope, and then John Bruce Lockhart, but meanwhile Liddell's dilemma was how much information should be sent to Washington, as he summarized on 27 June:

Dick has agreed a memorandum with SIS on the subject of Kim Philby, which is to go to the FBI. I have made various amendments, and in particular the exclusion of a reference in Goronwy Rees' statement to the effect that Burgess thought that Kenneth Younger would be sympathetic to his views about China.

Rees's remarks about Anthony Blunt have been allowed to remain, but I have said that I thought that Anthony's answer to them should also be included.

I am a little worried about the report, since it seems to me to be too categorical about matters on which there is no real evidence. Goronwy, in his statement, said that Burgess told him in about 1937 that he was working for an anti-Fascist organisation, which was a secret branch of the Comintern and was collecting information of a political kind. He had asked Goronwy and Blunt to co-operate with him. How far they actually did so has not emerged, nor indeed were they really in a position to give very much assistance. Blunt says that he never knew that Burgess was working for a Comintern organisation, but thought that it was something he was doing for our Secret Service to combat Nazi activities. Personally, I feel that, whatever the facts, Anthony would have been far more interested in his artistic pursuits than in politics, although his friendship with Burgess might well have led him into doing something rather stupid. I find it difficult, too, to imagine Burgess as a Comintern agent or an espionage agent in the ordinary accepted interpretation of these terms. He certainly had been Marxian and, up to a point, an apologist for the Russian regime, and would have been capable of discussing, in a highly indiscreet manner with anybody, almost anything that he got from official sources. He would have done this out of sheer political enthusiasm without any regard for security. Dick's report does not convey this, and it may be rightly so. In any case the Americans in these matters are incapable of assessing the finer points in a case like this: a man is either black or he is white. It seems to me that as a result of this report, Blunt will be blacklisted in America which, whatever the facts of his past, seems hardly justifiable.

The nature of MI5's rather-too-public investigation meant that it inevitably attracted a great deal of unwelcome media attention, and this created an unprecedented environment for the organization to go about its clandestine business. Furthermore, everyone who had ever met Burgess or Maclean seemed to have an informed opinion which, they felt, should be delivered to the appropriate authorities, and one such was Owen O'Malley, the former British ambassador to the wartime Polish government-in-exile. On 7 July Liddell learned that SIS's solution was to have an independent enquiry:

Dick was summoned to a meeting at Broadway at which C and Easton were present. They were extremely worried about Philby's position and anxious that his case should be further investigated before he returned from leave. Dick said that it would be difficult for him to carry the enquiry any further on the assumption that Philby was identical with ELLI in the Igor Gouzenko case, or that he was the 'counter-espionage officer' mentioned by Konstantin

Volkov. He suggested that Edward Cussen or Buster Milmo should be given all the evidence and conduct an enquiry. He doubted, however, whether any such enquiry could be conclusive: Philby would have to be told that the Americans suspected him of being ELLI and that it was up to him to do everything he could to produce factual evidence to the contrary. This might, however, be extremely difficult.

Meanwhile, O'Malley, late of the Foreign Office, has been to William Strang to say that he had positive evidence that Anthony Blunt had been a friend of Guy Burgess and that while at Cambridge he was a Communist. Strang thought this information should be given to Sir Alan Lascelles and thought that it should be transmitted through us rather than the Foreign Office. Dick thinks that the only way out is for me to see Lascelles.

Dick wants Anthony to see James Robertson and Arthur Martin on certain points which have cropped up in the Guy Burgess correspondence taken from his flat in Bond Street. I am going to arrange this.

The top-level meeting attended by White, Menzies and Easton was probably not minuted, but a few days later, but clearly the Deputy Chief had been unimpressed by MI5 because a few days later, on 12 July, Easton was in Washington where he saw Bedell Smith and informed the CIA's Winston Scott that he was convinced of Philby's innocence. Now the head of the CIA's Western European Division, Scott had until the previous year been the CIA's first station chief in London, serving for three years until his replacement by Dan Delabardelen.

Liddell did not make his views known regarding White's proposal that either Cussen or Milmo, who both had wartime MI5 experience, should conduct a review, but his solution to the issue about Blunt was to have lunch with him, which happened on 10 July:

I had lunch with Anthony Blunt. He told me about the recent activities of Jack Hewit, who seems to have sold himself to the *Daily Express* and to be in a highly neurotic condition. The *Daily Express* have been taking him on trips to Paris to try and obtain evidence about the whereabouts of Burgess and Maclean. Meanwhile, he has given them several highly indiscreet interviews. Both Anthony and Goronwy Rees have reprimanded him severely, as a result of which he is threatening to undermine Anthony's position. On one occasion he went so far as to say that he would commit suicide. Goronwy Rees informed the police, through a friend of his, and some action was taken by them to calm Hewit down.

I took the opportunity of asking Anthony again about his views on Marxian doctrine and the extent to which at any time he had been associated with Communist activity. He told me that in his early days at Cambridge he had been associated with a number of Communists, many of who were fellow Apostles. He has always been interested in the Marxian interpretation of history and art history, but he had never believed in the way the Russians applied it, nor had he ever accepted or been interested in the purely political aspects of the Marxian teaching. He was quite emphatic that when Burgess approached him, I think in 1937, to assist him in obtaining political information of an anti-Fascist kind, he was firmly under the impression that Burgess was working for the government. Burgess had never said to him anything which would imply that he was working for the Comintern.

I subsequently saw Dick, Robertson, Arthur Martin and Burbidge, and I think that what I had to tell them dispelled suspicions on a number of points which had been aroused through a number of conversations on the TC.

Five days later, following a meeting with Sillitoe, Liddell spoke to Lascelles about Blunt:

I saw Tommy Lascelles, at the D-G's request, in order to convey to him a report made by Owen O'Malley to William Strang to the effect that Anthony Blunt had been a Communist and might well be one today,

I told Lascelles that I had known Anthony Blunt for about ten years; that he had in his university days associated with a number of Communists; that he did believe in the Marxian interpretation of history and art history, and that he had no sympathy with Marxian theories as applied by the Russians. I was convinced that he had never been a Communist in the full political sense, even during his days at Cambridge.

Tommy said that he was very glad to hear this, since it was quite possible that the story might get round to the Royal Family; he would then be able to say that he had already heard it and looked into it and was satisfied that there was nothing in it. He told me that Blunt had on one occasion intimated to the Queen that he was an atheist – Tommy thinks he may well have said an agnostic – and that the Queen had been a little shaken by his remarks. He was certain that if he now went up and told her that Anthony was a Communist, her immediate reaction would be 'I always told you so'.

By mid-summer the situation remained unchanged and on 20 August Liddell reflected his unease about the prospect of an interrogation, but was coming under pressure from the CIA station chief in London, Dan Delabardelen:

I had a talk with Arthur Martin about the various entries in the Philby file. There seemed to me to be a few loose ends. He said that it was all being worked through again and most of my queries he had already answered. There is no doubt that he knows his cases inside-out and backwards.

I am still rather inclined to think that it was not a leakage which caused Maclean and Burgess to make their hurried departure. It seems to me quite possible that Burgess had discussed with Maclean on his return the two memoranda which he had put up to the Foreign Office on our policy in regard to China. Burgess had tried to get the embassy in Washington to forward them to London and, on getting a refusal, was anxious to put them in himself on his return. He would quite naturally have discussed the matter with Maclean as head of the American Department, who is a friend and would be likely to take a sympathetic view. Such a conversation, over a good deal of drink, might well have led both to express their innermost feelings about Russia, to vent their dislike of US policy, and to come to the conclusion that they must do something to prevent a third world war. At that stage Maclean might well have talked about his past and his apprehension that it might one day catch up with him. They might have decided to leave the country – Burgess taking the initiative. It this is true it would account for Burgess's remark that he was going to help a friend who was in difficulties.

Dan Delabardelen said that he had been asked by Washington whether we would be interested in their comments on our paper about Kim Philby, since Washington appeared to take the view that we were no longer investigating Philby's case. I said that I thought this misunderstanding had possibly arisen because we had expressed the view that an interrogation of Philby at this stage could not produce any useful results and might in fact dry up certain sources which could possibly help us to find a solution. We had in fact, and were still, making exhaustive enquiries. Meanwhile, it was useless to interrogate a man who had all the cards in his hands. Until we get some fresh cards, and some pretty high ones, there was nothing in the way of interrogation that would be profitable. I hoped that he would express this view, with which he agreed, upon his superiors in Washington, They have been urging us to interrogate immediately on the more sinister allegations against Philby arising from both the Igor Gouzenko and Konstantin Volkov cases. He asked whether we should be making any interim reports. I said that we might in a month or two's time when we should obviously have to take stock. This would be a normal procedure. We might then conclude that we had come to a dead-end and take a chance on interrogation.

By 1 October, when Liddell returned from his annual leave, he learned that MI5's research had uncovered the passport issued to Lizzie Philby a few days after her marriage to Kim in February 1934. This item would prove to be a key piece of evidence as the interrogation approached. Another discovery was a link with a senior Canadian diplomat, Herbert Norman, who turned out to have studied at the University of Toronto with Israel Halperin. Both men had then met subsequently at Harvard and socially in Ottawa, and Norman had already been investigated by the RCMP following a report that he was a Communist.

Since I have been away the case against Kim Philby seems to be somewhat blacker, although we are still working on what may be pure coincidences,

While all the points against him are capable of another explanation, their cumulative effect is certainly impressive. It now seems that his first wife made a number of journeys to the Continent at the time when Kim was living with her in London. The inference is that she was then acting as a courier. These facts were never revealed by Kim, although they must have been within his knowledge. His association with her only ended in 1940,

Dick White tells me that traces have now been found of Herbert Norman which show very clearly that he was one of the Cambridge group in 1934–36, and that at that time he was closely associated with Benjamin Bradley of the Indian Communist Group in London. Somewhat regrettably, this matter was not reported to the RCMP. Philip Vickery put a ban on it and Jane Archer acquiesced. Infantile Leftism was not, of course, at that time taken so seriously as it is now. We are, however, putting the RCMP in the picture, although I do not think the information adds a great deal to what they already know.

[XXXXXXXXXXXXXXXXXXXXXXX]

I saw the D-G who told me about his interview with Walter Bedell-Smith. Bedell Smith was given certain facts about the Kim Philby case, which he was told were still under investigation. It was, however, made clear to him that up to the moment these could only be regarded as a chain of coincidences, all of which might have a different explanation. He seems to have got a somewhat false impression of this interview and told C that we were now confident that Philby was identical with the man mentioned by Igor Gouzenko and Konstantin Volkov. This, of course, is far from the case.

The Herbert Norman connection was of potential interest because Norman's name and address at Charles Street, Toronto, had been found in Halperin's address-book, and Igor Gouzenko had revealed that his *rezident*, Nikolai Zabotin, had made enquiries in Moscow about someone named 'Norman', only to be informed that he was indeed known to his NKVD counterpart at the embassy, Vitali Pavlov.

MI5's research had also uncovered a link, apparently filed away by the omniscient pre-war entity Indian Political Intelligence (IPI), headed by Sir Philip Vickery, between Herbert Norman and a veteran CPGB activist, Benjamin Bradley, who had run one of the Party's fronts, the League Against Imperialism, and produced the fortnightly publication *Colonial Information Bulletin*. Trained as a metal-worker, Bradley was well-known to IPI and the Delhi Intelligence Bureau, having been convicted of sedition at the Meerut conspiracy trials in 1932. Clearly Norman had been moving among some very serious and committed Communists.

On 3 October Liddell noted that the investigation into Philby was widening, and the MI5 officers directly involved wanted to extend the surveillance to Blunt and Harris. This, Liddell considered, was 'distasteful', but he would not oppose the measure.

I had a discussion with Dick White, James Robertson and Anthony Simkins. Robertson and Simkins were anxious to get [XXX] going on Anthony Blunt and on Tommy Harris as they felt that something might emerge in regard to Kim. Distasteful as this would have been, I did not wish to interfere in any way with the enquiries now proceeding if any useful results were likely to be obtained. It seemed to me, however, inconceivable that either Anthony or Tommy, had they known that Kim had been a Soviet spy while he was working for SIS, would not have come forward and exposed him. The most, therefore, that they might discuss would relate to Kim's attitude and activities from the time of the war of intervention in Spain. Whether Tommy was associated with him at that time I do not know, but it would not be wholly improbable. In any case the picture of Kim at that time is a fairly clear one; it is his subsequent activities which really interest us.

Despite Liddell's scepticism, taps were placed on Blunt and Harris, although the redaction suggests that this was also an application of 'Special Facilities', thereby allowing the eavesdroppers to listen in on more than just telephone conversations. By 23 October, the electronic surveillance was operational, and providing results:

Tommy Harris telephoned to say that he had just got back from Mallorca. He asked me whether I could dine on Saturday, when Anthony Blunt would be there. I was unable to do this, so he then asked me to dine next week, which I accepted.

TC shows that Kim and his wife have both dined with Tommy. Kim explained his retirement from SIS: he said that he had been treated very generously and did not seem to have any recriminations to make against his old firm. His position in the matter he fully understood. Tommy, on the other hand, seems to be rather indignant about the whole thing and will doubtless tackle me when I see him. I have, therefore, asked Dick and B2 to consider precisely what line they wish me to take. We believe that Tommy could help us very considerably, but we have to be sure that in any discussion on the question of Kim it would be necessary to have a guarantee that nothing goes back. I am going to try and get Tommy to come up here so that we can go into the whole mention of Guy Burgess and his friends in some considerable detail. This will lead us on in the case of Kim.

Liddell's dinner with Tommy and Hilda Harris duly took place on 2 November, as he recorded the following day:

I dined with Tommy Harris and his wife last night. We did not get on to any discussion of office matters until after dinner when Tommy expressed anxiety about Anthony Blunt's indiscretions.

Anthony had told Tommy that the American, Bernard Miller, was returning to this country to study and that he intended to resume touch with him. Tommy had told Anthony that he considered this most unwise. He said that he had never been wholly satisfied with the peculiar story of Bernard Miller, who had become acquainted with Guy Burgess on board ship, had visited Geneva, been present when Burgess was packing his clothes to depart, and had returned to America immediately afterwards. Tommy thought it quite conceivable that Miller might have played some part on behalf of the Russians, or, alternatively, that he might have been an agent of the FBI. Even if he were wrong in both of these assumptions, it was quite possible that Miller might now be acting for the FBI, and that information detrimental to Anthony might go back to them. On all these grounds he had strongly advised Anthony to have nothing to do with Bernard Miller and had told him that if he, Anthony, had no objection he thought of mentioning the matter to me and asking my advice.

I told Tommy that he could tell Anthony that I entirely agreed with his, Tommy's, view, and I was sure that if Anthony did not pull himself together he might well be jeopardising the whole of his career.

We then talked about Anthony's relations with Jackie Hewit. Tommy, of course, knew about the latest incident and had strongly advised Anthony to break with Hewit and not to go on visiting him in St Mary's Hospital.

This led to a discussion about Guy Burgess, and of a hunch which Tommy had just after his disappearance that he might have gone behind the Iron Curtain. He recalled that he mentioned this at my first interview with him and Anthony, that I had asked him what made him think so, and that he had been unable to give any concrete reasons. I had then told him and Anthony that Burgess and Maclean had been traced to France. It was clear to me that Tommy now felt rather confirmed in his original belief, although he had always been worried by the idea that, whatever his potentialities, nobody could have seriously employed an individual who was so notoriously unreliable. He felt that if this had been a smoke-screen to cover up more sinister activities, Burgess was a far cleverer man than he had ever believed him to be.

During the whole evening PEACH was hardly mentioned and no reference was made to his dismissal. Tommy did say at one point of the conversation: 'I suppose you have seen PEACH and got all the information you want from him?'. It was quite clear to me that the idea that there could be anything wrong with PEACH had never entered the head of either Tommy or Hilda.

As I was going away, Tommy took me out to the car. I told him that we had no positive evidence of the whereabouts of Burgess or Maclean, but that there were a number of points where I thought he might be able to help us, I could not go into them now, as Dick had a good many of the details. Could he spare the time to look in on us one day neat week? He readily accepted and we fixed 11 o'clock on Monday.

In the course of this final conversation, Tommy did mention that he had driven Edouard Benes about at the request of Burgess and that this was in 1939 when Burgess was working for Section D of SIS.

During the whole of our discussion I could detect nothing that would suggest that Tommy was not being wholly frank and genuine.

The imminent reappearance of the medical student Bernard Miller, whom Burgess had encountered on the *Queen Mary* during his voyage home in disgrace in May, had seemed strange to both Harris and Liddell, but in retrospect this episode, with Blunt indirectly seeking Liddell's advice, was probably an attempt by him to find out if Miller really had been recruited by the FBI. Whatever Blunt's true motives in setting off this hare, Liddell gave an account of his dinner to his colleague, Anthony Simkins in 5 November, and then was joined by Harris and Dick White:

I told Anthony Simkins about my evening with Tommy Harris. He seemed quite happy about the position.

Tommy Harris came up and he Dick and I had a talk for about two hours. Tommy outlined his own position. He had run away from school at the age of fifteen and gone to the Slade. He did not go to either university but continued to study art and to take a certain amount of interest in his father's business. He first met Anthony Blunt he thinks somewhere about 1936, when Anthony on behalf of Victor was buying a picture. In 1938 he had somehow been placed in touch with [XXXXXXXXXXXXX]. It was not until 1939 that he first met Guy Burgess – he thinks through Anthony. His work consisted in driving people about in his fast car, in particular Edouard Benes. He abandoned this job as being more or less a waste of time and went to America to realise dollars on certain pictures which had been deposited in the United States. After the collapse of France he was approached to join Station XVII. There was a meeting between Commander Peters, Burgess and Kim, at which Anthony was also present.

This was the first occasion on which he had met Kim. Tommy's job was to get to know all the names of the camp, who were of various nationalities, and some of them highly intelligent people. He had to report on their morale and look after their welfare. His wife did the catering and cooking. The only points of interest that emerged were that Kim and Burgess were in fact responsible for the memoranda on policy, and in particular one which related to a proposal to assassinate Franco. There were innumerable rows, and finally Colin Gubbins had taken over and militarised the camp. It was at this stage that Tommy joined us and, presumably, when Kim went to MI6.

We then discussed Anthony. We told Tommy we thought that there were a number of matters on which he could help us, but that up to now his memory had been extremely hazy; we thought in fact that he could do better. Tommy said that Anthony was probably reluctant to tell us his whole life story, with allusions to his friends, unless the facts were really relevant. He could not, of course, know whether they were or whether they weren't without reference to our files, but his personal loyalties were such that he would be unlikely to disclose information unless he were convinced that there was a really important national interest. Tommy entirely saw our point and thought he could probably put Anthony in the right frame of mind. We said that we would like to think this over.

On 6 November, Harris visited Liddell to offer a story which was very reminiscent of the incident at Hugh Slater's party reported to the Foreign Office in January 1951. Considering that both Slater and Harris had both been taught at the Slade, and was also a painter, it is quite likely that the two men knew each other, and Harris's tale was probably about the same event.

At his own request Tommy Harris called to see me today. He said he had just heard from a friend of his the story of a party attended by Donald Maclean about a week before his disappearance at which, when exceedingly drunk, Maclean had made the comment 'You know I am the English Alger Hiss'. Harris was anxious for us to have the story as soon as possible and therefore came round with it immediately. Dick told Harris, but without, we hoped, discouraging him, that we already had this information and that it was reasonably well corroborated.

Tommy made no further mention of Philby.

I took the opportunity of telling Tommy that after careful consideration we thought it would serve a useful purpose for him to have the talk with Anthony Blunt which he had suggested.

Ten days later, on 14 November, Liddell had his meeting with Blunt, at which the latter announced that before his departure Burgess had entrusted him with a large quantity of what were described as personal papers:

Anthony Blunt called on me this afternoon, the visit having obviously been precipitated by an interview between him and Tommy Harris.

Anthony informed me that, in connection with the Guy Burgess case, he had just remembered being in possession of a further load of Burgess' personal papers and that these included, he found from a quick glance, an old passport. He therefore wished to know if we wanted to inspect them. This point was put to Dick after he had been summoned by me to join the discussion. Dick made it clear that we should certainly want to inspect every paper relating to Burgess that we could lay hands on. We therefore subsequently arranged that Anthony Simkins should accompany Anthony back to the Courtauld Institute where the papers were lodged in the basement and bring them back to this office for inspection.

The above point having been settled, Dick took Anthony once more over the Burgess story. The following points, not all of which may be new, were made by Anthony:

1. He is absolutely confident that Burgess must first have become a Communist while at Trinity College, Cambridge, between the dates October 1933 and February 1934. He asserts this because he was himself at Cambridge at the earlier date, at which time Burgess was certainly not claiming to be a Communist but, when Anthony returned from a Continental visit in February 1934, Burgess had certainly become converted to Communism. He therefore places the conversion as having taken place in the winter term 1933 and considers that the particular influence in persuading Burgess to Communism was probably James Klugmann, and that John Cornford may have had a hand in it. In any case, he remembers Klugmann and Cornford saying that Burgess was a very erratic Communist and that either their time or that of a competent Marxist was required almost every day to deal with his various deviations.
2. During the period that Burgess was doing historical research work at Trinity, Anthony remembers that he worked under Simpson and that he took as a special subject the Indian mutiny.
3. Anthony has a clear recollection of Burgess's break with Communism and places it as in the spring of 1935. The break appeared as a violent revolt against Party discipline and because this seemed to be entirely in line with Burgess' temperament, Anthony thought nothing of it. It was just another indication of Burgess' erratic enthusiasms. It also did not surprise him that Burgess threw up his job at Cambridge – he had never thought Burgess to have the right sort of personality to be happy as a don.
4. Anthony believes he can confirm that, on his return to London, Burgess tried for a job in the Conservative Central Office and wonders whether, during the period he worked for *The Times*, he was introduced to that journal either by Micky Burn or by E.H. Carr.
5. Regarding his Continental travels with Burgess in 1938, Anthony says that although he may have passed through Paris the spring tour was mainly to Italy.
6. As an indication of Burgess' political views, that they remained essentially Marxist, Anthony remembers that:
    (a) Burgess completely accepted the Russian purge trials on the grounds that the French had independent evidence of a conspiracy by the persons purged.
    (b) Burgess argued that the German-Soviet pact was not Russia's fault but that we had forced her into it by sending a low-level delegation to discuss a treaty with them which was never plenipotentiary.

7. Anthony remembers that Burgess' valet, George Stephenson, once told him that he had discovered a wad of pound notes in Burgess' property. He could not place the date of the discovery but thought it might have been three years ago though it, might have been much earlier. He also remembers that when the time came for Burgess to settle fairly large personal debts to him he would pay out £20 or £30 at a time in notes rather than pay by cheque.

The cost of the defections of Burgess and Maclean, codenamed BARCLAY and CURZON respectively in MI5 and Foreign Office files, would be high.[11] Liddell himself would resign from MI5 when he was passed over as Sillitoe's successor in May 1953 in favour of his protégé, Dick White. Nor was he the only casualty. David Footman retired from SIS in the same year and took up a fellowship at St Antony's College, Oxford. He was a prolific writer on Russian history and contributed many articles to academic journals. He retired from St Antony's in 1963 and died in October 1983 at the age of 88.

Chapter VI

PEACH

Apart from Anthony Blunt, the other loose end remaining from the events of 25 May 1951 was the conduct of Kim Philby, who had been summoned back to Broadway in June 1951 for a cross-examination by Dick White at Leconfield House. At the very least Philby was thought to have been unwise in his association with Guy Burgess, but there was a very much more serious case, albeit largely circumstantial, which was developing against him. MI5's investigation, led by Dick White and Arthur Martin but supervised by Liddell, was codenamed PEACH, and placed Liddell in an extraordinarily difficult position. As far as SIS was concerned, Philby had been suspended from duties upon his return, placed on leave and then required to resign, effective 18 September 1951. Liddell's references to these events are sparse, but on 11 October he recorded that:

> Victor Rothschild looked in. We discussed the Donald Maclean case. Victor thought that Tess could help quite a lot about PEACH. He thought, too, that there were others who could help in a general way, and he was prepared to press them to do so if the information about their past did not remain on the record to be used by future generations. It was clear that what these people might be willing to say would have to be handled by those actually working on the cases. It was agreed that Victor would give the matter further consideration and help us in any other way he could.

Thus Victor Rothschild and his wife were both tentatively volunteering relevant information, but on certain conditions. Six weeks later, on 30 November, Tess Rothschild had evidently agreed terms with Liddell, and begun denouncing underground CPGB members she had known at Cambridge:

> I saw Tess Rothschild last night. She told me that when she was at Cambridge, Judith Fisher-Williams, Jenifer Hart's younger sister, then aged about eighteen, was at the time, 1936, very much attached to a young Communist called Ian Henderson, aged about twenty. She had been approached and had become a secret – as opposed to an open – member of the Communist Party. Subsequently she had married David Hubback, who is now employed in quite an important post in the Treasury.

As far as is known, Judith Fisher-Williams is no longer active, and her husband is not believed ever to have had any connection with Communism – in fact he is recorded as wholly Tory in his outlook.

Tess would be prepared to approach Jenifer Fisher-Williams and ask her whether she can give the name of any other secret members with whom she was associated in her Cambridge days. I said that I would look up Jenifer Fisher-Williams and let her know. Meanwhile, I would say nothing about the case to anyone else.

This line of enquiry might have been fruitful, but it was not acted on for some years, perhaps because Jenifer Fisher-Williams was married to Herbert Hart, an Oxford academic and wartime MI5 officer. Jenifer would later admit to having been recruited by Arnold Deutsch when she worked in the Home Office, and her brother-in-law, David Hubback, would also become considered an espionage suspect. A senior civil servant, Hubback had been educated at Westminster School and King's College, Cambridge, before joining the Mines Department of the Board of Trade in 1939 and moving to the Cabinet Office in 1944. He was also known to be a member of the Leighton Group, a civil service discussion group based in the Home Office and regarded as a CPGB front organization.

Meanwhile, elsewhere in Whitehall, suspicions about Philby's true role were circulating. For example, the Foreign Office's Regional Security Officer at the Washington embassy, Bobby Mackenzie, registered his doubts on 30 October 1951 when he recalled a meeting that had taken place in Washington on 9 May attended by Philby, Sir Roger Makins and Geoffrey Patterson:

Philby spent the rest of the day sitting on a committee at Admiral Stone's Headquarters. During the day I dictated my letter and showed it to Sir Roger Makins and Mr Patterson.

Both approved its terms and, as Mr Philby had not returned by the time the bag closed, I sent it off and showed him a copy when he came back.

He was annoyed at my having sent it without consulting him and said that he thought that we should put the arguments both in favour of and against an early interrogation of Mr Maclean more fully, as he was not entirely convinced that this was the best course.

I was surprised, as I had understood him to concur in our conclusion that, despite the obvious disadvantages of such a course, we should interrogate as soon as possible. I agreed however that he should draft an aide memoire for me to take to London on May 11th. This was approved on the following day after some alterations had been made by Mr Patterson and myself.

You will remember that, when I was last in this country, I told you that both Mr Patterson and myself had been struck by the fact that Mr Philby had said so little to us about his personal knowledge of Mr Maclean. As far as I can remember he mentioned the fact that he knew him on one occasion only.

This was at the time when we in Washington, without being in possession of the facts, had come to the conclusion that Mr Gore-Booth was the most likely candidate. During a discussion in Mr Philby's room Esther Whitfield of SIS said that in her view Mr Maclean, whom she had known when he was in Washington, was equally likely to have been the culprit. She said that she came to the conclusion at that time that he was an idealist who lacked balance and sound judgment.

The aide memoire sets out the position with regard to the FBI in some detail. Admittedly it does not argue strongly in favour of postponing the interrogation, although some of the disadvantages are set out in paragraph 12. Nevertheless the impression left on my mind at the time was that Mr Philby was not in favour of early action. It is also my impression that Mr Philby told Mr Patterson and myself at the time that he still felt that Mr Gore-Booth was an equally good, if not a better, candidate than Mr Maclean. Perhaps there is nothing very much in this. It would be interesting to know whether Mr Patterson gained the same impression as I did.

She then asked whether any of us knew him. Both Mr Patterson and I replied in the negative but Mr Philby said that he thought that he had met him on two or three occasions but did not remember him well. The impression left on my mind then was that these meetings took place officially while Mr Philby was in government service.

In a conversation with Mr White before I went back to Washington I gathered that it had been established that Mr Philby did not know Mr Maclean well when they were at Cambridge. I now understand that it has subsequently been discovered that the opposite is true. If this is so, I think that it is highly significant that Mr Philby, from the time when he himself suggested that the person for whom we were looking might be identical with the 'Imperial Council' source, never told us that he knew, as he must almost certainly have done, that Mr Maclean was at one time a Communist.

Mackenzie's recollection at the end of October of the events on 9 May were significant because Admiral Earl E. Stone was the director of the Armed Forces Security Agency, the organization based at Arlington Hall that was responsible for producing the VENONA product.

The evidence assembled by MI5 was distilled into a dossier which was circulated on 30 November:

Ever since the disappearance of Maclean and Burgess the Security Service have been making a study of all available evidence in order to find out how Maclean was alerted just before he was going to be interrogated.

The main line of research has been to consider if the known records of all the people who were aware of the Maclean case warranted further investigation. PEACH, as a close friend of Burgess and because of his early history, naturally came under suspicion.

PEACH was born in India on 1st January, 1912. He was educated at Westminster School from 1924 – 29 and Trinity College, Cambridge from 1929 – 1933.

PEACH was interviewed on three occasions and provided two written statements. In addition evidence obtained from Russian defectors has been examined, as well as the information from intelligence sources arising out of a study of Russian espionage. A considerable volume of evidence has been collected most of which is circumstantial. The essential features are:

(a) PEACH's statements are false in regard to
    (i)   His first wife, who was a communist when he married her in 1934 and is believed to have been working for the Russians ever since. She is now married to a German communist and lives in the Russian sector of Berlin. There is evidence which suggests that PEACH remained friendly with his first wife until at least 1945.
    (ii) His relations with Guy Burgess. He denies that Burgess was a communist at Cambridge. He concealed close association with Burgess between 1933 and 1935. He told lies about how he was recruited into SIS when in fact he was recruited by Burgess.
    (iii) His own political views. He denies ever having been a communist, although he does not deny that some people will say he was one. As for Burgess, the truth or otherwise turns on the definition of the word communist. Nevertheless, five persons have stated that .each was a communist at Cambridge. PEACH's tutor described him as a 'militant communist' while at Cambridge and states that he had 'extreme views on social questions'. Professor Robertson of Cambridge found himself compelled to tell PEACH that he was unable to recommend him for the Indian Civil Service on the grounds of his extreme left-wing views.
    (iv) There are also a number or other false statements concerning certain persons about whom he was questioned.
(b) Information from the Russian defectors and Intelligence sources
    (i)   General Krivitsky, a defector from the Russian Intelligence Service of proved reliability, volunteered information that in 1937 the OGPU received orders from Stalin to arrange to assassinate General Franco. An Englishmen was recruited for this purpose and sent to Spain. He was a journalist of good family, an idealist and fanatically anti-Nazi. The plan to assassinate Franco did not mature, but Krivitsky says he is pretty certain that the 'imperial council source', namely Maclean, would have been amongst the friends of the young man sent to Spain.

PEACH did go to Spain in February, 1937 to General Franco's headquarters as a freelance journalist. He returned to England two months later when he was offered the appointment of *Times* war correspondent accredited to Franco. He held this position until 1939. Maclean was almost certainly known to PEACH, and the latter could be described as of good family and, at least while at Cambridge, as an idealist and fanatically anti-Nazi. In all respects, therefore, PEACH fulfils the description given by Krivitsky. So far as can be ascertained no other journalist accredited to Franco Spain does.

(ii) In 1945 Konstantin Volkov of the Russian Intelligence Service stated amongst other things that the NKGB had an agent in London 'who fulfilled the functions of head of a department of the British counter espionage administration'. PEACH was at that the head of Section 9 which was the counter espionage section.

(iii) In December, 1949 a fundamental change was made in the Soviet cypher system, as the result of which Soviet diplomatic telegrams became indistinguishable from one another. It had previously been possible to distinguish the telegrams of the Russian Intelligence Service and a successful break had been made which provided certain information, e.g. the source of the Washington leakage. The number of persons 'indoctrinated' into this cryptanalytic process is severely limited. PEACH was indoctrinated into the source of the Washington leakage in late September, 1949 immediately before being transferred to Washington. It is not unreasonable to calculate that the Russians would have required two to three months to devise and put into effect a change in their cypher system.

(iv) On 16th May, 1951 MI5 telegraphed their representative in Washington asking that a certain enquiry concerning the Maclean case should be made and, because time was short, asked that it should be completed by 23rd May. This telegram was seen by PEACH. The MI5 representative has since stated that he interpreted this telegram as meaning that the interrogation of Maclean would take place immediately after the 23rd May. In fact this interpretation was incorrect since the interrogation had been planned for the week beginning 18th June. If the leakage that Maclean did take place and if the flight of Maclean was as hurried as it would seem to have been, the date of the flight, 25th May 1951 would be more consistent with a leakage from Washington than from London.

(v) The Security Service have been able to establish with a fair degree of certainty that PEACH must have known Maclean at any rate in his youth. They were contemporaries at Cambridge, PEACH at Trinity and Maclean at Trinity Hall. It is known that Burgess and Maclean were the closest of friends at Cambridge. It is known too that PEACH and Burgess were close friends. On these grounds alone it is hardly conceivable that Maclean was not known to PEACH. Added to that they were both ardent communists at Cambridge. PEACH's reticence on this part of his youth at the height of the investigation of the Maclean case seems only explicable if he either wished to shield Maclean or to conceal his own past. In any ease PEACH knew that Burgess, while staying in his house in Washington, regularly visited Alan Maclean in New York. Clearly it was his duty to have reported on this as soon as he knew that Maclean was under suspicion. He did not do so.

Finally, mention should be made of the striking resemblance in the timing of Maclean's disappearance and the timing of the disappearance of a certain Russian defector, Konstantin Volkov, in Istanbul in 1945. Volkov had volunteered certain information and offered to defect in return for a large sum of money. PEACH had been selected to go out to Istanbul to interview him when Volkov suddenly disappeared in a Russian aircraft which was specially sent to take him away two days before the interview was due to take place. The number of people who were concerned with the Volkov case is very few and only one or two of these people were also concerned with the Maclean case. PEACH was one of them.

From all the foregoing the Security Service conclude that PEACH is the most likely person to have been responsible for alerting Maclean. I have studied all the evidence and I agree with this conclusion.

This document, distilled from three interviews with Philby and two written statements, includes the very first reference to what was to become known as 'Black Thursday', being the loss of the contemporaneous VENONA source. In reality, there was no one single day when the NKVD traffic dried up, but over an unspecified period of time, probably two or three months, the Soviets abandoned the compromised one-time pads constructed with duplicated pages that had appeared in previous pads, and adopted an entirely new system which could not be attacked by the same cryptanalytical technique, matching passages in the Soviet wartime trade messages with the identical fragments in the NKVD channel. Up until December 1949 some of the NKVD's cables had been read 'contemporaneously', which actually meant a delay of around three weeks, and this material had been prevalent on the Moscow–Canberra circuit, thereby allowing almost current exploitation in Australia. From a counter-intelligence perspective, this was an advantage that almost matched the ISOS and ISK triumphs during the war, and the Australian Security Intelligence Organisation (AISO) had been created in March of that very year precisely so the local authorities could reap the benefit of what was then termed 'the Source', a mysterious font of knowledge apparently only available to the British. Philby had been let into the secret at a private briefing given by Oldfield, then head of SIS's R5 counter-intelligence section, because the results of the work undertaken at Arlington Hall and Eastcote was developing dramatically, and was likely, as indeed it did, to dominate the Allied counter-intelligence approach to Soviet espionage. As the NKVD's Yuri Modin would later observe, the very unwelcome news 'caused a ripple of alarm at the Centre. We had no idea what the Americans might uncover and this information hung over us like a sword of Damocles.'

Although 'Black Thursday' served to terminate VENONA, there was nothing the Soviets could do about the past traffic, dating back to September 1940, which awaited study by the Anglo-American cryptographers. That project would continue until 1979 and prove a veritable treasure trove, but the opportunity to read any messages after 1949 was lost forever.

Although MI5 came to believe that Philby bore sole responsibility for what some perceived as a catastrophe, the more likely explanation is that a Soviet spy, William Weisband, already employed inside Arlington Hall as a Russian linguist, had provided the NKVD with the vital tip-off. However, from the British perspective, the burden of thinking that Philby had single-handedly sabotaged a hugely secret and fabulously productive intelligence source was too appalling to contemplate, and of course could easily undermine Anglo-American co-operation in a specialist, highly-compartmented field that had provided both countries with gigantic benefits. The consequences of Philby's betrayal of ACORN and BRIDE, the then-current VENONA codeword classifications, could be immense, and far beyond the transatlantic offence caused by the posting of a mole to a liaison role in Washington. However, those at MI5 and the Foreign Office who knew about VENONA were aware of something else that was relevant: although the FBI had been indoctrinated into the secret, the CIA had not. It was thought that Bill Harvey, the CIA's chief of Staff C (later the Counterintelligence Staff) and a former FBI Special Agent, knew of the project, but he had not been authorized to share his knowledge with anyone else at the CIA, an organization which, according to the preliminary VENONA breaks, was itself thoroughly penetrated by left-wing veterans of the Office of Strategic Services.

At the Foreign Office's Security Department, George Carey-Foster studied the MI5 document and immediately wrote to Dick White:

I have read your dossier on PEACH which I think has been extremely well assembled. I have a few comments which are mostly minor and perhaps I can discuss these with Martin. I have not yet had time to make a summary for the Permanent Under-Secretary but before doing so I would like to refer to my letter of the same reference of the. 27th November.

As I understand it, you propose to interrogate PEACH in the near future. You told me that you do not hold out any high hopes of success. I had not realised, however, the extent to which PEACH had lied in his interviews with you, and his written statement. It seems to me therefore that something may well come out of the interrogation which will enable you to take action against PEACH. I would therefore like to know what the subsequent form is likely to be since it is then that the Foreign Office may become seriously implicated. It seems to me that the following may occur:

(a) PEACH implicates himself sufficiently for you to have him arrested;
(b) PEACH gets away with it and is allowed to go home where he remains;
(c) PEACH gets away with it and is allowed to go home but takes fright and disappears.

Developments (a) and (c) would presumably fairly quickly become known and the Foreign Office would therefore become involved. Development (b) would simply mean the continuance of the present state of affairs. Are you at any stage proposing to warn the ports, because even that may leak and bring in the Foreign Office? For these reasons as well as for those referred to in my previous letter I think we ought to know how we are to act before we are overtaken by events. I should also like to ask you to keep me closely informed of any developments subsequent to your interrogation of PEACH. Will you please also let me know when this is going to take place.

Perhaps the best thing would be if you could spare the time to come to a meeting with Patrick Reilly early next week at which perhaps C ought also to be represented. I am bound to say that we may reach the conclusion that the Foreign Office should be formally consulted before the interrogation is allowed to take place.

While SIS, MI5 and the Foreign Office debated the issues surrounding the planned interrogation, the politicians had been kept largely in the dark, as Liddell discovered on 7 December, moments after he had returned from 10 Downing Street where he had been talking to Churchill about domestic topics, his employment of a Swiss chef and the four Swiss maids at Chartwell:

I had only been back from the Prime Minister a few minutes and reported to the D-G, when the D-G himself received a call from Downing Street. When he got there he found Anthony Eden and William Strang.

Eden was worried about the Kim Philby case; he had evidently been extremely badly briefed and had given the Prime Minister the impression that Philby might escape at any moment and that another scandal would ensure similar to that in the case of Guy Burgess and Donald Maclean, The D-G explained that on the fact of it this was not at all likely. Eden was evidently unaware that Philby had already been interrogated three times, although not quite on the lines of the proposed interrogation which is to take place on 19 December, on the basis of a number of subsequent enquiries.

Eden and Strang seemed to think that this interrogation was going to lead to a prosecution. It was explained to them that the chances of prosecution were extremely remote, since all the evidence amounted to was a chain of circumstances which pointed to Philby's guilt, and that all these circumstances were well-known to Philby himself on account of the appointment that he had formerly held in SIS. The odds, therefore, were strongly against any satisfactory conclusion of the case. It should, however, be understood that without a case and without a charge it was not really possible under the laws of this country to detain someone indefinitely upon a suspicion. If, therefore, Philby wished to go there would be nothing to stop him short of a withdrawal of his passport, which would not necessarily be effective.

The Prime Minister then said that he did not see why the interrogation could not take place at once. It was explained to him that all enquiries which seemed possible had only just been completed and that the brief was with the interrogating counsel, who, owing to previous engagements, could not place his services at our disposal until 19 December. Meanwhile there was no reason for supposing that Philby would attempt to leave, unless he was proceeding to India as a representative of the *Telegraph* to report on the Indian elections.

The Prime Minister gave orders that the interrogation was to be held within a week. It was a pity that he had been so badly briefed.

On the D-G's return, Dick got into touch with Buster Milmo and has fixed the interrogation for 12 December.

Thus it was on Churchill's orders that Philby was to be summoned to a formal, hostile interrogation. The case against Philby, with which he was to be confronted by 'Buster' Milmo on 12 December, appeared to be conclusive:

1. The Security Service has been carrying out an exhaustive investigation of PEACH as a sequel to the disappearance of Maclean and Burgess. As a result, there has emerged a very grave case of suspicion that PEACH is, and has been for many years, a spy for the Russians.

2. The stage has now been reached when, in the opinion of the Security Service, the next step to be taken is the interrogation of PEACH himself. It is proposed that this should be conducted by a distinguished member of the Common Law Bar, formerly an officer of this Service, and now on its reserve of officers. It is considered that this procedure offers the best chance of establishing PEACH's guilt, if he is guilty, and that it also has the advantage of bringing a trained and independent judgement to bear on a case which may prove impossible to resolve finally one way or the other.

3. There is at present no evidence on which PEACH could be prosecuted, and it is probable that this can only be obtained, if at all, in the form of a confession by PEACH himself under caution. The Security Service does

not exclude the possibility that such a confession will be forthcoming if PEACH is interrogated as proposed.

4. Inasmuch as PEACH is a former senior member of SIS, his prosecution would involve questions of public policy which the Foreign Office and SIS will certainly wish to consider. It is obvious that in the event of admissions being made by PEACH in a form admissible as evidence, action by the Law Officers might follow swiftly, and the Director of Public Prosecutions would need to know the Foreign Office views without delay.

5. The Foreign Office may also wish to consider whether there are any extraneous circumstances which should affect the timing of the operation. In this connection, it is relevant to recall that the United States intelligence authorities are aware of the grave suspicions against PEACH, and that we have undertaken to inform them of the conclusions which are reached about him. The CIA itself expressed anxiety about PEACH soon after the disappearance of Burgess and Maclean, and it is felt that the sooner the case is brought to a conclusion the better for Anglo/US relations where security is concerned. Furthermore, in view of the interest of the United States intelligence authorities, the Security Service thinks it essential that they should be given advance notice of the steps now projected, their attention being drawn at the same time to the legal considerations which govern them.

6. The interrogation of PEACH also necessitates immediate consideration of the possibility that he may flee the country. This question is examined separately in the appendix to this note.

7. Subject to the views of the Foreign Office, the Security Service considers that PEACH should be interrogated as soon as possible, viz: on or about December 19th 1951.

APPENDIX

1. If PEACH is a spy, it is to be presumed that he has for a long time had plans for escape prepared for use in case of need.

2. During the intensive enquiries into PEACH's case since his recall from Washington in June, the risk of his fleeing the country has been under constant review. Intelligence from a number of sources has been studied daily with this in mind. On the whole, the impression has been gained that, although PEACH is uneasy, he is possibly increasingly inclined to think that his explanations have been accepted as adequate. Ex hypothesi, he is a person of strong nerve. Moreover he is deeply attached to his family. While, therefore, he has been watched as closely as possible within the limits imposed by practical possibilities and the overriding necessity of not alerting him to his danger, the precautions so far taken have been limited to advising Special Branch officers at the principal ports of departure to the continent of our interest in him. The risk of leakage

involved in a wider state of alert has been considered unacceptable in the circumstances.

3. If he is a spy, the danger that PEACH will flee the country becomes acute from the moment that a request to attend for a further interview alerts him to the fact that he may be in imminent danger. The precautions at present operating will, of course, be maintained.

It is for consideration whether the following additional precautions should be taken:

(a) At the discretion of the examiners, PEACH should be asked at his interrogation voluntarily to surrender his passport as a sign of good faith.

(b) In the event of his refusal to do this, the necessary authority should be obtained in advance for the cancellation of his passport so that instructions may go out from the Home Office immediately to Immigration Officers instructing them that, if PEACH appears with his passport for travel purposes, it should be impounded and every reasonable step open to them taken to delay his departure.

In this connection it must be pointed out that such action does undoubtedly increase the risk of leakage and the presumption that the authorities are once more hiding a security scandal in the Foreign Service.

4. Unless evidence is obtained on which PEACH can be arrested and charged under the Official Secrets Acts, there is a risk that he will manage to flee the country notwithstanding the precautions outlined above. This might be done with false documents provided by the Russians, or even possibly without documents, for example by his being smuggled on board a Soviet ship or in a private aeroplane. It should be remembered that PEACH is a trained intelligence officer, skilled in clandestine operations.

If PEACH goes abroad, it may become known to the Press that a former member of the Foreign Service has left the country in suspicious circumstances. But there would be less opportunity for the Press to make a sensation out of this than in the case of Burgess and Maclean, and more scope for manoeuvre by the Foreign Office.

It must also be accepted that the cancellation of his passport and the circulation of his name to the ports involves some risk of leakage.

5. There is a likelihood that if interrogation is delayed beyond the end of this month, PEACH will in any case leave the country and a possibility that he will do so earlier. It is probable that he will be offered and accept a post with the *Daily Telegraph* newspaper, to which he has obtained introductions

He has suggested that he might visit India for this paper as a special correspondent to cover the elections which are now in progress, and he anticipates that if this does not materialise, the paper will be willing to engage him as a correspondent for special assignments abroad.

The Security Service has considered the possibility of approaching the *Daily Telegraph* to secure postponement of PEACH's appointment. It is felt that such action must be ruled out:-

(a) because of its obvious impropriety, which carries serious legal implications, and -
(b) because of the risk of leakage.

On the basis of this summary a new document was prepared by Patrick Reilly on 6 December as a brief for the Foreign Office which was presented to the Foreign Secretary who then obtained the Prime Minister's approval for an interrogation to be conducted as soon as possible:

THE PEACH CASE
1. Since the disappearance of Maclean and Burgess the Security Service have been carrying out an extensive investigation of a former senior officer of SIS called in this memorandum by the codename of PEACH. As a result there has emerged a grave suspicion that PEACH is, and has been for many years, a Soviet agent and that he was responsible for the disappearance of Maclean just as we were about to interrogate him. The attached memorandum summarises the case against PEACH. It should be noted that it is not based on material from the special source which aroused our suspicion of Maclean. The case is based essentially on information about PEACH's known Communist associations in the past: on the lies he has told about them and about his association with Burgess and Maclean: and on the fact that he fits information about a Soviet agent in British Intelligence given by Soviet defectors.
2. This investigation has now reached the stage when the Security Service wish to interrogate PEACH. PEACH held local diplomatic rank as a First Secretary at Istanbul from March, 1947 to September, 1949 and as First Secretary at Washington from October, 1949 to June, 1951 when PEACH terminated his employment because of his close association with Burgess, who lived with him in Washington. The Foreign Office is thus closely concerned. Any publicity is bound to reawaken interest in the Maclean and Burgess case, in the Foreign Service and in British Security generally. Further, should the case result in a prosecution the facts about Maclean will almost certainly have to be revealed in court.

   In addition, there are bound to be repercussions on relations with both the United States and Turkish Governments. Sir Percy Sillitoe therefore very properly wishes to have Foreign Office agreement before proceeding with the interrogation. Meanwhile he is not informing the Prime Minister about the case.

3. In order to clarify the points on which a Foreign Office decision is required, Mr Reilly held a meeting on the 5th December with Mr Dick White and Mr Carey-Foster. The following statement of the issues involved has been agreed by the Security Service. It has not been seen by C who is in France and will not be back till the 10th December. The recommendations are submitted jointly by Mr Carey-Foster and myself.

PRESENT POSITION.

4. (a) Precautions taken.

PEACH is being watched as closely as possible without running any risk of alerting him, and Special Branch officers at the principal ports are aware that the Security Service is interested in him. The risk of leakage involved in a wider state of alert, namely warning Immigration Officers, is considered unacceptable. In any case, the Security Service wish to make it clear that so long as there is insufficient evidence on which to base a prosecution, they have no legal power whatever to prevent PEACH from leaving the country, and it is impossible to make absolutely certain that he cannot escape.

(b) American knowledge of the case.

The Federal Bureau of Investigation know that an investigation into PEACH is being made, but they do not know how far it has advanced. The CIA suspected him after the disappearance of Maclean and Burgess and told the FBI of their suspicions. Consequently both Services have been promised the results of our investigation. The Security Service will wish to inform the FBI in advance that an interrogation will take place. They will do this as soon as they obtain the Foreign Office decisions on the points referred to later in this paper. C will probably also wish to inform General Bedell Smith in view of the latter's strong interest in the case. As in the Maclean case, HM Ambassador and Sir Kit Steel should also be informed at this stage, and kept informed, by the Security Service representative.

THE INTERROGATION.

5. Procedure proposed.

After informal consultation with the Director of Public Prosecutions, the Security Service have decided to brief a distinguished member of the Common Law Bar with wartime experience in counter-espionage work and in the prosecution of spies, to carry out the interrogation. They consider that this procedure offers the best chance of establishing PEACH's guilt, if he is guilty, and that it also has the advantage of bringing a trained and independent judgement to bear on a case which may prove impossible to resolve finally one way or the other. The date at present proposed is the 19th December. The interrogator would not be ready much earlier, but the date might be advanced to the 17th December.

Questions for decision
A. Do the Foreign Office agree to an interrogation taking place?

6. C has already been consulted and has agreed to an interrogation. We submit that since the Security Service are satisfied that the results of their investigation now justify an interrogation, it is out of the question for the Foreign Office to object, provided the timing is acceptable.

B.   Do we agree to the date proposed?

7. The timing is awkward
   (a)   The interrogation will almost certainly raise issues requiring immediate high-level decisions, which it may be difficult to obtain just before and during the Christmas holidays.
   (b)   Once the interrogation has taken place, the risk of publicity is much greater. If PEACH is arrested immediate publicity is inevitable. If arrest is not possible, he might try to escape. Whether he succeeded or not might well cause publicity depending on the circumstances. Is it right to risk publicity on such, a matter just before the Prime Minister goes to Washington?
8. There are however strong arguments for not postponing the interrogation 'till later:
   (a)   The longer the delay the greater the danger that he may be alerted.
   (b)   PEACH is expecting to go to India soon after Christmas as a correspondent for the *Daily Telegraph*.
      (The Security Service, after careful consideration, have ruled out the possibility of persuading the *Daily Telegraph* not to employ him). This might mean delaying the whole enquiry for several months till he returned, if he ever did.
   (b)   We are bound to be severely criticised by the Americans if PEACH is allowed to go abroad without being interrogated.

Recommendation.
9. We submit that in all the circumstances the right course is to interrogate at the earliest possible date. If anything went wrong just before, during or immediately after the Prime Minister's visit, and especially if PEACH escaped and this became known, the effect would surely be very bad.

We submit that rather than run any such risk, it is better to grasp the thistle and let the Americans see that we are resolute in clearing up Soviet espionage in the United Kingdom.

Precautions to prevent PEACH's escape after the interrogation.

10. Unless, which is highly unlikely, PEACH clears himself completely, the Security Service intend to ask him, at the end of the interrogation to surrender his passport.

   They do not expect him to refuse. If he does, they would like to be able to tell him that the Foreign Office have already agreed to cancel his passport, and that all ports will be warned accordingly. They therefore ask now for Foreign Office agreement that his passport should he cancelled if he refuses to surrender it.

Recommendation

We see no objection and recommend that authority should be given to proceed accordingly.

11. Since PEACH will have been alerted as a result of this interrogation the watch on him will thereafter be stepped up, if necessary with the help of Scotland Yard.

   The Security Service wish to make it absolutely clear, however, that unless PEACH can be arrested and charged under the Official Secrets Act, in the final resort he cannot be prevented from leaving the country. The Security Service will of course do everything possible to prevent this.

PROSECUTION.

As stated above, the Security Service think it most unlikely that PEACH will clear himself. They think it also unlikely that the interrogation will produce a confession on which he can be prosecuted. Although suspicion against him is very strong, he has of course exceptional experience, ability and nerve. The Security Service think that the most likely result is a stalemate. If, however, they do get evidence on which a prosecution is possible, they will almost certainly wish to prosecute.

   In that case there will be two stages:

   (a)   The Director of Public Prosecutions, probably after reference to the Attorney General, will decide whether there is a case for prosecution.

   (b)   If the decision is that there is a case, the Foreign Office and C will he asked whether they wish to represent that there are any overriding grounds of public policy to make a prosecution undesirable,

12. The Security Service consider that the Foreign Office cannot decide in advance of the interrogation, but must do so in the light of the evidence on which it would be necessary to go into Court. The sort of points which may require consideration are:

   (i)   The effect our relations with the United States authorities.

   (ii)   The effect on the Turkish Government and on C's valuable relations with the Turkish intelligence service. (PEACH was in open liaison with the latter.)

   (iii) The effect on C's organisation generally of the publicity which the case would involve.

   (iv)   We agree that no decision can be taken until the upshot of the interrogation is known. We submit however that, on general grounds of public policy, the presumption should be that a prosecution, if it is possible, should take place unless the arguments against it are of quite exceptional force. We suggest that in the long run at least it would be better for our relations with the United States, and for the reputation of the Foreign Office, that there should be a prompt and efficient prosecution, rather than that we should run any risk of appearing to be hushing up a scandal.

13. There is thus bound to be an interval, though possibly a short one, between the interrogation and the decision whether to prosecute. If it is decided to prosecute, PEACH would normally be arrested at once and would have to be brought before a Magistrate within 48 hours.

   If all went well, publicity could be avoided up to this stage, but once the case came into Court it would of course be public. (Parts of the evidence might be taken in camera, but the trial as a whole would certainly be in public.)

14. It would therefore be necessary for us

   (a)   to have ready some form of statement to answer press enquiries and for the guidance of posts abroad. (Since the case would then be sub judice this might be kept quite short, e.g. to the effect that PEACH was a temporary member of the Foreign Service from 1946 to June, 1951 when his employment was terminated.)

   (b)   to warn HM Ambassador in Turkey in advance and if he thinks it desirable, to prepare some communication to the Turkish Government.

   (c)   to decide what should be said to the US authorities. The subject can be mainly handled by normal MI5 and MI6 liaison channels, but HM Ambassador may also wish to say something to the State Department.

15. To sum up:

   (i)   decisions are required now on the following points;

(a) May the Security Service interrogate PEACH, on or about the 19th December?

(b) If so, may authority be given for his passport to be cancelled, and for the Security Service to inform him of Foreign Office agreement to do this, in the event of his refusing to surrender it?

No decision on the question of prosecution is possible now, but one may be required at short notice. It is submitted that the Foreign Office could only object to a prosecution if there were altogether over-riding grounds for doing so; no such grounds are at present apparent.

This remarkable document, setting out the tactics to be deployed against the wily Philby, who was acknowledged to be a formidable adversary, prompted some comment from Sir William Strang, in manuscript:

My chief misgiving in all of this is the delay in interrogating PEACH. I understand that the reason for this is that the member of the Bar selected requires this period for briefing and rehearsal, in the absence of which the interrogation may fail to achieve its purpose. The Secretary of State may wish to send for Sir Percy Sillitoe to discuss this point. I will only add this. If we wish to avoid embarrassment the best course would be to let him slip away. He is no longer in government employment and his departure from this country, eg to take up his appointment in India, need cause no public comment. I do not recommend this course. From the point of view of our own security and our relations with the Americans we must pursue this case and face the music, if need be.

This case summary mentioned General Bedell Smith as having a strong interest in the case, which was no exaggeration. When the defections had occurred the Director of Central Intelligence (DCI) had asked two of his staff who knew Philby, Bill Harvey and James Angleton, to write up their views on Philby's role, if any. Harvey's five-page memorandum dated 15 June outlined Philby's friendship with Burgess, his connection with the Volkov episode and his part in the failure of joint CIA–SIS operations in Albania. In short Harvey, who harboured some personal animosity towards Philby after a very drunk Burgess had been insufferably rude to his wife Libby during a dinner party at Philby's home in January 1951, denounced Philby as a Soviet spy. Four days later, Angleton submitted his report, suggesting that Philby had been duped by Burgess, and recommended caution in any accusation of espionage against him.

Carey-Foster, having obtained approval for the proposed strategy from Foreign Office colleagues, wrote to Dick White on 11 December, the day before Philby's interrogation:

We have been considering what line to take with the press if a prosecution is inevitable.

We do not at this stage propose to brief the head of our News Department. We shall not do it until we hear from you that a prosecution is likely. We should therefore be most grateful if you would let us know about this as soon as a decision is reached.

If there is to be a prosecution we shall give the head of our News Dept a very brief outline of the background of the case but all we propose to say to the press is that PEACH was a temporary member of the Foreign Service from 1946 to June, 1951 when his employment was terminated. We shall refuse to comment further on the grounds that the case is sub judice. The fact that PEACH was connected with Burgess and is therefore linked to the Maclean/Burgess affair is almost certain to leak out, at any rate from America. We shall not be able to deny this but again we shall refuse to comment.

The fact that somebody who is connected with the Maclean/Burgess affair has been arrested and is to be charged under the Official Secrets Act will put the worst construction on the disappearance of Maclean and Burgess, a fact which we have not so far admitted. We are bound therefore to have some awkward questions but we shall do our best to stave them off. I know however, that the press will be very persistent and we shall certainly be pestered.

I hope you agree with the foregoing and I take it that Robertson will be in a position to give me any further guidance in answering questions. I shall keep in close touch with him. I should perhaps add that the press are capable of keeping me going at all hours of the night, therefore if the worst (or is it the best) occurs I hope your duty officer will be in a position to help.

The epic confrontation between Philby and the legendary interrogator, 'Buster' Milmo QC, took place as planned on 12 December but, as predicted, it was inconclusive, although nobody present believed Philby to be innocent. Milmo's report, now reproduced in a slightly redacted form, made harrowing reading for the few who were allowed to glimpse it:

Terms of Reference
By letter dated 3rd December 1951, I was instructed to undertake an official enquiry into the possibility of there having been a leakage of information to Mr Burgess and/or Mr Maclean resulting in their subsequent disappearance. My terms of reference were as follows:

(a) to enquire as to whether there did in fact occur a leakage of official information to Mr Burgess and/or Mr Maclean which leakage resulted in their sudden disappearance;

(b) if you are satisfied that such leakage did in fact occur, you are to enquire as to the identity of the officials or official responsible for such leakage and the motive which prompted such leakage.

Introduction

For the purpose of the enquiry I was provided with a very full dossier on the case, together with a large number of appendices consisting of records of interviews with material witnesses, statements taken from witnesses and other papers and documents bearing upon the subject matter of the enquiry. The conclusions which I have reached are based on a study and appreciation of the material contained in this dossier, my interviews with officers of the Security Service and my questioning of Mr H.A.R. Philby.

My enquiry has not therefore been conducted in accordance with the law of evidence which would be applied in a Court of Law, nor would it have been practicable in the circumstances to conduct the enquiry on any such basis. I have proceeded upon the footing that unless a particular witness had any prima facie motive for lying or there was some reason to believe that his recollection might be at fault, or there were intrinsic grounds in the statement itself to make one doubt its reliability, I accepted the statements in the dossier as being truthful.

Findings

There is no room for doubt that it was as a result of a leakage of information that Burgess and Maclean disappeared from this country on 25th May, 1951. There is no evidence in law to prove the source of the leakage or to establish the identity of the person or persons responsible for the leakage. Subject to this important qualification, I find myself unable to avoid the conclusion that Philby is and has for many years been a Soviet agent and that he was directly and deliberately responsible for the leakage which in fact occurred.

Reasons

In reaching the conclusion that Philby is and has for many years been a Soviet agent and that he was directly responsible for the leakage which in fact occurred, I have been influenced principally by the following facts which I consider are established:

1) Philby has for some twenty years been a close friend of Burgess and, for the major part of that period, Burgess was a Soviet agent.
2) Philby and Burgess share the same Cambridge Communist background and the development of their political careers has followed the same pattern.
3) From July 1950 to April 1951 Burgess stayed in Philby's house, though latterly, according to Philby, as an unwelcome guest. Thereafter the two

were in communication prior to the disappearance of Burgess and Maclean. During this period Philby had access to and was kept up-to-date and fully informed as to the steps which were being taken to apprehend the agent who was known to be operating in the Foreign Office. Everything points to Burgess having been the channel through whom Maclean received his warning that an immediate escape was necessary.

After the news of the disappearance of Burgess and Maclean had reached Washington, Philby deliberately refrained from informing the authorities of the following material facts which were well known to him:

a) that Burgess had in the past been a Communist and a member of the Communist Party;
b) that he knew Burgess to have been a close friend of Maclean.

Instead, Philby sent a report to London representing that he thought it important that the authorities should know that Burgess owned such objects as a sun-lamp and a camera and that he sometime worked out of office hours.

Philby has played down the importance of his Communist associations and beliefs at Cambridge. His denial that he knew that Burgess when at Cambridge with him had been a Communist cannot be accepted and was, in my opinion, a deliberate lie. His denial that he knew the notorious Communist Klugmann when at Cambridge and his denial that he knew Maclean when at Cambridge, or that Maclean had been a Communist at Cambridge, are equally unacceptable.

The whole history of Philby's married life with his first wife is fraught with the highest suspicion. At the time when he was desperately poor and their joint means were no more than £3 a week, she was making constant journeys to the Continent for reasons which Philby must know but is unwilling to explain.

Having regard to this woman's proven connection with the Comintern before her marriage it is difficult if not impossible to resist the conclusion that these trips were made on behalf of and were financed by some Communist or Soviet organization. Moreover I am quite unable to accept Philby's statement that he knows nothing about them or the source from which the necessary funds were obtained.

8) [XXXXXXXXXXXXXXXXXXXXXXXXXXXXXXXXXXXXXXX]
9) In forming an opinion on the case of Philby as a whole there are two further matters which cannot be wholly excluded from consideration though their probative value is small. They are:-

a) A report from Krivitsky, a source which has proved itself over and over again to be reliable that early in 1937 the Soviets had enlisted and sent to Franco territory of Spain a young Englishman of good family who was a journalist, an idealist and was fanatically anti-Nazi, and who was almost certainly the 'Imperial Council Source' in the Foreign Office. Not only does this description fit Philby like a glove, but no other candidate has been found who fills the bill.

b) [XXXXXXXXXXXXXXXXXXXXXXXXXXXXXXXX][1]

The detailed reasons for my findings are set out in an appendix.

Appendix

At the time of Maclean's disappearance he was the subject matter of enquiry and within a very short time would undoubtedly have been picked up and interrogated.

He had been, it is known, a Soviet agent of long standing and the fact that he made what was obviously a hastily prepared escape, leaving his wife and family at the particular time at which he did, establishes in my mind quite conclusively that the reason for his precipitate departure was that he had suddenly received information which made it imperative for him to disappear without a moment's delay.

There are various possibilities as to the source from which Maclean derived his information. It might have been from a London source; it might equally well have been from a Washington source, since a limited number of people in the Washington Embassy, including Philby, were fully in the picture as to the progress of the investigation and the intentions of the authorities. The fact that Burgess, who had only very recently arrived from Washington in circumstances to which I will revert later, organised the escape and is now known to have been a Soviet agent and to have been one over at least as long a period as Maclean, is a strong pointer to Washington as having been the site of the leakage. Although I have not completed a full enquiry into the point, I came to the conclusion at an early stage that Washington was the probable source of leakage and thereafter concentrated my attention on the personnel at that end.

Philby as a witness

I asked to be given an opportunity to question Philby which I did at considerable length on 12.12.51.

He did not impress me as at all a reliable or satisfactory witness. He is a highly intelligent individual, very clever and was no doubt fully alive to the fact that in practically every peace-time espionage case the authorities have to rely upon admissions by the agent charged in order to make good a case against him. He had, moreover, been trained whilst in the service of the Crown in resisting interrogation.

I formed the opinion that Philby was determined at all costs to avoid making any incriminating admissions and rather than do so was content either to give no answer when it was obvious that he must have an answer or else to adhere to a false story, even when he realised that its falsity was apparent on the face of it. As hereafter appears, I am satisfied that he lied deliberately on a number of material matters and I strongly suspect that he was not telling the truth on many others.

Burgess and Maclean – Communist agents

I am satisfied that Burgess has been a Communist agent since not later than his visit to Moscow which took place in 1934.

The record shows that Burgess was a prominent Communist when at Cambridge where he was a contemporary and a close friend of Philby. He was at Trinity from 1930 to 1935. Philby was there from 1929 to 1933.

In July 1934 Burgess visited Moscow and on his return went to Brittany with Maclean and either one or two other persons who have not been identified. One of the two was probably a certain Klugmann, to whom I will refer later, a notorious Communist who exercised an over-riding influence in Communist circles at Cambridge. There is no evidence as to the identity of the fourth member of the party, if there were a fourth, but I think it improbable that Philby was there. The importance of this visit to Brittany is that a decision appears to have been reached on that occasion by both Burgess and Maclean that they should sever their ostensible connections with Communism. This decision was in each ease implemented within the ensuing twelve months. It is now evident that it was purely a cover move and that by it the conspirators, for such they were, far from abandoning their Communist beliefs and allegiance, were dedicating themselves to the furtherance of the Communist cause throughout the careers which they were subsequently to adopt.

Maclean, on his return from Brittany, told his mother that he had ceased to be a Communist and intended to proceed with his projected Foreign Office career which he in fact did. Burgess left the Party and appears to have been at pains to let everyone know that he had done so and thereafter became closely associated with Right Wing politics. He sought employment in the Conservative Central Office and he became an intimate associate of Jack Macnamara MP. That this device was successful in achieving its purpose is evidenced by a letter dated 27th December 1935 sent by one Derek Blaikie to the *Daily Worker* informing that paper that 'Burgess is a renegade from the Communist Party of which he was a member while at Cambridge'. The letter contains the following highly significant passage: 'In "going over to the enemy" Burgess followed the example of his closest friend amongst the Party students at Cambridge who abandoned Communism in order successfully to enter the Diplomatic Service'.

It may be remarked that Blaikie himself was Burgess's companion on his visit to Moscow the previous year.

A statement made by one Goronwy Rees reveals that Burgess in the period immediately preceding the war, was in touch with at least one Russian agent and was himself a recruiting agent for the Soviet Intelligence service.

Firstly, the circumstances of Burgess's disappearance with Maclean leaves no room for doubt but that Burgess was still, in May 1951, in the employ of the Soviets.

It is of course now known that Maclean was a Soviet agent in the Foreign Office. It is regarded as highly probable that he was the 'Imperial Council Source' whom Krivitsky reported to have been operating in 1936. For the present purposes it is unnecessary to embark upon the grounds for this deduction and I will confine myself to a few remarks concerning Maclean's early history which I have already touched upon in dealing with Burgess.

It is established that Maclean was a Communist when at Cambridge and that Maclean at Cambridge was a close friend of Burgess. What is particularly revealing is a letter which Maclean sent to the *Granta* and which was published in the issue of that paper for the 7th March 1934 in which he reveals himself not only to be a Communist but to be an outspoken disciple of Communism who is not afraid to voice his beliefs with the maximum publicity in undergraduate circles.

It is fair to point out that this letter only appeared in the *Granta* the year after Philby had gone down from Trinity but it is unlikely that the man who wrote such a letter in March 1934 made any secret of his political views during the two immediately preceding years.

Philby's Communism at Cambridge

I am satisfied that Philby was not only a Communist in the sense that we understand that term nowadays, but a notorious Communist when at Cambridge where he remained for four years from 1929 to 1933. It is possible that his Communism developed in the latter part of his residence but it was so well known to the authorities that he was refused a reference for the Indian Civil Service because of it and his Tutor in writing to the Appointments Board on his behalf felt himself obliged to draw attention to Philby's extreme views on social questions. The same Tutor has described Philby as having been a 'militant Communist' whilst in residence.

Philby's answers when questioned on these matters have not been satisfactory, though it is fair to say that his initial leak of frankness can easily be accounted for on the grounds that he was reluctant to admit to political beliefs which were inconsistent with his service in SIS. In the early stages of the investigation he endeavoured to create the impression that although influenced by Marx he was not a Communist at any time and had nothing to do with Communists. By almost imperceptible degrees he departed from this line and when I questioned him, which was after he had ceased to be in the service of SIS, I think that his attitude may be fairly summarised by saying that he admitted that he held very advanced Marxist views, views more advanced than Burgess himself held at the time, but that it would be wrong to call him a Communist only because he had never been a member of the Party,

The fact remains that on his own admission Philby, whilst at Cambridge, was an avowed and convinced Marxist.

He was not only politically minded but politically active in that he was a member of the Cambridge University Socialist Society (CUSS) whose meetings and debates he attended. He says, and indeed he complains, that after 1931 the CUSS consisted of about one sixth Communists who exercised an influence in the Society disproportionate to their number. In this setting Philby steadfastly denied that he knew Klugmann who was a contemporary of his in the same College and was far and away the most active and influential Communist of the day at Cambridge. The influence and prominence of Klugmann at Cambridge at that time can fairly be described as remarkable and I have found it impossible to accept Philby's statements that he did not know Klugmann and that he did not know that Klugmann had been up at Cambridge at the same College and at the same time as Philby himself.

Philby's Association with Burgess and Maclean at Cambridge

For some reason Philby, at the early stage of the investigation, endeavoured to play down the intimacy of his association with Burgess in their Cambridge days. The evidence shows that the two were on the closest possible terms and at least one witness, a fellow Communist, has stated that Burgess, oven in those days, was his closest friend.

Philby has stoutly and steadfastly denied that he knew at the time when they were both at Cambridge that Burgess was a Communist. This denial I am unable to accept. Burgess led a hunger march at Cambridge and if, as seems probable, this happened during Philby's period of residence, it is inconceivable that it could have occurred without Philby knowing about it at the time. Philby would have us believe that he only learnt about it several years afterwards. Philby's Tutor recalls an occasion when Burgess, Philby and one Jim Lees, a known Communist, endeavoured to expound and to convert him (the Tutor) to dialectical materialism.

It is impossible to believe that Philby, one of Burgess' closest friends, if not his closest friend, should not have been fully aware where Burgess stood politically at that time.

Philby has asserted and continues to assert that he did not know Maclean at Cambridge, Originally his story was that he believed he might have met Maclean on one or two occasions at the Foreign Office where he attended from time to time during his career as *Times* correspondent in Spain. When I questioned him, he went a little further and said that when he first met Maclean in the above circumstances, he recalled that he had seen him somewhere before – he now concedes it was probably at Cambridge – but he had no recollection where.

There is no direct evidence that Philby did know Maclean at Cambridge, but it is extremely difficult to accept Philby's denial on this point. Maclean was a close friend of Burgess. Philby was a close friend of Burgess. Maclean, like Philby, was a Marxist whilst at Cambridge and was an active Marxist as is evidenced by his letter to the *Granta* to which I have already referred. However while Burgess and Philby were members of the same college (Trinity), Maclean was at Trinity Hall. One further pointer deserves mention. Philby was interviewed on three occasions since the disappearance of Maclean and a verbatim transcript of what he said is available. Throughout these interviews he referred to Donald Maclean as 'Maclean' or 'Donald Maclean' with one exception. The exception was no doubt a slip of the tongue in an unguarded moment when he referred to him as 'Donald'. It was precisely the sort of slip which one would have expected him to make if he in fact knew Donald Maclean well and was on Christian name terms with him.

The importance of the Cambridge Maclean connection can hardly be exaggerated for Philby knew at a relatively early stage that Maclean had fallen under suspicion. If he knew Maclean to have been a member of the Communist Party in his Cambridge days, there is no acceptable excuse for his having omitted to convey to his organisation this vital piece of information with the minimum of delay.

Association with Burgess after Cambridge

The initial line taken by Philby, as I have already mentioned, was to play down his intimacy with Burgess in the early days, and to represent that he only become closely associated with Burgess after 1940. I think that he modified this attitude considerably as investigation proceeded, but all the evidence shows that they have been intimate friends from 1930/31 onwards. It is not without significance that there were found amongst Burgess' possessions Philby's Cambridge degree dated 20th June 1933, and also a statutory declaration which had been made by Philby's grandmother on the 14th February 1934 in connection with Philby's impending marriage. Another pointer is to be found in an early denial by Philby that his first wife knew Burgess well, when asked, he stated in terms that she did not know Burgess well and only accepted him as a friend of Philby himself. That this is untrue is proved by a letter in 1937 from Lizzie Philby to Burgess inviting him to come and see her in Paris and indicating that Burgess was at that time a class friend of both Lizzie Philby and her husband.

Philby's first wife

Some of the most unsatisfactory answers given by Philby in the course of this investigation concern his first wife, a sinister figure who throws a revealing light upon Philby's past.

Lizzie Philby, whom Philby married in Vienna on 24th February 1934, was, on his own admission, a Communist at the time and he knew her to be such. She was, moreover, an active Communist. Philby would have us believe that her activity was restricted to charitable or semi-charitable works in the form of collecting clothes for children, etc. It seems extremely unlikely that her work for the Communists was of such a praiseworthy or innocuous nature. It is known that her present husband is also a Communist and that the pair are now living in the Eastern Sector of Berlin in circumstances which leave no doubt that they enjoy the full confidence of, and are working for, the Eastern German Communists and the Russians,

Philby asserts that he met his first wife in Vienna fortuitously as the result of putting an advertisement for lodgings in a paper. It is indeed an odd coincidence if this were so and that a person who held the advanced views which Philby admits he held at the time should have met a person of similar opinions in such a way. There is no evidence at all to disprove Philby's story in this connection, but a more likely explanation is that he received an introduction to Lizzie from one of his Communist friends in this country such as a certain Mrs Tudor Hart, who is known to have worked for the Communists. Mrs Tudor Hart appears to have been in touch with Lizzie in 1930 and is known to have been in touch with her again in 1944. It is further known that Mrs Tudor Hart had in her possession in August 1951 a negative of a photograph of Philby and that she intended to destroy it, because for some reason she felt apprehensive lest the police should become aware of the fact. Philby purports never to have heard the name of Mrs Tudor Hart previously. He is quite unable to account for the negative in Mrs Tudor Hart's possession. This pretended lack of knowledge of Mrs Tudor Hart does not carry conviction and it is not easy to think of any innocent motive he could have for wishing to conceal his knowledge of her.

It may or may not be significant that when Philby was originally questioned on the subject, he put a wrong date upon his marriage to Lizzie. He gave the date as April 1934. The marriage in fact took place on 24th February 1934, at or about the time of the Leftist rising in Vienna, and it is possible that Philby was anxious to divert attention from the connection between the two. It is fair to say, however, that he subsequently conceded frankly that the timing of the marriage was in order to get his wife the protection of British citizenship lest she should be arrested by the Austrian authorities. One cannot, however, lose sight of the possibility – particularly in the light of subsequent events – that Communist discipline entered into the matter and that Philby married Lizzie, and married when he did, because he was told to do so. He admits that he was already living with her as his mistress when he married her.

The period immediately following Philby's marriage to Lizzie is unsatisfactory and most suspicious. At that time Philby concedes that he was extremely poor and that he was living on an income of some £3 a week. He further concedes that his wife had no resources of her own and was earning no money. Nevertheless, it appears that between 6th March 1934 and 15th April 1934 Lizzie Philby made no less than three journeys into Czechoslovakia from Vienna on her British passport which she obtained two days after her marriage. Philby is unable to explain the purpose of any one of these visits. On their return to England, she went to France on 4th September 1934 and entered Spain on the following day.

Ten days later she left a French port and on 21st September 1934 she entered Austria where she remained over a month.

On 8th April 1935 she paid a week's visit to Holland and on 16th August 1935 she arrived in France, entering Spain on the following day. On 3rd April 1936 she entered Austria and a week later went on to Czechoslovakia, returning to Austria again on 22nd April. Between 25th May 1936 and 22nd July 1936, she made a visit by air from this country to Paris and on 22nd July and 28th December 1936 she made further journeys across the Channel.

With the exception of one of the visits to Spain, which Philby asserts was a holiday, he is wholly unable or unwilling to offer any explanation of any of these journeys.

He is, moreover, unable to offer any explanation of how they were financed and concedes that he would have been quite unable to finance any of them save for the one visit to Spain which he says was a holiday. On his income at the time it is difficult to see how he could have paid for the so-called holiday in Spain.

As hereafter appears, Philby asserts that he and Lizzie separated permanently and finally early in 1937.

After that date her passport shows that she continued her unexplained travels. She went to Algiers in March 1937 and made a trip in July of that year to Greece, Jugoslavia, Italy, Austria and France. She made further journeys from time to tine across the Channel, to which it is unnecessary to refer in detail at this stage. Once again Philby is unable or unwilling to offer any explanation of these journeys, though for this period he endeavours to excuse his inability to do so by relying upon the alleged estrangement. This excuse is, however, unacceptable for it is known that throughout the period of alleged estrangement, Lizzie Philby had authority to draw on Philby's banking account, and it is known that she did in fact draw sums of £30 both in Greece and in Austria.

The foregoing facts are, in my opinion, indicative of one thing and one only: Philby is lying when he states that after their marriage his wife lost all her contacts with Communism. He must have known the purpose for her journeys and he must have known the source from which she was obtaining the money to finance them. He chooses not to tell us. I believe that all these journeys were, to the knowledge of Philby, undertaken by Lizzie Philby on behalf of the Comintern or whatever other conspiratorial organisation she was working for, and were paid for by such organisation.

Philby's story is that his association with his first wife ended finally when he left for Spain early in 1937 and that thereafter their very occasional meetings were of the shortest possible duration and tinged with embarrassment. I am satisfied that these statements are untrue and that long after the separation Philby and Lizzie remained on good terms. As I have already stated, he continued to authorise her to draw up to £40 per month upon a joint banking account. Correspondence in the possession of the Security Service dating from this period is inconsistent with existence of the strained relationship of which Philby has spoken. Lizzie's mother, in an application to the Aliens' Tribunal for release from restrictions, stated that Philby was paying £12 per month towards her maintenance.

What I regard as particularly important and significant in this connection is a letter which Philby wrote to the Passport Office on 26th September 1939 in order to enable Lizzie to obtain the requisite facilities to get to France, If Philby's story is to be accepted, at that time he did not know what his one-time Communist wife had been doing with herself in the course of the previous 2½ years. I have already suggested that in fact he must have known that during the period that they were living together she had been working for and was being financed by some Communist organisation on whose behalf she had made frequent journeys to the Continent. September 26th 1939 was approximately one month after the announcement of the German-Soviet pact. I do not believe that any loyal subject of the Crown would, at that time, have reconciled it with his allegiance to assist a person whom he knew to have been a Communist agent to travel in and out of the country when we were then at war with Russia's ally. This is, however, precisely what Philby did. The letter which he wrote to the Passport Office contains a number of falsehoods and of course could only have been written because Philby was still Lizzie's husband in name. This is the second occasion on which Lizzie, the Communist agent, is making use of the fact that she is married to Philby. A third occasion when she does the same thing is to be found in December 1939 when she obtained permission to make a journey to Paris in the New Year for the alleged purpose of meeting Philby there. She in fact obtained the requisite exit permit and went to Paris though Philby says, probably quite correctly, that she never met him there and it was never intended that she should do so.

The fact that Philby's marriage to Lizzie was not dissolved until 1946 is odd and may not be without some significance. The reason which Philby has given for not obtaining a divorce have varied at different times and one of them at least is manifestly false. There is little doubt that the divorce which was ultimately obtained was collusive and, in these circumstances, if they were prepared to act collusively in 1946, it is not readily apparent why they would not have been prepared to do so in 1940 when Philby started to live with his present wife and when he states he first became interested in a divorce. Nevertheless, nothing was done and Philby thereafter had a number of children by his present wife who were born illegitimate and will continue for all time to be so. One wonders whether the real reason there were no divorce proceedings prior to 1945 was because it was felt that Lizzie's position as a Communist agent required her to remain the wife of Philby. This suspicion is reinforced when it is known that from 1942 onwards Lizzie was in fact living with the man to whom she is at present married.[2]

[XXXXXXXXXXXXXXXXXXXXXXXXXXXXXXXXXXXXXXXXX XX]

Similarity of careers of Burgess, Maclean and Philby

It is worth drawing attention to the striking similarities of the careers of three men, two of whom are conclusively proved to have been Communist agents. The three careers follow the same pattern, which is one with which anyone who has had to deal with Soviet espionage is familiar.

All three were Communists at Cambridge; all three at or about the same time purport to drop out their Communist affiliations. Burgess renounces his membership of the Party and does so with the maximum of ostentation, so much so that he incurs the anger and contempt of his Communist friends. He is then found association with the Right Wing. Maclean also washes his hands of the past and enters the Foreign Office.

Philby, on his return to England from Vienna, at almost precisely the same time as the apparent defection of the other two, becomes associated with the Anglo-German Fellowship, and this at a time when he has just married a Jewish woman who was a Communist and who, there are the strongest possible grounds for thinking, was continuing to act as a Communist agent.

Events leading up to the disappearance of Burgess and Maclean

As a general proposition it can be stated that all the information concerning the progress of the investigation of the Foreign Office sources which was available in London was also available to Philby in Washington. Philby would therefore have known in the early part of 1951 that the hunt was on and the pace was quickening, The name of Maclean was not mentioned at that stage but anyone who was aware that Maclean was in fact a Soviet agent, and who had access to the information at Philby's disposal, would have known that Maclean was in great and increasing jeopardy. In this setting one finds that Burgess, a Soviet agent, is living with Philby in Philby's house. At the end of February 1951 Burgess commits a series of ridiculous speeding offences and the suggestion initiated with Philby himself that this may well have been done deliberately in order to engineer his (Burgess's) return to London. If Burgess did in fact know at that stage of the danger of Maclean's position, he would have been only too conscious of the danger in which he himself stood, for if Maclean, who had had a nervous breakdown in Cairo at the time of the Fuchs case, had been interrogated, Burgess could not have entertained any great confidence that Maclean would not have given him away.

If one assumes that Philby was also a Soviet agent, the obvious course was to get Burgess, who was not suspect, to London as soon as possible, for then both ends are covered. Philby is stationed at the listening point in Washington and will know exactly what is planned; Burgess is in London to take the necessary action on the information which Philby can easily transmit to him. Before Burgess left it was known to Philby that Maclean was on the short list of Foreign Office officials under suspicion.

On 16th May Philby had access in Washington to a telegram from which it might erroneously have been concluded that drastic action was planned to take place very shortly after 23rd May.

The behaviour of Philby after the disappearance is significant.

On 30th May he saw the telegram announcing what had happened and according to those who witnessed his reaction it was evident that he was dumbfounded. At first sight this is a bull point in Philby's favour but when looked at more closely it is nothing of the kind. On any view the disappearance of Burgess with Maclean was a grave error on his part and is something to which Philby could never have consented since it necessarily compromised him, Philby, most seriously. On the hypothesis therefore that Philby is himself an agent, the news of the escape of Burgess must have been a shattering blow to him. It is Burgess's disappearance that has landed Philby in his present plight. If Burgess had arranged for Maclean to escape on his own no suspicion would have fallen on Burgess and Philby's personal position would have remained secure.

Philby's behaviour at this point is, in my opinion, highly suspicious. Even if one accepts, though I am not prepared to accept, his denial that he knew Burgess to have been a Communist at Cambridge, he admits that he knew Burgess had been a Communist and a member of the Party between 1933 and 1935. He also admits that he knew that there were people who in 1940 regarded Burgess as a Communist. When I questioned him, by a slip of the tongue which I formed the opinion he recognised at once to have been an error on his part, he admitted that Burgess had told him in Washington that Donald Maclean was a close friend of his (Burgess).

Quite obviously the information referred to above was vitally important and the significance of it must have been fully appreciated by Philby. It at once provides a prima facie Communist background for one of the top suspects in the Foreign Office, evidence of which was otherwise lacking in the case at this stage. It was clearly his duty to communicate the information immediately to London but he did nothing of the kind even after the disappearance.

Instead, on 1st June 1951, one finds Philby sending a telegram containing the following statement: 'I assume Burgess knew Maclean well. He was certainly a good friend of Alan Maclean.' This was grossly misleading and, in my opinion, was intended to be so. He was well aware that Burgess did in fact know Donald Maclean well and that it was only because he knew Donald Maclean well that he knew Alan Maclean at all. More significant still is a telegram which Philby despatched on 4th June 1951 in which he reports to London on a number of matters stating: 'I feel that their possible combined significance is such that I could not fail to report them.' He goes on 'There is, I am afraid, very little doubt that Burgess had available the essential requirements of an espionage agent.'

One finds that the 'essential requirements' to which Philby is referring and which he considers it important to report, are the possession of a sun-lamp and a camera, the fact that on occasions Burgess worked at home after office hours, the fact that he travelled frequently to New York and the fact that he left behind a Marxist book. What Philby did not report was the information already referred to, the importance of which cannot be exaggerated and the significance of which cannot have escaped him.

In the same telegram on 4th June 1951 Philby purports not to have known all about Maclean at Cambridge and to reconstruct Maclean's and Burgess's joint careers at the University on a basis of assumption and surmise when it is virtually certain that he knew all about them first hand.

Other possible espionage activities

a) Spain

In 1940 a Soviet intelligence defector, Krivitsky, is recorded as having made the following oral statement to an interrogator:

'Early in 1937 the OGPU received orders from Stalin to arrange the assassination of General Franco. Hardt was instructed by the OGPU chief Yezhov to recruit an Englishman for the purpose. He did in fact contact and send to Spain a young Englishman, a journalist of good family, an idealist and fanatical anti-Nazi. Before the plan matured Hardt himself was recalled to Moscow and disappeared.'

Krivitsky was 'pretty certain' that the Foreign Office (Imperial Council) source would have been amongst the friends of the young man who went to Spain. Krivitsky has proved an extraordinarily accurate source of information.

There is no proof that Philby was in fact the agent referred to in the above statement but the information fits him like a glove and no other alternative candidate has been found. Early in 1937 Philby went to Spain as a free-lance journalist. It is possibly significant that he adopted the very means of getting to Spain which had been indicated to Burgess in a letter from Jack Macnamara MP, at the end of 1936. Philby admits that although at the time he was a member of the Anglo–German Fellowship, he had no sympathy with the political aspirations of that body and was an anti-Nazi. He has himself further stressed that there were very few English journalists on the Franco side at the time and has been unable to suggest any candidate who would fit Krivitsky's statement other than himself. If the fact be that Philby did know Maclean at this time, the pointer towards Philby becomes even more striking. In Philby's favour it should be said that the journalist was himself to assassinate Franco or that the journalist necessarily knew the real object of his mission.

When questioned about this matter Philby was obviously surprised and, I think, gravely disturbed. It is possible that these reactions on his part may be accounted for by the fact that this was the first occasion when it was directly suggested to him that he was a Soviet agent. I, however, formed a different opinion. Although the suggestion that he was a Soviet agent may not have been made directly to him at any earlier stage in the interview, I do not think that he can have had any doubt in his mind that he was suspected as such. I strongly suspect that Philby's discomfiture was due to the fact that the cap fitted and he knew it.

b) [XXXXXXXXXXXXXXXXXXXXXXXXXXXXXXXXXXXXX][3]

This woman, who was Philby's secretary in Washington, at all material times, has fallen under some suspicion as a possible source from which Burgess might have obtained advance information of the projected action. She had access to the information in question and I will assume that nothing which was relevant and which was known to Philby was not also known to her. She lived with Philby and Burgess in Philby's home in Washington. There existed, at any rate on her part, a sentimental attachment between her and Burgess who appears to have toyed with her affections in a discreditable manner. In short, she had the information and she had both the motive and the opportunity to pass it on to Burgess.

Whilst the negative is certainly not proved, viz: that she did not warn Burgess, I consider that the probabilities are all against her having done so and, having reviewed the case as a whole, I have come to the conclusion that there are no reasonable grounds for entertaining any serious suspicions against her.

The possibility that Esther Whitfield being herself a Soviet agent can, I think, be rejected. There is nothing known of her background which would support such a possibility.

If Whitfield was responsible for the leakage but is not herself an agent, it must mean that she was guilty of an indiscretion, conscious or unconscious, in her conversation with Burgess. Satisfied, as I am, that Philby was a Soviet agent, I can see no legitimate grounds for suspecting

Miss Whitfield of indiscretion. Why should Burgess rely in indiscretion on the part of an innocent secretary to obtain second-hand information which he could have obtained first-hand from her principal who was an agent.

I did not question Miss Whitfield herself but I had the advantage of discussing the case with her interviewer who believed that she was telling him the truth and satisfied him of her innocence. Nothing which I have seen causes me to think that his conclusions about her were wrong; everything which I have seen tends to show that he was right.

A Summing Up After The Cross-Examination

On 12 December 1951 Philby was cross-examined on the evidence set out in the Security Service brief. At the outset he was told that certain statements he had made earlier were unacceptable and he was invited to correct any conscious falsehoods he had then told. Philby denied that any of his earlier statements were consciously false and, showing complete self-possession, maintained this attitude throughout four hours of hostile questioning.

On 28th December 1951 Philby volunteered a further oral statement in which he commented on much of the evidence which had been used at his cross-examination.

Milmo's forensic analysis of the PEACH case had been aided by the moments when Philby had been caught unawares. He had slipped up by referring to Maclean as 'Donald' and had been stunned when MI5 presented him with Lizzie's original British passport. Quite how MI5 had acquired this document is unknown, but his inability to explain her expensive peregrinations across Europe at time when they were supposed to be scraping an existence on £3 a week was utterly compelling. MI5's satisfaction at the outcome could not be concealed, and the Milmo Report was circulated to the few entitled to see it with the final comment:

It is not for the Security Service to pass judgment on a case which it cannot prove. Investigation will continue and one day final proof of guilt or innocence may be obtained. Advice must be given now, however, on the urgent practical issues which arise and on this aspect the Security Service accepts without qualification the independent judgment found by Mr Milmo; it must recommend that for all practical purposes it should be assumed that Philby was a Soviet spy throughout his service with SIS.

Two days after the encounter, which lasted a gruelling four hours, a memorandum was circulated on the event:

There is no legal evidence on which PEACH can be prosecuted (the DPP has been consulted and concurs) and little hope that it will now be possible to obtain it.

We do, however, possess the opinion of the Barrister appointed to enquire into the intelligence evidence and this is to the effect that 'PEACH is and has for many years been a Soviet agent and that he was directly and deliberately responsible for the leakage which in fact occurred' (i.e. in the Maclean and Burgess cases).

DECISIONS REQUIRED

In the above circumstances decisions are required on the following points:

a) PEACH's passport has been voluntarily surrendered to the Security Service pending further enquiries. It cannot be held indefinitely and is likely to be re-applied for early in the New Year in order to enable PEACH to take up an assignment for the *Daily Telegraph* reporting the General Elections in India.

   If it is considered desirable that he should be prevented from holding a passport for a period longer than one month action must rest with the Foreign Office to cancel the passport and so inform him.

b) The temporary withdrawal of PEACH's passport does not of course prevent the possibility of an illicit escape from the country. On the Prime Minister's instructions the Security Service has kept day and night watch on PEACH with a view to seeing that he does not escape from the country without being questioned. He has now been questioned and no evidence has been produced which would enable us to institute a criminal prosecution against him.

It is assumed that, in these circumstances, the surveillance which ties up considerable resources and in any case can never be more than partially effective – can now be withdrawn. The Security Service will in any event continue their enquiries.

a) Should a report on the PEACH case now be furnished to the US authorities? If so, by what channels and in what form?

b) What other authorities or persons if any should also be informed – e.g. former friends of PEACH's in the Intelligence Services and the Foreign Service?

This was the highly unsatisfactory result from the event that some optimists had hoped would be the opportunity to extract a confession but Philby simply stonewalled, on awkward moments pleaded ignorance, and flatly refused to make any incriminating statement. Years later, from the safety of Moscow, Philby observed that the interrogations had given him a chance to assess the weight of any evidence against him:

> I enjoyed three great advantages. Many senior officers of SIS – from the Chief downwards – would be greatly embarrassed if it were proved that I was working for the Soviet Union. They would certainly want to give me the benefit of any doubt. Second, I knew the SIS and MI5 archives in great detail. I knew the sort of evidence they could bring against me. I had recognized myself several scattered references in the files. For instance, Krivitsky had said that the Soviet Intelligence had sent a young English journalist to Spain, Volkov had said that a Soviet agent was working as head of a counter-espionage section in London. So I had time to prepare my answers. Third, I knew British security procedures inside out, having been involved in many cases involving German, Italian and Soviet agents. I knew that much of the information in the possession of the security authorities cannot be made the basis of a charge in the courts as it either cannot be corroborated or comes from sources too delicate to be revealed. In such cases the Security Service interrogate suspects with the object of extracting a confession. As soon as they started on me, I knew that the information in their possession was not enough to start a court action against me. So I knew that provided I stuck to stout denial of a connection with the Soviet Intelligence, I would be all right. It was a long battle of nerve and wits, lasting – on and off – for five years.

Evidently Liddell, fully aware of the predictable stance adopted by Philby, was concerned about the failure to make progress. On 2 January 1952 he confided to his diary:

> I had a long talk with Dick White and James Robertson about the PEACH case. It is difficult to see how it can be done, but it seemed to me if it were possible to take Tommy Harris fully into our confidence and give him the whole dossier, he might, on looking back on his association with PEACH, be able to supply us with some quite significant information. It would have to be only borne in mind that his association with PEACH only began in 1940. Personally, I do not think we can 'open the ball' with Tommy, unless he says something to me. He has certainly seen PEACH since the latter's interrogation, and it would of course be of the greatest importance to know precisely what PEACH had told him. He has probably told him part of the story, but I should doubt whether he told him everything.

The situation was made rather more complicated when General Sinclair expressed some reservations about the Milmo report while the issue was discussed at a conference held on 14 December, prompting Sillitoe to write to Strang a month later, on 14 January:

I have myself had further discussions with C and, as the result of a conference between Mr. Milmo and senior representatives from C's organisation, the former has accepted certain amendments to his report. I enclose a copy of the final version. Despite the amendments which Mr. Milmo has agreed to, C is still not entirely satisfied with this report and I am therefore sending you a copy of his comments. While I would agree that Mr. Milmo's report sounds at times a professional note of advocacy, the evidence it contains seems to me damning in its own right and without reference to its presentation.

Since the cross examination by Mr. Milmo, PEACH has been interviewed on three further occasions by Skardon of my department and once by senior officers of his own department but no new facts have come to light as a result.

A final summing up of the evidence has now been prepared by my department and I am glad to say that this has been agreed by C. I am sending you a copy of this document also.

I have sent copies of the above-mentioned documents to the FBI, together with the case-book of the investigation. I am further arranging for Dick White to visit Washington and to be at hand for discussions on the case with Mr. Hoover and his officers, and for the briefing of General Bedell Smith. Patterson consulted Steel as to the advisability of such a visit and tells me he found him much in favour of it.

I am sending a copy of this letter to C.

On the same day Sinclair wrote to the DCI, General Walter Bedell Smith:

I fancy you would wish to have my personal reactions on the Philby case, as it has now emerged. Dick White will have given you an account, together with the interim conclusions so far drawn on the accumulated circumstantial evidence against Philby.

Needless to say, I have given this matter my maximum attention, and have come to the conclusion that, in law, with a well-briefed defending counsel, Philby would be acquitted – certainly in Scottish law it would, at the worst, be a case of 'Not proven'.

While I appreciate the difficulty in producing real proof of guilt, I see that it is no less difficult for Philby to prove his innocence.

I cannot bring myself to believe that an enemy agent would sit in our midst and fool MI5 and my Service for so long a period, unless one accepts the view that his activities were confined to protecting himself.

I admit to certain unsavoury matters connected with his first wife, and if only these could be completely probed, much of the remainder of the story might be seen in its proper perspective.

Naturally, I am profoundly disturbed lest I should be mistaken in which case I should have to offer you professionally my profound apologies that Philby has been in a position to do serious damage.

It is, therefore, only right that we should accept the interim verdict and treat Philby with all the suspicion he deserves for having closely associated with so undesirable and dangerous an individual as Burgess has proved himself to have been.

An intensely decent man, Sinclair found it hard to accept that Philby could have engaged in betrayal on such a colossal level, and was also conscious that, in the absence of a confession, MI5's case had been entirely circumstantial. Nevertheless, the General was reluctant to accept what ultimately would turn out to be the truth. Indeed, on 17 January Sinclair made his views known to Strang:

Further to Sir Percy Sillitoe's letter to you dated the 14th January, reference PF.604584 Supp.A/D,G, with a copy to me, the main reason why I was not satisfied with Mr. Milmo's report was that it presented the case for the prosecution against PEACH, but nowhere in the dossier which went to America was there a comparably full case for the defence.

While, for all practical purposes, I naturally have to act on the worst assumption against PEACH, I questioned the wisdom of sending this damning and circumstantial story to the Americans on a case which is still admittedly incapable of proof in law.

It may perhaps turn out that in the future further information will come to light in PEACH's favour or show that we have been on the wrong track. If this were so, it could be embarrassing, as far as the Americans are concerned, that emphasis had been put only on the prosecution side. Perhaps you would care to see how I feel about it as shown in the attached copy of a letter which I have recently sent to Bedell Smith.

The correspondence continued in a three-cornered match between Sinclair, anxious not to do Philby an injustice, MI5 convinced of his guilt, and the Foreign Office reluctant to do anything that might be construed as misleading the Americans. Meanwhile, Dick White was in Washington, providing the FBI with his own version, as Liddell recorded on 22 January:

Dick White has telegraphed from Washington about his interview with J. Edgar Hoover, which seems to have gone well. Hoover seems fairly convinced about the case against PEACH, but understands that no action is possible. He did, however, ask how it was that PEACH got a clearance for work in SIS. Dick pointed out to him that PEACH came into SIS in the early stages of the war when cases of his kind were not looked at with the same scrutiny as they would be in the present situation.

Two days later, on 24 January, Liddell attended the weekly meeting of the JIC and told the chairman, Pat Reilly, that Philby had been in touch with Skardon:

I had a word with Patrick Reilly after the JIC meeting about a letter which PEACH has written to Jim Skardon. PEACH says that he may get a job with a firm in Egypt and wants to know if there would be any difficulty about his passport. We propose to tell him that there will be no difficulty. Meanwhile, we are retaining the passport; we should, however, like to have the Foreign Office view as to whether we should send it back now or retain it until the occasion for its use arises. Reilly asked me to write him a letter. C has no objection to the return of the passport.

On 6 February Liddell talked to Menzies about Philby who, in an interview with Skardon, had nominated six people from his university days who, apparently, could act as referees. However, in the aftermath of the Burgess and Maclean disappearances, enquiries of this kind could not be conducted with any degree of confidentiality.

I spoke to C about his letter, in reply to ours, regarding the six people named by PEACH as acquaintances of his during his university days, and particularly the statement 'I can see no other risk … '. I pointed out to him that in our view there was a considerable risk of a leakage of information, to the effect that another member of the Foreign Office was under suspicion. Bearing in mind that out of the six people named by PEACH as acquaintances of his during his university days, five had Communist traces, I made it clear that it would not be possible to interrogate these individuals without it being apparent to them that we regarded PEACH with considerable suspicion. If there were a leakage, it seemed to me that the Foreign Office would be seriously embarrassed.

C readily accepted this point. He then asked John Sinclair to come in, when we continued the discussion about the case. I made it quite clear there was no reluctance on our part to carry out the interrogations, provided SIS, on their behalf and on behalf of the Foreign Office, were prepared to accept the risk. We did not, however, anticipate that we should be much nearer a positive solution: We had all heard from PEACH that short of holding a Party card, he was a near being a Communist as no matter. If, of course, it was felt that in fairness to PEACH the interrogations should be carried out, we would go ahead.

Sinclair thought it was possible that someone might be in a position to say or to deny that PEACH was a close associate of James Klugmann or of Donald Maclean, and that this would be a material point worth getting at. Both C and Sinclair, however, realised the risks involved and suggested that we should select one of the six individuals whom we thought to be the least likely to talk. C hoped that it might be possible to start the interrogation by discussing Burgess and Maclean and leading from them to PEACH.

On 22 February Cary-Foster weighed in, having been instructed by Strang to challenge the evidence on which MI5's assumptions were made about Burgess and Maclean:

Sir William Strang has drawn attention to the statements about Maclean and Burgess in the MI5 reports by Mr Milmo in the PEACH case. These state categorically that both Maclean and Burgess were Soviet agents and Sir W Strang therefore assumes that this has been established. Sir W Strang has asked

(a) what precisely is the evidence on which these statements are based;
(b) whether it is the view of the Security Service that both have been proved to be Soviet agents;
(c) whether, if Burgess and Maclean returned now, they could be prosecuted under the evidence presently available.

I have consulted the Security Service and the following are the answers to Sir W. Strang's questions:-

Maclean.
The evidence against Maclean is derived from the investigation into the leakages to the Russians from HM Embassy in Washington in 1944/45. It is not evidence which could be produced in a court of law, largely because of the source of the information about the leakages. The following is a brief summary of the facts and reasoning which form this evidence:

(i)   information derived from the source material showed that the agent had almost certainly decyphered at least one telegram in the Churchill/ Roosevelt series,
(ii)   all the telegrams in this series were decyphered, at the Washington end, in the British Embassy on behalf of United Kingdom interests and by certain American authorities on behalf of the Americans,
(iii) the possibility that the leakage was from American sources in Washington was virtually eliminated since the Russians received from the agent texts of Foreign Office telegrams which would not have been passed to the Americans even unofficially,
(iv)   in looking for the agent in the British Embassy it was argued that since he/she must have been closely concerned with decyphering of telegrams he/she must be found either in the cypher room or in Chancery. It was further argued that since he/she certainly had access to one non-cypher document of which the Russians were made aware and was apparently also well informed on general political matters, in particular post-hostilities planning, he/she was more likely to be in Chancery,

(v)   a piece of information from the source material which appeared to refer to the agent stated '... to go frequently to New York where his wife lives ...'. Of the Chancery staff in Washington only Maclean had a wife living in New York and whom; he used to visit. Maclean therefore is the only person who can be found to fit all the circumstantial evidence. In the view of MI5, It can be accepted that he was responsible for the leakages from Washington and was therefore a Russian agent. Their conclusion is reinforced both by his sudden disappearance and by the following supporting evidence:

   (a)   The information provided in 1940 by the Russian defector Krivitsky concerning an unidentified Russian agent in the Foreign Office in 1936/37 would fit Maclean.

   (b)   Investigations into Maclean's early history have revealed that he was a Communist at Cambridge.

The statement that Burgess was a Russian agent is based on the testimony of Goronwy Rees who said that in 1937 Burgess told him that 'he was working on behalf of an anti-Fascist organisation and that his task was to collect confidential political information,' and he said later that this organisation was in fact 'the Comintern, or rather a secret branch of it'. MI5 accept Rees's statement on this subject:

   Their conclusion is reinforced by the evidence that Burgess was a Communist while at Cambridge.

   With regard to Sir W. Strang's point (c) whether Burgess and Maclean could be prosecuted, should they now return, MI5 say:

   (a)   that in the case of Maclean there is no legal evidence at present available which would justify any prosecution against him for espionage:

   (b)   that as regards Burgess, there is no legal evidence at present available which would justify a prosecution against him for espionage. There is, however, legal evidence that Burgess retained in his possession, when he had no right to retain them, various documents which had been issued to him or to which he had had access during the course of his employment, and that therefore should he return, evidence exists upon which, in the opinion of MI5, a successful prosecution could be launched against him under Section 2(b) of the Official Secrets Act, 1911, as amended by the Official Secrets Act, 1920.

In retrospect it does seem odd that at this late stage, two months after Milmo's inquest, the Permanent Under-Secretary should be manifesting ignorance of the VENONA evidence that had been used by, among others, Carey-Foster, to single out Maclean. In manuscript, Pat Reilly added to the file: 'I think it is very unlikely that Mr Milmo was wrong. But I do not think that the known facts justify language so categorical as used on page 2 of his report, and pages 1, 2 and 4 of the annex to it.' Dick White's reply, dated 4 March and delayed until after his return from Washington, was comprehensive:

I hope that this letter will bring you and the Foreign Office up-to-date on the PEACH case.

1. American reactions.

FBI. As you know, I visited Washington in January and February with the primary purpose of informing the two US intelligence authorities, the FBI and CIA, of the results of our enquiries to date in the PEACH case. Before my arrival in Washington, the Director-General had sent Mr. Hoover a full case history and the FBI case officers had already studied this and briefed Mr. Hoover before my first interview with him. Mr Hoover was therefore able to deliver the official FBI verdict on the case. His actual words were: 'For my part, I conclude that PEACH is as guilty as hell, but I don't see how you are ever going to prove it.'

In a subsequent discussion of the matter he did not ask what restrictions could now be put upon PEACH, nor did he express alarm at the damage which might have been done by PEACH to FBI security. Indeed, on this point, Mr Ladd – Mr Hoover's Head of Intelligence – had already hinted to me that it was not thought likely that PEACH had spied for the Russians while in the USA. In this hint of Ladd's, and in Mr Hoover's obvious lack of curiosity to hear more about the PEACH case, I discerned a fear that it would do the FBI no good to have to admit that they had had a Russian spy going in and out of the Bureau and enjoying excellent relations with many of its senior men.

On the DG's instructions I asked Mr Hoover for an assurance that the documents we had submitted to the Bureau would be accepted as the frank submission of one technical investigative body to another and that the information in them would not be disseminated to other US authorities. Mr Hoover agreed to this and, for reasons I have given above, I am inclined to think we need not fear that he will attempt to represent it as a further catastrophe on the British security front. I make these observations, of course, subject to there being no subsequent public revelations for, in that event, I have no doubt at all that Mr Hoover will take such action as he sees fit to defend his own position at the expense of ours.

My interview with Mr Hoover was extremely cordial and I believe that he is now sincerely anxious to enjoy close working relations with us. I naturally reported all this at the time fully to Sir Christopher Steel and, in a brief word or two, to the Ambassador.

CIA. For the purpose of reporting to General Bedell Smith I represented both my own DG and C and I was accompanied to my first interview with the General by John Bruce Lockhart, C's representative in Washington.

Much more plainly than Mr Hoover, General Bedell Smith took the line that this was essentially a British matter, that he did not wish to pry into the detail of it and that, despite the possible damage his organisation might have suffered therefrom, he was anxious that it should not affect the close working relations between his organisation and C's. He showed himself very appreciative of our frankness in informing him of the interim verdict we had reached and argued that such frankness gave him increased rather than less confidence in the British alliance.

He also admitted ruefully that what had happened to us today might, after all, happen to him tomorrow. Unlike Mr Hoover, he has a mind which remembers and connects related facts on the US side – for example, the Alger Hiss case and the wide penetration of US Government Departments by the Silvermaster Group. He can therefore see our disasters in due proportion to the American ones.

To sum up US reactions: I think we were certainly wise to be frank with both the FBI and CIA. I do not think that either Mr Hoover or General Bedell Smith harbours bitter reflections against us and I think that the former has probably a personal interest in regarding the case as a purely British one and in not advertising it to a wider public in America. In any case, both realise that PEACH's guilt is not proven though I think that, on the facts available, both consider him guilty.

2. Current position in the case.

Since PEACH was interrogated by Mr Milmo in the middle of December 1951, he has had interviews with Mr Skardon and with General Sinclair. He has also supplied two memoranda dealing with some of the matters raised against him and has given permission for the inspection of his bank account. Routine checks have been in operation. But the case has not been advanced in any way by any of these means beyond the point reached by Mr. Milmo. PEACH has given no hint that he might be guilty, even to those closest to him, while in our opinion the case against him is in essentials untouched by his representations. Although we shall continue to pay attention to PEACH's activities while he is in the United Kingdom, we think it very unlikely that this will advance the case in any way and the final verdict will probably have to await the discovery of entirely new evidence. This might be forthcoming from current enquiries arising from the Burgess/Maclean case which are by no means exhausted, from the acquisition of new sources, or from successes in the field of crypt-analysis.

PEACH has pursued the search for a new job with rather more energy. Through the intervention of former colleagues in SIS, he now considers that he has a fairly good chance of being appointed as Public Relations Officer to the Shell Mex Group in Egypt, and that if he obtains this post the *Observer* may be prepared to appoint him as its Special Correspondent.

PEACH's passport is in our possession. He has been informed that he can have it back when he requires to travel for the purpose of taking up employment.

While the Foreign Office continued to be preoccupied with Philby, MI5 had made progress against another espionage suspect, John Cairncross. On 4 March Liddell confided to his diary:

> There seems to be a strong case against John Cairncross, now in the Treasury and was at one time in Section V.
>
> A piece of paper in his handwriting, giving notes on interviewing in 1939 with various officials in the Foreign Office and other departments, was found among documents belonging to Guy Burgess. As Cairncross is of the same Cambridge vintage as Burgess and Maclean and knew them both, it looks very much as if he was at one time an agent of Burgess.

Cairncross had been identified as the author of incriminating documents found in a suitcase left under Burgess' bed in his flat after his defection, and although they were unsigned, a sharp-eyed MI5 officer, Evelyn McBarnet, had recognized the distinctive, spidery handwriting which she had seen recently in a routine security questionnaire. He was placed under surveillance, and on one occasion it rather looked as though he had aborted a rendezvous outside Acton Town Tube station at the last moment in very suspicious circumstances. Although the Watchers did not spot any Soviets in the area, Yuri Modin had been on the scene, but had escaped detection when he sensed danger. On 3 April, Liddell had more to say about Cairncross:

> John Cairncross has been seen. He was extremely perturbed when confronted with the document in his own handwriting which had been found amongst the papers of Guy Burgess. His statement is somewhat contradictory; on the one hand he says that he gave Burgess the information because he thought that he was working for some Government organisation and that it would be in his, Cairncross', interests to keep in with him. On the other hand, he says that he was extremely nervous when he tried to get his notes back and was told by Burgess that he had either lost or destroyed them. A further point which is not in his favour relates to an incident reported by the Watchers. He apparently deposited in a wastepaper basket in one of the parks, a copy of the *Communist Review* of current date. This would have been understandable in the circumstances if the copy had been an old one, but it is difficult to see how a man who describes himself as having given up his Communist ideas and as

having become a Churchillian, would go on wasting his time reading such turgid material as the *Communist Review.*

Within a fortnight, the Cairncross case was over, as Liddell noted on 15 April: 'The Treasury have considered the case of John Cairncross and are requesting him to resign. They seem to feel that the case has been extremely well handled by Jim Skardon.'

Terrified at the prospect of being linked to Burgess, Cairncross had resigned from the Civil Service and forfeit his pension. In 1955 his PF listed his past career, noting that he had

entered the Diplomatic Service on 6 October 1936.On 1 October 1938 he had transferred to the Treasury and on 23 September 1940 he was appointed Private Secretary to Lord Hankey (Chancellor of the Duchy of Lancaster and Postmaster-General). From 11 May 1942 to 31 May 1943 Cairncross was employed by GCHQ. On 14 June 1943 he joined Section V of MI6 and remained there until June 1945 when he was released in order to return to the Treasury. He served in the Treasury until 1 May 1951 when he was transferred to the Ministry of Supply. In December 1951 he was transferred back to the Treasury and his resignation from the Civil Service was accepted on 19 April 1952.

It is evident from the details of his record that although of brilliant promise his work was not of a high order and he was never a particularly satisfactory employee.

Cairncross came to the notice of the Security Service prior to the disappearance of Maclean and Burgess. In 1938 an unsigned letter ending 'fraternally' addressed to Cairncross, was misdirected and handed to the police. The letter referred to the death of one of Himmler's staff officers. No explanation as to the significance of this letter has ever been obtained. In February 1939 Cairncross sponsored the arrival in England of Victor Herman Haefner, a German of doubtful reputation who had been convicted of espionage on behalf of the French in Germany in 1925 who had later been involved in arms dealing both in Spain and in Greece.

After the disappearance of Maclean and Burgess Cairncross's name and telephone number were found in Maclean's office diary under the date 30 April 1951. Cairncross was interviewed and admitted that he had known Maclean since 1937 when they were both in the same department in the Foreign Office and had continued to see him intermittently from that time. Cairncross said that the diary entry referred to a party to which he had invited Maclean. Cairncross said that he had also known Burgess vaguely since 1937 but since he did not like him had seen little of him.

In 1952 a manuscript document written probably in about March/April 1939 which had been found among the personal possessions of Burgess, was identified as having been written by Cairncross, This document consisted of a fifteen-page report on conversations on international affairs and on British foreign policy which Cairncross had had with nine different government officials.

In a formal statement dated 2 April 1952 Cairncross admitted being the author of the document but claimed that it was the only official information he passed to Burgess either orally or in writing; in mitigation Cairncross said that he thought that in 1939 Burgess worked in a secret Government department, the implication being that he was therefore justified in reporting to him as he did.

In the same formal statement Cairncross admitted having been attracted to Communism and having associated with certain well-known Communists in Cambridge. At an interview in 1951 he had denied associating with Communists at Cambridge, although admitting his political views at Cambridge were slightly to the left.

During the course of the investigation of Cairncross in 1952 he was seen on one occasion soon after the interrogation to adopt what appeared to be methods of evasion from surveillance such as might be used by a spy. When asked to account for this, he gave an explanation which on the following day he altered finally explaining his actions by a story that he had a rendezvous with a woman. The truth of this story could not be proved or disproved and some possibility therefore remains that Cairncross may have been in touch with the Russian Intelligence Service as recently as April 1952.

Security Service enquiries established that Cairncross had been a Communist sympathizer while at Trinity College, Cambridge in 1934 and 1935. In 1947 Cairncross was reported by a reliable and delicate source to belong to a group of 'near Communists' and to hold left-wing views of a fairly advanced nature.

Cairncross has recently been employed as a correspondent for the *Observer* news service and also for the Canadian Broadcasting Corporation.

Cairncross's case is unsatisfactory but the prolonged investigation into it has failed to produce evidence on which a charge of espionage could be based. There is no indication that he is now a Communist.

It would later emerge that he had shared a room in the Foreign Office's Western Department with Donald Maclean, without realizing he too was a spy. Indeed, the KGB archives reveal that Maclean had recommended Cairncross for recruitment, unaware that he was already in harness, and had been warned off by his NKVD contact. Cairncross would also work alongside Philby in Section V in St Albans, unaware that he was the originator of what is now notorious as the Cambridge Ring-of-Five.

Years later, when Arthur Martin reinterviewed Cairncross in the United States, where in 1964 he held a teaching post at Case Western University in Cleveland,

Ohio, he incriminated James Klugmann as his recruiter, MI5 would realize that a vital opportunity had been missed. If he had been placed under sufficient pressure by Skardon in 1952, Cairncross admitted he would have cracked.

On 7 March 1952, when the Foreign Office began to draft a brief on the Philby saga for the Foreign Secretary, Sir John Sinclair sent a note to Carey-Foster:

> I would not go so far as Dick White, in saying that Bedell Smith thinks that on the facts available, PEACH is guilty. At the time of Dick White's visit, I wrote to Bedell Smith and gave him my personal opinion, which is, briefly, that the case is non proven. I concluded my letter, by saying:
>
> 'It is only right that we should accept the interim verdict and treat Philby with all the suspicion he deserves for having closely associated with so undesirable and dangerous an individual as Burgess has proved himself to have been.'
>
> I have now received a reply from Bedell Smith, saying that he agrees with my conclusions regarding the Philby matter. He goes on to say:
>
> 'From our point of view, of, course, this is one of those cases where one hopes for the best and expects the worst, as this is the only safe thing to do. We have taken such precautions as are possible and, in the event of the worst, I doubt if we would find ourselves very hard hit.'
>
> As regards the future of PEACH, I should omit any reference to his future occupation, as I understand that he will not receive an appointment with the Shell Mex Group in Egypt. I should confine yourself to saying that he is seeking business employment.

When Sir William Strang came to sum up the situation for Anthony Eden on 27 March 1952, he adopted the line taken by Sinclair, and also introduced the new suspect, John Cairncross:

> You may care to know the present position and the general conclusions reached in the Maclean/Burgess case and the PEACH case. The last note which you saw on the former subject is attached for reference.
>
> After the receipt of the letters from Maclean of last July and August, nothing more was heard about either Maclean or Burgess, until we recently received the report from an American source quoted in the letter from MI5 consider that this is probably low grade information to which they do not attach great importance. They have asked the Central Intelligence Agency for information about the source, but on previous form, they are unlikely to get it. We have no reason to suppose that there is any foundation for the reference to a further defection from the Foreign Office.
>
> MI5 have recently produced a restatement of the reasons why they still do not want to publish any further information about the background to the

disappearance of Maclean and Burgess. You may care to read this paper. I agree with MI5's conclusions.

Intensive study of the papers left behind by Burgess has produced a good deal of information about his contacts and intelligence activities. In particular it has been established that some notes made in March 1939 just after the German invasion of Czechoslovakia, of conversations with junior officials, mostly in the Foreign Office, were written by Mr John Cairncross, who had recently been transferred from the Foreign Office to the Treasury (where he still is) because he was found unsuitable for the Diplomatic Service. It is now known that Mr Cairncross, a contemporary of Maclean, was a member of the Communist Party at Cambridge. The papers are going to the Director of Public Prosecutions, but it seems likely that after this lapse of time, he will advise against a prosecution; in that case the standing purge procedure will be used. We are lucky to have got rid of Mr Cairncross when we did.

The present position about Maclean, Burgess and PEACH can be summed up as follows:

Maclean.
It is virtually certain that Maclean was a Russian agent in Washington in 1944/45. It is extremely likely that he was one in the Foreign Office in 1936/37. It is not known whether he continued to be a Russian agent after 1945.

If Maclean should return, he could not be prosecuted on available legal evidence, but it is of course always possible that he might provide the necessary evidence himself under interrogation.

Burgess.
Burgess was certainly a Russian agent in the 1930s. Material which he collected and inexplicably left behind makes it virtually certain that he continued to work as an agent at least during the war and possibly thereafter, but there is no positive proof that he did so. It is also virtually certain that he was the channel for the arrangements for the escape of Maclean and himself, which creates the presumption that he was still in touch with the Soviet Intelligence organisation.

If Burgess should return, he too could not, on available legal evidence, be prosecuted for espionage.

He could, however, be prosecuted under the Official Secrets Act for having retained in his possession, when he had no right to them, various secret documents to which he had had access during the course of his employment.

PEACH
The Security Service's summing up of the PEACH case after his cross-examination by Mr. Milmo, which has been agreed by C, ends as follows:

'The Security Service must recommend that for all practical purposes it must be assumed that PEACH was a Soviet spy throughout his service with SIS.'

C wrote to General Bedell Smith in January 1952 saying that it was only right to accept this, interim verdict but that the case was not proven. General Bedell Smith replied agreeing with this view.

Mr D.G. White of the Security Service has recently been to Washington and has given a copy of the complete case history to Mr. Edgar Hoover, the head of the Federal Bureau of Investigation (FBI). Mr. White also, with C's approval, gave an oral account of the general conclusions of the case to General Bedell Smith, the head of the Central Intelligence Agency (CIA).

Mr White summed up United States reactions by saying that he considered that we had been wise to be frank with both the FBI and the CIA. He does not consider that either Mr. Hoover or General Bedell Smith harbours any bitterness against us and he thinks that the former has probably a personal interest in regarding the case as a purely British one and is not advertising it to a wider public in America. In any case they realise that PEACH's guilt is not proven though Mr White thinks that both consider him guilty. (C however infers from his own correspondence that General Bedell Smith does not believe PEACH guilty).

The current position of the case itself is that PEACH has been interviewed twice by the Security Service and once by General Sinclair since he was interrogated by Mr Milmo, and routine MI5 checks have been in operation. The case, however, has not been advanced and MI5 do not think it can be unless new evidence comes to light,

PEACH is looking for a job in business, but has not yet found one. MI5 has his passport but he has been told that he can have it back when he needs to travel for the purpose of taking up a job.

From this point, in March 1952, the trail went cold and MI5 effectively gave up the entire investigation, with some of the key participants, such as Arthur Martin, being preoccupied with other duties. In his case, he was transferred first to Singapore, then engaged in counter-insurgency operations during the Malayan Emergency which had been declared in June 1948, and then to Kuala Lumpur as Director of Intelligence. With no criminal proceedings likely against Cairncross, and Philby living quietly in a rented house near Rickmansworth in Hertfordshire, there seemed every likelihood that the saga had finally run its course. However, for Liddell the PEACH problem had become a preoccupation, as is apparent from his diary entry for 10 April when he dined with Tommy and Hilda Harris, and encountered Philby:

I arrived at Tommy's house at about 7.30 pm. He met me at his garden gate, and said nothing about PEACH. Hilda and PEACH met me in the hall and I greeted PEACH in the normal way. I asked him what he was doing and he told me that he was going to Spain, where he would be doing journalistic work and writing a book. He thought that at this moment, when there seemed to be a change of attitude towards Spain by both America and ourselves, the situation would be an interesting one on which to report.

At no time during the evening was PEACH's case discussed. The conversation rang on a whole number of other topics, including war reminiscences. The only hint that I got as to the extent or otherwise of the Harris' knowledge of the PEACH case was when I was alone for a moment with Hilda. She remarked that she thought it was such a good thing that PEACH was going to Spain as she thought it would do a lot to restore his morale. She added that he was 'such a fine fellow'. She then mentioned that Mrs. PEACH would not be going with him at the outset, but might possibly join him later if he settled down in Spain.

The relationship between Tommy and Hilda seemed to be absolutely normal. He seemed in very good form, but has recently been so worried about the restrictions on business matters, in particular the export of pictures to the United States, that he has more or less decided to wind up his business and acquire a permanent residence in Lincoln's Inn Fields. He, Hilda, and PEACH are leaving on 22 April; PEACH going to Spain and the other two to Mallorca, as far as I can understand. Tommy and Hilda will be returning in September when he is to have another operation, but not, I gather of a serious kind.

During the evening Tommy was drinking only wine. PEACH was looking reasonably well and only drank in moderation, but I should say in a general way he was drinking quite a lot.

On re-reading the TC I am a little inclined to think that the Harris' are not fully informed about the case against PEACH; I doubt otherwise whether Tommy would have been quite so sanguine about throwing me together with PEACH in the way he did. PEACH himself was evidently somewhat worried at the prospect, and although he was a little uneasy at the start, very soon became normal. He made on half-hearted attempt to go home before dinner, but was easily persuaded by the Harris' to stay on.

The dilemma for Liddell who, as we have seen, was initially reluctant to believe the worst of Philby, was the weight of evidence developing against him, and the increasingly disagreeable nature of the investigation into which he had now inserted himself. In effect, by dining with Hilda, Tommy and Kim, Liddell was playing the role of agent provocateur, interrogator and agent, also aware that all the conversations in the house were being monitored. MI5's problem of course, that it was dealing with a highly professional adversary who knew all the tricks of the trade, and rarely put a foot wrong.

Chapter VII

Exposure

With the PEACH case quietly consigned to MI5's top security Y Box Registry and Percy Sillitoe preparing to retire, Guy Liddell persuaded himself that he had every hope of succeeding him as Director-General. Indeed, he was interviewed for the top post when he attended an Appointments Board at the Cabinet Office on 14 April, and recorded the event in his diary:

I attended the Appointments Board which was considering the D–G's successor. Sir Edward Bridges was in the Chair, the other members of the Board being William Strang, Frank Newsam, Harold Parker, General Sir Nevil Brownjohn, Norman Brook, and a representative of the Civil Service Commission. Bridges took me through my curriculum vitae, when I explained the various appointments I had held. He then asked me what qualifications I thought were appropriate for the Director of this Service. I said while this was a little difficult for me to answer, I felt strongly somebody was needed who had a fairly intimate knowledge of the workings of the machine. While one expected ideas to germinate in all stratas of the organisation, it was necessary for the head to do quite a lot of thinking on the subject, particularly in the direction of improving our methods of obtaining information.

Strang asked me about our foreign relations. I explained how we met our opposite numbers in Europe in the SIC [Security Intelligence Committee] every three months, and how we had facilities to go over and discuss matters with them when cases of mutual interest arose. I also explained our relations with the Dominions and the extent of our organisation overseas.

Newsam suggested to me most of our information came from the police. I said this was a complete misconception; that the bulk of the information was obtained from our own sources, and it was we who were directing the police to fill in the gaps or to make special enquiries in regard to particular cases. He then asked me whether I did not think the most important function of the D–G was not in the choosing of staff. I said it was an extremely important function, but I thought we had a good staff and that we had been recruiting the right sort of people. I might, of course, have said the D–G has only attended one Appointments Board in the last six years, but I felt this was rather too personal!

Norman Brook asked me about languages. I said that I had found French and German very valuable to me in the days when I had a good deal of it to read, and that it was, of course, extremely useful when discussing matters with the French and Belgians, and that I had used my German quite a lot in the visits that I had paid to that country over a period of years.

General Brownjohn asked me about relations with the police, which I explained in some detail, making it clear it was we who gave them instructions and direction, but that from the point of view of action, namely prosecutions, we did not use them very often. The reason was that our work was much more long-term: it was our business to learn about the enemy's intelligence organisation and subversive movements in order that we might advise on appropriate action at a time of crisis. [XXXXXXXXXXXXXXXXXXX]

Harold Parker asked me what I thought we ought to be considering during the next five years. I said that one of the things was the improvement of technical means for obtaining intelligence. Working within a democracy against a totalitarian state, whose security precautions were pretty watertight (I gave examples) was by no means an easy matter. I explained how difficult it was to follow a man who was on the look out for it. It was for this reason we were turning more and more to scientific means. He remarked that SIS were tending in the same direction.

Bridges asked me at the end whether I had any other points which had not been covered, and on reflection I rather regret that I did not say something about the morale of the staff and the importance of making people feel that it was possible for them rise to the top. However, this is a point which I know has been well drummed into Bridges by J.C. Masterman and others.

There were many other things which I feel I might have said, but this I am afraid is inevitable. The meeting lasted half an hour.

Dick followed me, and although I think he is despondent about his performance, he may have done a good deal better than he thinks. He got in one very good crack at Newsam. He said he thought the head of the organisation ought to be a technical man, to which Newsam replied: 'Surely you do not suggest that your previous Director-General had an intimate knowledge of the workings of the machine?' Dick said 'No, they did not!', at which all those present roared with laughter.

The other candidates were Kenneth Strong, Ferguson, Dunn of Ryton, Ronnie Howe, and Sir William Johnson of the Colonial Police. The impression that both Dick and I had is that Kenneth Strong will get the job. He will certainly be backed by Brownjohn and Harold Parker, and may be regarded as the Chiefs of Staff candidate. Dunn is Newsam's candidate, and Ferguson and Johnson are, I believe, the D-G's. Ronnie Howe probably made his application through the Home Secretary, whom he knows fairly intimately.

The Cabinet Office took a month to deliberate, and then announced that Liddell's protégé, Dick White, had been selected. Aghast, Liddell promptly resigned.

Liddell's final departure from Leconfield House might have been expected to bring down the curtain on the immediate post-war era in the counter-intelligence world that had been dominated by loose ends left over from espionage cases directly linked to atomic research or high-level penetration of the Foreign Office, but it was not to be. Four months later, on Friday, 11 September 1953, Melinda Maclean vanished from her new home in Switzerland and, accompanied by her three children, was thought to have joined her husband in the Soviet Union. Her disappearance rekindled interest in the Burgess and Maclean defections but, from a security aspect, the episode had little significance except that it served to cast suspicion on Tommy Harris, with whom she had recently seen at his home at Camp de Mar in Mallorca. Melinda had flown to Spain on 23 July with her three children to stay for five weeks with an American friend, Douglas MacKillop, at his home at Cala Ratjada.

Scarcely a week had elapsed from her return on Friday, 4 September to her mother's apartment in Geneva's rue des Alpes, when she announced that she was driving to see an old friend, Robin Muir, that same afternoon, and was going to stay the weekend at Territet. She then drove away in her 1952 black Chevrolet which was found a week later, parked in a Lausanne garage. A police investigation established that she had visited a bank to draw £50, and then had walked to the railway station where she and her children had caught a train to Zurich. There they had changed for another to Austria, and had alighted at Schwarzach Saint-Velt where they had been met by a large limousine which had whisked them away to continue their journey to Moscow.

A close friend of Liddell, Blunt and Philby, Harris had given up his famous art gallery at 6 Chesterfield Gardens and retired to the Balearic Isles to paint. Had he been the means by which Melinda had received her apparently elaborate instructions on how to elude Swiss surveillance and slip out of the country undetected?

Suddenly, more news emerged from an unlikely source. The SLO in Canberra, Derek Hamblen, reported to Leconfield House on 6 April 1954 that the NKVD *rezident*, Vladimir Petrov, had defected two days earlier.[1] Although Petrov had been cultivated for months, his ASIO case officer had not been certain of his precise status until after he had accepted political asylum on 4 April.

During his debriefing conducted by ASIO, Petrov had revealed that one of his colleagues in Moscow, Filipp Kislitsyn, had confided to him in a moment of canteen gossip that he had supervised the escape from London of Burgess and Maclean. He claimed that he had been familiar with their cases because he had been posted to the London *rezidentura* as a cipher clerk between 1945 and 1948, but the bombshell was his confirmation that both men had been Soviet spies since their recruitment at university. He also claimed that both Burgess and Maclean suspected that MI5 'had been on their track'.

Whilst this news was no great surprise to MI5, it was interpreted in rather a different way by SIS which noted that Petrov had nothing to say about the existence of a wider spy-ring, or even about Philby. In the absence of any derogatory information concerning Philby, SIS undertook a review of the PEACH case, and the results were disclosed by Sinclair to the JIC Chairman, Pat Dean, on 23 September 1955:

> As I told you during our conversation on Wednesday I do not wish to prejudice the current reassessment by the Security Service and ourselves of the suspicions surrounding PEACH by giving my views on those aspects of the case which are the subject of special study and upon which differences of opinion exist. There are, however, certain facts not open to doubt, which in my opinion reduce very considerably the suspicion that PEACH was a Soviet agent. We are examining these points among many others with the Security Service. How much weight the Security Service will give to them I cannot say at this stage. Very briefly they are:-

> (a) A careful recent review of his record with this Service has failed to reveal any indications of his having been other than loyal in his conduct of the many cases which he handled.
> (b) PEACH was in the confidence of the FBI in regard to a number of cases which had been linked to that of Klaus Fuchs (e.g. Julius Rosenberg) and all of them were successfully concluded by the Americans.
> (c) PEACH has remained in this country. During this time he has not, so far as this Service is aware, been detected in any clandestine activity.
> (d) There has been no mention of PEACH by any of the recent defectors from the Russian Intelligence Service. The absence of any reference to him by Petrov seems to me especially significant.

> In my view PEACH should also be given due credit for the part he played in the investigation of the Washington leakage, for which Maclean was found to have been responsible.

Sinclair's extraordinary intervention was actually no more than a reflection of views quite widely held within SIS, where some officers believed that MI5 did not fully appreciate the differences in culture between the two organizations. A good example was the appointment of Milmo, a devout Roman Catholic, who had expressed in his report his personal revulsion of Philby's sordid private life. He had drawn attention to Philby's three illegitimate children with Aileen (Josephine, John and Tom) whom he did not marry until September 1946, only a few weeks before the birth of their fourth child, Miranda. Milmo also seemed personally offended by Philby's long-standing affair with his secretary, Esther Whitfield, and his failure to report his previous links to Maclean. On the other hand, some of Philby's SIS colleagues entirely understood his reluctance to acknowledge previous unwise connections, and did not see such behaviour as indicative of involvement in espionage. Four years older than Philby, Milmo had also been an undergraduate at Trinity College.

Milmo's wartime service in MI5 had been in B1(b) where he had handled the investigations of dozens of suspected enemy agents, most of whom had been compromised by signals intelligence. He had interviewed any number of nationalities, and had gained a reputation, reflected in his nickname 'Buster', of extracting confessions, but there was a big difference between confronting a foreigner in detention, who would be at an obvious disadvantage, and challenging a highly sophisticated and experienced intelligence officer who fully understood the very limited nature of the evidence.

Oddly, Milmo had ridiculed Philby's telegram to his Chief in June 1951 in which he had recalled Burgess's ownership of a sun-lamp. Clearly Philby had offered this fact, linking it to Burgess' camera, as possible evidence of the illicit copying of documents. SIS officers fully understood the problems of photographing papers in poor light, and possession of a sun-lamp could represent an ingenious solution to the problem. This was surely the very practical point being made by Philby, whereas Milmo had dismissed it with derision.

Sinclair's doubts about Milmo's one-sided analysis concentrated on operational issues where, according to a lengthy internal review of the cases Philby had handled, there was no evidence of any espionage. According to the Chief, the examples of Klaus Fuchs and Julius Rosenberg counted in Philby's favour, as he had been indoctrinated into both investigations and neither of the suspects appeared to have been tipped off.

Sinclair, of course, was overlooking the Volkov episode and could not know that in fact Philby not only had tried to warn the Soviets in September 1949 that MI5 was closing in on an unnamed atomic physicist, but actually thought that he had done so. He had been called in to Broadway to be briefed on VENONA just the day before he was due to embark on the Cunarder RMS *Caronia*, and just *after* he had held his final rendezvous with his Soviet contact in London. His next meeting, in the United States, was not scheduled for some months, so Philby entrusted Burgess with the task of alerting the Soviets to the danger. Burgess, for whatever reason, failed to pass the message on, so no warning could be given to Fuchs, with predictable consequences, By the time Philby met his contact, Ivan Makayev, alias Ivan Kovalik, the New York illegal *rezident* in November 1950, it had been too late to save Fuchs.

When Philby had been indoctrinated by Maurice Oldfield into VENONA at the very end of September 1949 he had never heard of Fuchs, and was therefore unaware that the scientist had been under MI5 surveillance since 7 September 1949 when he had been identified as the spy in the traffic codenamed REST and CHARLES. In fact Fuchs would not be interviewed by MI5 for another three months, on 21 December, which would have given the London *rezidentura* plenty of time to arrange for his exfiltration.

In the example of Julius Rosenberg, he had not fallen under suspicion until 16 June 1950 when he had been named as his controller by his brother-in-law, David Greenglass. Actually, the Rosenbergs had been warned to flee to Mexico but had decided not to go, and he had been arrested at their eighth-floor apartment in Manhattan. In his statement to the FBI Greenglass revealed that several months earlier, and some weeks before the arrest of Fuchs on 2 February 1950, Julius had warned him that 'something had happened' to jeopardize the network, and that he should prepare for his escape. This had suggested to the FBI that the NKVD had issued some kind of warning in around January 1950, and it also implied that Sinclair had not learned that the arrest of the Rosenbergs was not necessarily evidence of Philby's integrity.

In fact the threat to the Rosenbergs had come from another defector, Elizabeth Bentley, who had approached the FBI in September, and then made a formal statement on 30 November in which she named dozens of her contacts. On 15 December 1945 Aleksandr Feklisov had warned Julius Rosenberg of the danger and instructed him to suspend all his activities until his next rendezvous, now rescheduled for the third Sunday in March 1946. In anticipation of trouble, Feklisov's colleague Anatoli Yakovlev, working under consular cover in Manhattan, received orders in October to withdraw to Paris, and he sailed on a delayed voyage aboard the SS *America* in December. Feklisov himself would return to Moscow in October 1946.

With the benefit of hindsight one can appreciate that Sinclair was quite mistaken about Philby, but the issue that brought the whole embarrassment back into the public's attention was the leak from Australia about Petrov's debriefing. This was indeed the very first news that Burgess and Maclean were alive and well in the Soviet Union, and prompted much press speculation, forcing the British government to draft a White Paper scheduled for release in September 1955.

The White Paper, drafted by Graham Mitchell, now Director of a reorganized MI5's D (counter-espionage) Branch and endorsed by the D-G Dick White, was short and largely untrue. It was riddled with errors, and even asserted that Maclean had been an undergraduate at Trinity College. In a more sinister vein, regarding the defectors, it alleged that 'the security authorities had been on their track' thereby falsely implying that Burgess also had been under investigation, when of course it was only Maclean who had come under suspicion. Remarkably, the value attributed to Petrov's testimony was undermined by his description as 'Third Secretary at the Soviet Embassy in Canberra', omitting the very relevant detail that he was actually the NKVD *rezident*, and of equal status to the ambassador. The media rejected the White Paper as a cover-up, and the government prepared for a House of Commons debate, in the midst of speculation about the likely existence of a 'third man' who had tipped off the missing diplomats. Meanwhile, in Whitehall, the exchanges continued, and on 30 September Pat Dean wrote to Sinclair:

2. We have always understood that the case against PEACH is not conclusive. It is based on circumstantial evidence and circumstantial evidence may be misleading. Throughout the investigation of the Maclean and Burgess case we have borne in mind the possibility that Maclean, or Burgess, or both, may have discovered through means other than a 'tip off' that Maclean was under investigation. In the White Paper we make it clear that although the possibility of a 'tip off' exists there were other ways by which Maclean alight have been warned. It is also possible that the 'tip off', if any, came from some other source, perhaps inadvertent.

3. In your letter you have given four facts which in your opinion reduce very considerably the suspicion that PEACH was a Soviet agent. I do not think I can usefully comment on these points except, as regards (c), to agree that the fact that PEACH has remained in this country may be (but I would not go further than may be) an indication of a clear conscience. Whether his record with you was entirely satisfactory and whether he was of service to the FBI in cases in which they were concerned are points of fact on which I can have no comment and which much less I could dispute. what is more arguable, if I may say so, is your view that these considerably reduce the suspicion against PEACH.

4. In my assessment of this man's loyalty one should, I suggest, start with his background and if the information in our hands is accurate there can be no doubt that his background was unsatisfactory and that in present circumstances he would have been considered wholly unqualified for a position of trust. If you will be good enough to look through the criteria handed down to us by the Official Committee on Security for assessing an officer's suitability for a certificate of positive vetting, I think you will agree that PEACH comes far short of meeting these criteria both on political and general grounds. It now seems clear (as, had the positive vetting procedure then existed, field enquiries would have made clear) that in his University days at Cambridge PEACH was an active Communist.

His tutor later described him as 'militant' and stated that he had 'extreme views on social questions'. These are strong words from a don. Professor Robertson of Cambridge, who is no McCarthy, found himself compelled to tell PEACH that he was unable to recommend him for the Indian Civil Service on the grounds of his extreme left-wing views. What is more, I understand PEACH's first wife, whom he married in 1934, was a Communist when he married her and that after their separation he remained friendly with her at least until 1945. On the evidence known to me, I cannot avoid the conclusion that PEACH's married life with this woman was highly suspicious. At the time he appears to have been desperately poor, she was making constant unexplained journeys to the Continent.

Subsequent investigation revealed this woman's connection with the Comintern before her marriage. There are fairly good grounds for believing that the marriage, which took place at the time of the leftist rising in Vienna (1934), was timed in order to give the woman the protection of British nationality lest she should be arrested by the Austrian authorities. I believe that I'm right in saying that when questioned PEACH gave a false date for this marriage.

5. [XXXXXXXXXXXXXXXXXXXXXXXXXXXXXXXXXXXXXXXXXXX]

6. Having said all this, I must make it clear that I understand your desire to ensure that PEACH will not be branded as a traitor on the basis of circumstantial and inconclusive evidence. As I have said above we accept the fact that Maclean may have been warned by some other means, and even if he was in fact 'tipped off' we do not necessarily accept that it was PEACH who was responsible, or, if he was responsible, that he did it deliberately or knowingly. In advising ministers, as we will shortly have to do, on what they are to say in the House, we are bound to put all the possibilities before them, as indeed we have already done in, the White Paper. We are bound also to give them all the material we have to enable them to form their opinion and give our own views on the way Maclean was warned. We are bound to tell Ministers of the case against PEACH including his early Marxist record, his long friendship with Burgess and, as subsequent investigations have revealed, his unsuitability for a position of trust. We shall have to say that we believe that, on the evidence available, he lied to your organisation when he was recruited and we shall have to admit that although the then normal standards of recruitment may have been followed and the then normal precautions taken, these standards and precautions fell far short of what should now be required before a man were recruited into a position of the high trust and confidence, and Ministers will ask – as the Foreign Secretary has already – 'if it was not PEACH, who was it, or how did Maclean and/or Burgess spot that they were under suspicion?' The other possibilities mentioned in the White Paper are to my mind very thin, if they were the sole reasons for the disappearance, so well timed, and organised as it was. If we are to exonerate PEACH, we all badly need the true answer and we want it very soon.

Sinclair did not attempt to undertake any further research into Philby's background, but on 24 October attended a meeting with Dick White at which preparations were agreed for the imminent Parliamentary debate in which the Foreign Secretary, Harold Macmillan, would defend the White Paper and, when challenged about Kim Philby, whose name had been leaked, gave a guarded response which had the effect of clearing him from suspicion.

Despite Macmillan's highly legalistic answer when Philby's name was uttered in the House of Commons by a backbench Labour MP, Marcus Lipton, Sinclair went on the offensive and on 22 December set out the case for his defence. Perhaps with gritted teeth, White had given a qualified endorsement to the document:

> I regard the memorandum as a paper worth putting alongside others in the case. I think that it brings out a number of points which are fair to Philby and that the effect of it is decidedly to reduce the case of his being the 'third man'. At the same time I cannot but note that the memorandum neglects to deal with his early record and consequently that it does not purport to contain a full intelligence assessment of the case.

Sinclair explained that his memorandum, addressed to Ivone Kirkpatrick at the Foreign Office, was not intended to deal with Philby's background, but to rebut the allegation that his organization had been comprehensively penetrated.

> With regard to Philby's early record, the memorandum is of set purpose confined to examining the period of Philby's service with SIS. No attempt has been made to deal with his early record, since a satisfactory examination of that period would require background information which this Service does not possess and which is, generally speaking, outside its normal competence. The memorandum sets out to examine the assumption that Philby was a Soviet spy throughout his period with SIS and nothing more.

The document, intended to challenge some of the assertions made by Milmo, was quite unambiguous in tone and content:

> The Secretary of State's speech on the affair of Burgess and Maclean in the House of Commons on 7th November 1955 included a passage on the subject of H.A.R. Philby. This represented views on the content of a public statement which were jointly reached by the Security Service and SIS after a discussion between the two Directors and their staffs on 24th October.
>
> 2. This passage, in which Mr Macmillan stated that he had no reason to conclude that Philby had at any time betrayed his country or that he was the so-called 'third man', is at variance with the view expressed in certain documents dating from 1951 and 1952 held in the Foreign Office to the effect that 'for all practical purposes it must be assumed that Philby was a Soviet spy throughout his service with SIS.'
> 3. By the Spring of 1954 SIS felt that although more than two years had elapsed since the original investigation no new evidence had been produced and that the time had come for a re-appraisal. Since then SIS have been minutely examining all those aspects of the Philby case which lie within their competence in an endeavour to reach a firm conclusion,

favourable or unfavourable, upon the case. This has involved a reconsideration of all Philby's activities while in SIS, including the part which he played in the investigation of the Washington leakage.

It was from the outset the intention of SIS to submit their findings to the Security Service so that if a new assessment were possible it should be made by them or with their full concurrence. The investigations were of necessity prolonged and it was an unhappy chance that they were brought to fruition and submitted, after 17 months of work, to the Security Service only a short time before preparations began for the debate in the House. No one could have foreseen this coincidence when work started in May 1954.

4. The SIS investigation began from the assumption, current since 1952, that Philby was a Soviet spy. As it proceeded however the case against Philby grew weaker rather than stronger and factors favourable to him which had not been given due weight by the Security Service in 1951/2 acquired greater force when looked at after the passage of time. Thus, when the SIS 'reassessment' was presented to the Security Service on 20th July, 1955 its conclusions were that the charge hitherto held against Philby, viz. that he was a Soviet spy while in SIS service, would not stand scrutiny. It was upon their discussion of the SIS case that the Directors of the Security Service and SIS based their submission for the Secretary of State's speech.

5. In this short paper it is proposed to do no more than relate the facts discussed between the Security Service and SIS to the documents which are held in FO Security Department, copies of which are in SIS files. The documents are as follows:-

Document (A)

6. On 30th November 1951 Carey-Foster issued a memorandum on *The PEACH Case*. A copy of this was sent to C by Patrick Reilly on 8th December 1951. Carey-Foster's minute of 30th November 1951 contained much which requires modification, in particular an allegation that Philby blew BRIDE to the Russians immediately after his own indoctrination.

Document (B)

7. On 13th December 1951 Milmo issued a report, in accordance with his instructions of 3rd December to enquire whether the disappearance of Burgess and Maclean was the result of a leakage to them and, if so, who was responsible and from what motive.

Document (C)

8. On 10th January 1952 the Security Service issued a *History of the Investigation of H.A.R. Philby* together with 'A Summing-up after the

Cross-examination' the last paragraph of which stated that, in regard to the urgent practical issue which arose, 'the Security Service accepts without qualification the independent judgement formed by Mr Milmo; it must recommend that for all practical purposes it should be assumed that Philby was a Soviet spy throughout his service with SIS'.

Document (D)

9. On 12th March 1952 Carey-Foster submitted a draft to C (who reluctantly approved it) of a minute from the PUS to the Secretary of State quoting the Security Service recommendation 'that for all practical purposes it must be assumed that Philby was a Soviet spy throughout his service with SIS.'

10. Mr D.G. White (as he then was) of the Security Service had at that time recently visited Washington, where he had given Mr Edgar Hoover (FBI) a copy of the complete case history. With C's approval he had also given a verbal account of the general conclusions to General Bedell Smith (CIA). Both realised that Philby's guilt was not proven, though Mr White thought both considered him guilty.

C, however, inferred from his own correspondence with General Bedell Smith that the latter did not believe Philby guilty.

Document (E)

11. [XXXXXXXXXXXXXXXXXXXXXXXXXXXXXXXXXXXXXXXXX]
    [XXXXXXX]

12. [XXXXXXXXXXXXXXXXXXXXXXXXXXXXXXXXXXXXXXXXXX
    XX]
    [XXXXXXX]

13. [\[XXXXXXXXXXXXXXXXXXXXXXXXXXXXXXXXXXXXXXXX
    XX]

14. [XXXXXXXXXXXXXXXXXXXXXXXXXXXXXXXXXXXXXXXXXX
    XX]

15. [XXXXXXXXXXXXXXXXXXXXXXXXXXXXXXXXXXXXXXXXXX
    XX]

16. [XXXXXXXXXXXXXXXXXXXXXXXXXXXXXXXXXXXXXXXXXX
    XX]

The Case against Philby as the 'Third Man'. The Milmo Report

17. It is well understood in SIS that the Milmo document is not and was never intended to be an impartial assessment of all the facts in the Philby case. It was in effect a brief for the prosecution. If in the course of this paper criticisms are advanced against Milmo's report it is with full realisation of its special character. Milmo's investigation of Philby

was undertaken as a corollary of the preliminary to his brief, which laid down that he should first be satisfied that there was in fact a leakage of official information to Burgess and/or Maclean which resulted in their disappearance. Milmo found that 'there is no room for doubt that it was as a result of leakage of information' that they disappeared. He found also 'Philby is and has for many years been a Soviet agent and that he was directly and deliberately responsible for the leakage which in fact occurred.' It is now recognised that no leakage of official information did necessarily occur and, if any leakage of information did take place, it was not necessarily deliberate

18. The means other than through Philby, by which Burgess and/or Maclean might have been alerted to Maclean's danger are various; they have already been considered elsewhere and will not be repeated here.

19. The case built up by Milmo against Philby therefore rested in the first place upon the assertion that Burgess and Maclean disappeared because there had been a leakage of information. There is no more support for that assumption now than there was four years ago. In the second case Milmo concluded that 'Philby was directly and deliberately responsible for the leakage which in fact occurred', (a) because he was in any case a Soviet agent and (b) because 'he had had access in Washington to a certain telegram from which he might have deduced that action against Maclean was planned for soon after 23rd May'.

20. It may be seriously doubted whether in law or in logic it is admissible to conclude that Philby was directly and deliberately responsible for the leakage simply because he was in any case assumed to be a Soviet agent. Because Philby seemed to Milmo to be the sort of man who leaked information to the Russians it was inadmissible to conclude without further evidence that he was the man who in fact did leak this particular piece of information to the Russians. In any case the 'fact' of a leakage was in itself an assumption on Milmo's part.

    As will be shewn later Milmo's conclusion that Philby was a Soviet agent was in itself based upon a mass of selected circumstantial material without a crumb of positive evidence. The argument is circular.

21. Before turning to the question whether Philby could legitimately be assumed on general grounds to be a Soviet agent it will be as well to consider the possibility that Philby learnt of the date of the proposed action against Maclean through the medium of a telegram to which he had access in Washington. Since this is in fact the only piece of evidence ever produced to shew not indeed that Philby did tip off Maclean but that he was in a position to do so, it is of the utmost importance.

22. In the Appendix to his report Milmo wrote:

'There are various possibilities as to the source from which Maclean derived his information. It might have been from a London source; it might equally well have been from a Washington source, since a limited number of people in the Washington Embassy, including Philby, were fully in the picture as to the progress of the investigation and the intentions of the authorities.'

23. It is not true that anyone in Washington was fully in the picture about the progress of the investigation and the intentions of the authorities in London. In fact the intentions of the authorities were only decided at a meeting which was held in the Foreign Office on 24th May 1951, (the day before Maclean's disappearance) to discuss a paper entitled *Considerations affecting the action to be taken in the case of D.D. Maclean.* On 25th May 1951 the Security Service wrote a letter to their representative (which was to be made available to Philby) enclosing a copy of the above mentioned *Considerations,* the minutes of the meeting and an 'anticipated programme of events up to the date at the end of June upon which Maclean is to be interviewed, this being at present provisionally fixed for 19.6.51' Of course this letter to Washington was overtaken by events before its despatch, owing to Maclean's escape on May 25th. Milmo asserted that because Burgess, who engineered the escape, had arrived from Washington under the circumstances now about to be described, the leakage must have occurred in Washington. The alleged circumstances were:
    (a) that in the early part of 1951 Philby would have known all that London knew about the investigation, and that the hunt was now on and the pace quickening. That Philby informed Burgess who, though not suspect himself, would have been apprehensive that Maclean might give him away if interrogated.
    (b) that Philby therefore decided to get Burgess to England, so that he would be ready to take the necessary action in London on information of the progress of the leakage which Philby would transmit to him from Washington.
    (c) that at the end of February 1951 Burgess therefore deliberately committed a series of motoring offences in order to engineer his return to London in accordance with this plan.
    (d) that before Burgess left the States Philby knew that Maclean was on the short list of suspects.
    (e) that on 16th May Philby saw a telegram which might have led him (mistakenly) to think action was planned for soon after May 23rd.
24. As regards (a) above it is, of course, untrue to say that Washington knew all that London was doing in regard to the investigation.

In any case, in February 1951 Maclean had not been considered as the chief suspect. If Philby was at that time familiar with all that London knew of the investigation he would have known that the hounds were at fault and shewed no signs whatever of finding.

Nothing at that date could have led him to suppose that Maclean was in any particular danger. The theory in (b) and (c) that Philby decided to get Burgess to England in order that the latter might be ready to take action and 'engineer the escape' is far-fetched.

Philby, if he were a Soviet agent, could not have taken such decisions on his own authority. If he had been instructed to do so by the RIS it could only have been because they already knew what no one else knew that Maclean was ultimately to be impugned. Philby certainly did not know it in February 1951. It does not accord with Petrov's evidence, according to which 'after Burgess and Maclean had notified the RIS that they were under security investigation the 1st Directorate of the KI organised their escape'. It was not the RIS who informed Burgess and Maclean; it was they who informed the RIS. The statement in (d) seems of little importance to Milmo's case as Milmo elsewhere stressed the sudden nature of the flight, stating that 'the fact that he made what was obviously a hastily prepared escape leaving his wife and family at the particular time at which he did, establishes to my mind quite conclusively that the reason for his departure was that he had suddenly received information which made it imperative for him to disappear without a moment's delay.'

25. Milmo's case is that it was Philby who deliberately and directly was responsible for Maclean suddenly receiving this information which, it is assumed, made flight imperative, and that, on May 16th, Philby had access to a certain telegram from which he might have concluded that drastic action in regard to Maclean was planned in London for very shortly after May 23rd.

26. Thus this telegram becomes the very heart of the whole argument that Philby warned Maclean. We have the alleged placing by Philby of Burgess in London to await the moment for action, the sudden flight of the suspect on 25th May on the receipt of information which made flight imperative, the transmission somehow of this information to Burgess from Philby, all of these suppositions being based on the assumption that Philby interpreted in a certain way, and acted upon, a telegram from London dated 16th May 1951.

27. What was the nature of this telegram from which Philby might erroneously have concluded that drastic action was planned to take place very shortly after 23rd May? In fact all the telegram, which was addressed to Patterson, said was 'Anxious you see Thomas before May 23rd. If necessary you must visit his home but suggest you first confirm

that he will not be back at the office before this date.' (Mr W.L Thomas had been head of the Cypher Room in the Washington Embassy, 1944–45). The argument in the Milmo report that from this Philby concluded that 'drastic action was planned to take place very shortly <u>after</u> 23rd May' may have fitted very nicely to the fact that Burgess and Maclean fled on 23rd May. But is it possible to conclude that Philby could only assume that the telegram referred to action after the 23rd? If any conclusion is really to be read into the words of this telegram it would surely be that if Philby were desirous of safeguarding Maclean he must assume that action was planned to take place on 23rd May, not 'very shortly' after that date. The telegram cannot explain the flight occurring on <u>May 25th</u>? If, as has been alleged, though with little accuracy, Philby was aware of what the investigators were doing in London, it certainly cannot be believed that he could have counted on Maclean not being under continual surveillance at this stage. Therefore it is not logical to believe that had he been a Soviet agent he would have waited until this stage (i.e. until the consultation of Thomas) to give a warning which he could have given earlier.

28. The reason for consulting Thomas was to ask him about the conditions under which a certain Churchill–Roosevelt telegram had been decyphered. The background of this bit of the investigation was that in August 1950 Philby had reported to SIS in London that he had discussed certain new cryptanalytical recoveries with his colleagues Patterson and Mackenzie in Washington. Philby suggested that as a Churchill–Roosevelt telegram was concerned in the new recoveries it might be possible to narrow the field of suspects, because of the more limited distribution of this class of telegram. As a preliminary step therefore Philby had listed all those who handled these special folders during 1944. This did not cover cypher personnel, etc., but, for what it was worth, he gave a list of about a score of names, one of which was D.D. Maclean. Of course this provoked no particular action in London in August 1950 so far as Maclean was concerned, but, in view of the reference to Thomas, it should be noted that Philby had already, in August, linked Maclean's name, among others, to the Churchill–Roosevelt telegram.

29. In April 1951 Carey-Foster asked Washington to see if there were any record of journeys by Maclean to New York and to find out what work he had been on at the relevant time. On 13th April Mackenzie answered that 'from an examination of the Churchill–Roosevelt telegrams which were marked to Maclean it would appear that the countries with which he dealt included France and Italy.'

30. Why should Philby, if he were a Soviet agent, not have given the warning at this time rather than later? He clearly did not. Further, it was Philby

who drew attention to Maclean's connection with this particular class of telegram when the investigators were checking this aspect of the case.

31. What might perhaps be called the commonsense view of all this is that since full information regarding the proposed action against Maclean was held in London and not in Washington and since Burgess, an undetected Soviet agent, was at liberty in London at the material time it is probable that if a leakage occurred it occurred in London rather than in Washington. To prove, as against common sense, that a leakage occurred in Washington and that Philby was the source of that leakage requires powerful, positive evidence. In the submission of SIS, Milmo's construction, including the incident of the telegram referring to Thomas, is in the highest degree strained; it does not provide the evidence required.

The General Case Against Philby as a Spy
Milmo

32. Milmo assumed that when Philby carried out the elaborate plans for warning Maclean of which he was accused, he did so in his capacity of an RIS agent. Prom this point Milmo argued that 'if one accepts the hypothesis that Philby had been a Soviet agent of some years' standing, at least three other Soviet espionage problems are solved.'

Soviet Cyphers
(a) One of these three cases was a charge that Philby, on being initiated into our cryptanalytical successes, betrayed his knowledge of them to the Russians. This charge has now been completely refuted.

Plot to Assassinate Franco
(b) The second case was a supposition that Philby had been enlisted by Paul Hardt early in 1937 to assassinate General Franco. Milmo's report admitted, however, that 'there is no proof that Philby was in fact the agent referred to in the above statement but the information fits him like a glove and no other alternative candidate has been found.' At the present date there is still no proof.
[XXXXXXX]
(c) [XXXXXXXXXXXXXXXXXXXXXXXXXXXXXXXXXXX]

B. The MI5 History of the Investigation' and 'Summing-Up
47. Of the Milmo Report the Security Service states that it 'accepts this report as a most valuable contribution to the case. Nevertheless, it recognises, as does Mr Milmo, that the evidence upon which it is based falls short of proof, both in law and by logic'.

The Security Service declared their intention 'to remain in direct contact with Philby and to employ every other form of investigation for as long as any possibility remains of proving his guilt or innocence.' During the four years which have elapsed since those words were written nothing has emerged to prove Philby's guilt either as the outcome of the investigations of the Security Service or from researches carried out by SIS. Neither has any proof or even faint indication been forthcoming from Soviet defectors or from cryptanalytical sources.

C. The Philby–Burgess Relationship in Washington

49. Philby's evidence, which has not been refuted, is that when Burgess was posted to Washington he wrote to Philby asking to be accommodated with him while searching for a flat. To this Philby as an old friend acceded. Philby has been severely blamed for this and for not reporting earlier that Burgess was a Communist. His answer to these charges are (a) that if Burgess was fit to represent Great Britain in the USA he was fit to live in Philby's house and (b) be did not know that Burgess was a Communist, sharing in this respect the ignorance of many of Burgess' innumerable friends and acquaintances

50. To SIS the fact that Burgess who is now known to have been a Soviet agent was permitted by his Masters to share a house so long with Philby makes it highly improbable that Philby was himself a Soviet agent. Nothing could have been more insecure from the Soviet point of view. It was almost inevitable that what did happen should have happened i.e. that when Burgess was exposed Philby would come under suspicion. What unique folly could have induced the RIS with its high security standards, to have placed two such high–grade agents in such a posture that if one were 'blown' the other would inevitably be blown also or brought under intense scrutiny? It may plausibly be argued that Burgess was attempting to use Philby as an unconscious sub–source while in Washington. If he did so he was doing no more than he had done with many other well–informed contacts.

D. Philby's Service while in SIS

51. The Security Service 'Summing–Up' of January 1952 contains a note of the essence of the case against Philby, and also a paragraph showing on what lines Philby answered the case against him. It is also added on his behalf that 'There are no signs that many of the secrets with which he was entrusted have been compromised.'

52. [XXXXXXXXXXXXXXXXXXXXXXXXXXXXXXXXXXXXXXXXXX XX]

53. [XXXXXXXXXXXXXXXXXXXXXXXXXXXXXXXXXXXXXXXXXX XX]

54. [XXXXXXXXXXXXXXXXXXXXXXXXXXXXXXXXXXXXXXXXX
     XX]

Conclusions

55. The case against Philby is familiar to the Foreign Office through the
     Security Service's History of the Investigation and Summing-Up
     (Document (C)) and the Milmo Report (Document (B)). The latter
     contains the essence of the unproven charges held against him.

     (a) By concentrating, all available evidence for the purpose of a hostile
          attack to cause Philby to 'break' and confess.

     (b) To enable a case for submission to the Director of Public Prosecutions.
     Both purposes were of course completely legitimate at the time and as
     such were acceptable to SIS. But it will be remembered that on the one
     hand the Director of Public Prosecutions did not consider that there was
     a case to go forward to the Courts and on the other that Philby's hostile
     interrogation, which could not in the nature of things both attempt to
     'break' Philby and at the same time give him credit where credit was
     due, failed in fact to shake him.

56. The Milmo Report, which produces no single piece of direct evidence
     to shew that Philby was a Soviet agent or that he was the 'Third
     Man', is therefore a case for the prosecution inadmissible at law and
     unsuccessful in Security intelligence. It is constructed of suppositions
     and circumstantial evidence, summing up in a circular argument
     everything the ingenuity of a prosecutor could devise against a suspect.
     It seems likely to remain as a permanently accusing finger pointed at
     Philby unless some at least of the arguments which were not included in
     it are given their due weight.

     Philby was in fact convicted of nothing by the investigation in 1951
     and despite four years of subsequent investigation is still convicted of
     nothing. It is entirely contrary to the English tradition for a man to have
     to prove his innocence even when the prosecution is in possession of
     hard facts. In a case where the prosecution has nothing but suspicion to
     go upon there is even less reason for him, even if he were able to do so, to
     prove his innocence. But if documents summarising the suspicions are
     permanently to play a part in our assessment it is only just that others
     which offset those suspicions should lie beside them. The case set out
     in this present paper was sufficient to lead to agreement between the
     Directors of SIS and the Security Service as to what should be submitted
     for the Secretary of State's speech. It is submitted that the argument of
     this paper should be considered as balancing, for reasons of justice, the
     material in the Foreign Office's possession.

Sinclair's paper went down badly at the Foreign Office where, on 10 January 1956, Pat Dean wrote to Ivone Kirkpatrick and sought to demolish it, concentrating on his arguments about 'the Third Man':

In paragraphs 17 to 31 inclusive C attempts to destroy the case against PEACH prepared by Mr Milmo in January 1952. Firstly, he argues that there is no proof that a third man ever existed. We have always accepted this possibility and the Secretary of State accepted it in his speech in the Burgess and Maclean debate in the House of Commons on November 7th, 1955.

In his paragraph 18 C, however, refers to 'the other means by which Burgess and/or Maclean might have been alerted to Maclean's danger'. He says that these means have been considered elsewhere and he does not repeat them. It has never been explained to us what these means could be. Whatever the strength of the legal case against PEACH on this score, what we really should like to know is what are the other possible explanations and how likely they seem to be.

4. C then goes on to argue that there is no proof that Maclean and Burgess' disappearance was due to a leakage of information. If there was no leak the only possible explanation for the flight must be that Maclean spotted that he was under observation. This is, of course, possible. It is also possible that there was a leak to and a spotting by Maclean or Burgess.

5. In paragraphs 21 to 24 inclusive C argues that PEACH did not tip off Maclean because he was unaware of the date when it was proposed to interview him. This argument ignores the fact that although he may not have known the exact date when action against him was proposed, PEACH had throughout been privy to the investigations in Washington. It is unlikely that he did not know that Maclean was on the 'short list' and indeed the principal suspect. C argues, however, that he did not know even this.

6. In his covering letter C refers to the criticism of his paper made by the Director-General of the Security Service. The main criticism is that the paper does not deal with PEACH's Communist background and his somewhat undesirable past (for instance, his first marriage). C argues that PEACH's background has nothing to do with the case against him for tipping off Maclean. As a matter of legal evidence this is true, but PEACH's background shows him as unfitted entirely for employment in SIS and is consistent with his having been a spy,

7. C proposes that a copy of the document attached to his letter should be sent to the Head of the Central Intelligence Agency and to the Head of the Federal Bureau of Investigation. The Director-General of the Security Service does not object to it being sent as it stands to Allen Dulles but

he has not yet decided whether he agrees to it being sent to Mr Edgar Hoover.

8. Since the CIA and FBI received the documents in the case against PEACH, either in full or in summary, it is fair that they should receive this paper also. If, however, Sir Dick White has objections to it being sent in its present form to Mr Edgar Hoover, his views should be rejected. It is up to him to send it to him in the form he wishes.

9. Generally my conclusion is that if the case against PEACH was inconclusive it is certainly equally true that C's present defence of PEACH is also each inconclusive. At the moment we just do not know.

In April 1956 the players in Whitehall all changed, a transformation prompted by a disastrous SIS operation in Portsmouth Harbour that resulted in the death of a freelance diver employed to undertake a covert survey of the hull of a visiting Soviet cruiser. The incident led to Sinclair's retirement and, most pointedly, his replacement by Dick White. At Leconfield House, White's deputy, Roger Hollis, was promoted to Director-General, with Graham Mitchell appointed as his deputy. As far as Philby was concerned, he accepted a job with the *Economist* and the *Observer* as their correspondent in Beirut, where he remained for seven years before he finally defected to the Soviet Union in January 1963.

Following his resignation in May 1953, Guy Liddell was an outside observer of these events, but he must have been astonished at White's unparalleled ascent through MI5 to become the SIS Chief. His reactions are unknown, for he died of heart failure at his flat in Sloane Street on 3 December 1958, aged 65.

Postscript

Jane Archer	Having interviewed Walter Krivitsky in January 1940 Archer was transferred to SIS in November, but returned at the end of the war. She retired in 1958 and died in Dorset in September 1982.
Vladimir Barkovsky	Withdrawn from New York in 1950, Barkovsky returned as *rezident* in 1956. He retired from the KGB in 1984 and died in July 2003.
Charles Bedaux	Arrested in Algiers in January 1943, Bedaux committed suicide in Miami in February 1944.
Walter Bedell Smith	Having left the CIA in February 1953 to serve in the State Department, General Bedell Smith died in Washington in August 1961.
Cedric Belfrage	The founder of the *National Guardian*, Belfrage was deported in 1955, moved to Mexico and died in Cuernavaca in June 1990.
Anthony Blunt	Having confessed in April 1964, in return for an immunity from prosecution, Blunt was exposed in November 1979 and stripped of his honours. He died in London in March 1983.
Engelbert Broda	After his return to Austria in 1947, Broda was appointed Professor of Physical Chemistry at the University of Vienna, and died in October 1983.
Earl Browder	Replaced as the CPUSA's General Secretary in June 1945, Browder gave evidence before a Senate committee in 1950, was indicted and acquitted on a charge of contempt. He died in Princeton in June 1973.
John Bruce Lockhart	After serving as the SIS station commander in Washington for two years, Bruce Lockhart was appointed Director Middle East and Africa, and then in 1961 Vice Chief. He retired in 1965 and died in May 1995.
John Cairncross	Interviewed by Arthur Martin in Cleveland, Ohio, in 1964, Cairncross confessed his espionage and finally returned to England from France in 1994. He died in October 1995 and his memoirs were published posthumously.

George Carey-Foster	Posted from the Security Department to the British embassy in Rio de Janeiro in 1953, Carey-Foster later served in Warsaw, Hanover and The Hague before retiring in 1968. He died in January 1994.
Carter W. Clarke	Between January 1949 and May 1950 General Clarke was Chief of the ASA. He was then posted to Japan and in 1953 was appointed a special assistant to DCI Allen Dulles. He retired in 1954 and died in Clearwater, Florida in September1987.
Arnold Deutsch	Withdrawn from London in September 1937, Deutsch died when his ship, the *Donbass*, was torpedoed by a U-boat in November 1942 while on a voyage to New York.
Martha Dodd	Subpoenaed by the FBI in July 1956, Dodd fled to Mexico and settled in Moscow. She died in Prague in August 1990.
Jack Easton	Appointed Deputy Chief of SIS in 1951, Easton resigned in 1958 to become consul-general in Detroit. He retired in 1968 and died in October 1990.
Trilby Ewer	Ewer continued to assist MI5 after his first interview with Max Knight in 1950, and died in January 1977.
Peter Floud	Made a governor of the National Museum of Wales in 1955, Floud died in January 1960. His brother Bernard committed suicide in October 1967.
David Footman	Footman retired from SIS in 1953 and took up a fellowship at St Antony's College, Oxford. He died in October 1983.
Lizzie Friedmann	After her marriage to Georg Honigmann, Lizzie returned to Vienna where she died in 1991.
Klaus Fuchs	Released from prison in June 1959, Fuchs returned to East Germany where he died in January 1988.
Gustav Glück	Never convicted of espionage, Glück died in Santa Monica, California, in November 1952.
Harry Gold	Sentenced to thirty years' imprisonment in 1951, Gold was paroled in May 1965 and died in Philadelphia in August 1972.
Igor Gouzenko	Resettled as a Czech immigrant, Stanley Keysac, in Port Credit, Ontario, Gouzenko went blind and died in Mississagua in June 1982. Svetlana died in September 2001.
Israel Halperin	After his acquittal in 1947 Halperin returned to academic life and retired from the University of Toronto in 1976. He died in March 2007.

Tommy Harris	Implicated in the disappearance of Melina Maclean, Harris was killed in a car accident in Llucmajor in January 1964.
Jenifer Hart	A self-confessed Soviet spy, Hart wrote an autobiography, *Ask Me No More*, and died in April 1991.
Roger Hollis	Investigated as a suspected Soviet mole, Hollis retired to Wells in Somerset and died in October 1973.
J. Edgar Hoover	The FBI's director remained in his post until his death in Washington in May 1972.
V.J. Jerome	A member of the CPUSA's Control Commission, Jerome was the alias adopted by Jerome Romain. The editor of *Political Affairs*, he was imprisoned under the Smith Act between 1950 and 1953 and died in 1965
Rolf Katz	Arrested in Prague in 1952, Katz endured a show trial at which he was convicted of espionage, and hanged in December 1952.
Eric Kessler	Appointed press attaché at the Swiss embassy in Washington DC in 1945, Kessler was later promoted chargé d'affaires in Bucharest. He died in 1981.
James Klugmann	The CPGB's official historian and editor of *Marxism Today*, Klugmann declined to co-operate with MI5 and died in September 1977.
Max Knight	Having retired from MI5 in 1956, Knight took up a career as a BBC radio naturalist and died in January 1968.
Walter Krivitsky	Interviewed by MI5 in London in January 1940, Krivitsky returned to the United States and was found shot dead in the Bellevue Hotel in Washington in February 1941.
Freddie Kuh	Retiring as head of the *Chicago Sun-Times* Washington bureau in 1964, Kuh died in Rockville, Maryland in February 1978.
Mickey Ladd	Appointed Assistant Director of the FBI's Security Division (later renamed the Domestic Intelligence Division) in 1941, Ladd was promoted head of counterintelligence in May 1949. He retired in 1954 but was killed in a car accident in Sanford, Florida, in July 1960 while running for Congress.
Bob Lamphere	Having resigned from the FBI in 1955 to join the Veterans Administration, Lamphere died in Tucson in January 2002.
Tommy Lascelles	The King's private secretary between 1943 and 1952, Lascelles then served the Queen until 1953 when he retired from Buckingham Palace. He died in August 1981.

Josef Lemmel	After the war Lemmel opened a travel agency in London but returned to Vienna in 1962 and died in July 1980.
Guy Liddell	Employed as a security adviser by the Atomic Energy Authority, Liddell died at home in December 1958.
James MacGibbon	A successful publisher, MacGibbon died in February 2000.
Bobby Mackenzie	Having retired from the Foreign Office in 1966, the 12th baronet died in Westminster in July 1990.
Donald Maclean	Maclean died of heart failure in Moscow in March 1983.
Melinda Maclean	Melinda returned to the United States and died in Manhattan in February 2010, having refused to be interviewed by the FBI.
Theodore Maly	Withdrawn to Moscow from London in June 1937, Maly was executed in September 1938.
Arthur Martin	In May 1964 Martin was transferred to SIS. He retired to Gloucestershire and died in February 1996.
Alan Nunn May	Released from prison in 1952, May finally returned to Cambridge in 1978 and made a deathbed confession in January 2003.
Stewart Menzies	Having retired as SIS's Chief in July 1952, Menzies moved to Wiltshire and died in May 1968.
Helenus Milmo	Appointed a High Court judge in 1964, Milmo died in Chichester, Sussex, in August 1988.
Yuri Modin	In London continuously from June 1943 to his withdrawal in May 1953, Modin was promoted in Moscow and later served in Delhi. He died in 2010.
Herbert Norman	Appointed the Canadian ambassador to Cairo in 1956, Norman killed himself in April 1957 by jumping off the roof of the Swedish embassy rather than return to the United States to face interrogation.
Maurice Oldfield	Appointed SIS Chief in 1973, Oldfield retired in 1978 and died in London in March 1981.
Vladimir Petrov	Resettled in Melbourne as Sven and Maria Allyson, Petrov died in June 1991. Evdokia died in July 2002.
Edouard Pfeiffer	Never questioned about his Soviet contacts, Pfeiffer died in France in 1966.
Kim Philby	Following his defection to Moscow from Beirut in January 1963, Philby married for the fourth time, and died in Moscow in May 1988.

Bruno Pontecorvo	Accompanied by his wife and three sons, Pontecorvo defected to the Soviet Union in August 1950. He died in Dubna in September 1993, reportedly having made a deathbed statement acknowledging his espionage.
Ronnie Reed	Posted to New Zealand as SLO in 1957, Reed retired from MI5 in 1976 and died in January 1995.
Goronwy Rees	Forced to resign his academic posts because of his anonymously-written newspaper articles about Burgess, Rees died in December 1979.
Trudie Rient	Wed to Walter Mansfield in January 1947, Trudie Rient died in New Canaan, Connecticut, in March 1978.
Tess Rothschild	Having agreed to supply confidential information to MI5 about Communists she had known at Newham College, Cambridge, Tess died in May 1996.
Victor Rothschild	Often accused of having spied for the Soviets, or of having remained silent about traitors known to him, the 3rd Baron Rothschild died in March 1990.
Percy Sillitoe	After his retirement in 1953 Sillitoe opened a sweetshop in Eastbourne, where he died in April 1962.
Jim Skardon	Having retired to Torquay in 1964, Skardon died in March 1987.
Jack Soble	Convicted of espionage and sentenced to seven years' imprisonment in October 1957, Soble tried to commit suicide while in custody, but died in 1967, following his release.
Claud W. Sykes	Sykes left MI5 in 1944 to resume his work based in Letchworth as a translator, and died in Malta in August 1963.
Dick Thistlethwaite	After his retirement from MI5 Thistlethwaite emigrated to the United States and died in Pennsylvania in April 2003.
Philip Toynbee	Employed by the *Observer*, Toynbee succumbed to alcoholism and died at his home in St Briavels, in Gloucestershire in June 1981.
Edith Tudor Hart	Edith moved to Brighton to be near her institutionalized son, Tommy, and opened an antiques shop. She died in May 1973.
Philip Vickery	When the IPI was closed down in 1965 Vickery retired. He died in January 1987.

Valentine Vivian	Vivian retired from SIS in March 1951 and lived in Lymington, Hampshire, where he died in April 1969.
Konstantin Volkov	Abducted in Istanbul and returned to the Soviet Union in 1945, Volkov was interrogated and executed.
Dick White	Appointed Chief of SIS in 1956, White retired in 1968 to become Intelligence Co-ordinator to the Cabinet. He retired to Arundel and died in February 1993.
Esther Whitfield	Philby's secretary and lover resigned from SIS and went to live in Alicante. She returned to England to live in Fareham and died in Mere, Wiltshire, in April 1989.
Peter Wright	Having joined MI5 as a scientific officer in 1954 Wright debriefed Anthony Blunt after his confession in 1964 and retired in 1976. He published his memoirs, *SpyCatcher*, in 1987 and died in Tasmania in April 1995.
Courtenay Young	MI5's SLO in Canberra until March 1951, Young later served in Kuala Lumpur, retired in 1964 and died in Surrey in September 1974.
Kenneth Younger	Elected a Labour MP in 1945, Younger served as a Home Office minister and remained in the Commons until 1959. He was knighted in 1972 and died in May 1978.
Nikolai Zabotin	Withdrawn from Ottawa in September 1945, Colonel Zabotin was imprisoned in the gulag but released after Stalin's death.
Vasili Zarubin	Withdrawn from the Washington *rezidentura* in 1944, having been denounced to the FBI by a subordinate, Vasili Mironov, Zarubin was promoted to Deputy Chief of Foreign Intelligence but retired because of ill-health in 1948. He suffered a stroke in 1968, recovered partially but died in 1972.

Appendix I

Walter Krivitsky on Soviet Spies
in the Foreign Office

In 1936, while Theodore Mally [*sic* Maly] alias Paul Hardt was the illegal OGPU *rezident* for the United Kingdom, the INO [Foreign Department of Soviet State Security] of the OGPU began to receive what Krivitsky called 'Imperial Council' information of high Naval, Military, Air Force and political importance. From his description of photographic prints of documents he saw in Moscow on two or three occasions in 1936 and 1937 there is no doubt that printed reports of the proceedings of the Committee of Imperial Defence and other highly confidential reports available to the same source were regularly made available to and photographed by OGPU agents in London. Krivitsky recalls that one of the latest of such reports dealt with defence measures and an appreciation of the situation in Germany by the British Ambassador in Berlin.

Reports supplied by the 'Imperial Council' source were especially dealt with in Moscow. The printed report, which ran into a very large number of pages, was translated literally into Russian. When the translator was not sure of the Russian translation the English word was put in brackets after it. Extracts were made of the more important passages and bound up in the form of a book, typewritten on pale green paper. Only five copies of this book were made – one each for [Chief of Defence] [Klement] Voroshilov, [Assistant Chief of Defence] [Vladimir] Orlov, [Chief of NKVD] [Nikolai] Yezhov, [Chief of NKVD Foreign Department] [Abram] Sloutski and [General Secretary of the Communist Party] [Josef] Stalin. Photographic prints of the original report and the full Russian translation were always attached to Stalin's copy.

In the last days of April, or in the beginning of May 1937, when Krivitsky was in Moscow for the last time, he called on Sloutski, head of the Foreign Department of the OGPU. Sloutski was Krivitsky's friend as well as chief of the OGPU

[Line missing]

… side of the commission with which he had been entrusted in 1935. Sloutski handed him the latest book of extracts of information from the 'Imperial Council' source and asked him particularly to read a report bound up with it which dealt with a special meeting of the Politburo at which [Foreign Minister] [Maxim] Litviinoff was present. From this report Sloutski deduced that the British Intelligence must have a source in the Narkomindel (Soviet Foreign Office). The man in the English section of the INO who actually received the material made the same comment. This report although bound up with extracts from the usual printed 'Imperial Council' report was additional to and not part of the report.

At that time Sloutski was not at all certain of his own position and he wanted Krivitsky to think over the report with a view to making any possible suggestions as to where the leakage in the Narkomindel could be. Sloutski felt that if he could discover this it might save his own position. Krivitsky says that he could not give his attention to the report although he skimmed through it. At that time he was only anxious to get out of Moscow. He told Sloutski he would return and go into the matter thoroughly but in fact he never did.

As regards the source of the 'Imperial Council' information, Krivitsky has little definite knowledge.

He is certain that the source was a young man, probably under thirty, an agent of Theodore Mally, that he was recruited as a Soviet agent purely on ideological grounds, and that he took no money for the information he obtained. He was almost certainly educated at Eton and Oxford. Krivitsky cannot get it out of his head that the source is a 'young aristocrat', but agrees that he may have arrived at this conclusion because he thought it was only young men of the nobility who were educated at Eton. He believes the source to have been the secretary or son of one of the chiefs of the Foreign Office.

Krivitsky reported the following incident in support of his recollection that the young man in question obtained his information from the Foreign Office.

Krivitsky had as his agent at The Hague an old Dutchman and Social Democrat. He cannot recollect his name but says he was sent by *The Times* to act as their correspondent in Hungary during Bela Kun's time there.

In 1936 this old man reported that he had had meetings with an employee of the British Foreign Office who was offering to supply Japanese information. Krivitsky sent a message to Hardt to have the man looked up in the Foreign Office List and is sure that in reporting that he was unable to find any record of him, Hardt said he had consulted his other agent (not King) in the Foreign Office regarding the proposed new recruit. Krivitsky recalls that in connection with this incident he forbade the engaging of another agent in the Foreign Office as there were two there already and a third might be prejudicial to the other two.

Krivitsky cannot say whether since the disappearance of Mally (alias Hardt) this young man is still working. He is quite certain that although they would almost certainly drop the remainder of Hardt's organisation in London, the OGPU would not willingly give up the 'Imperial Council' source because his information was of vital importance. He thinks it more likely that since the Stalin-Hitler alliance the young man will have tried 'to stop work' for he was an idealist and recruited on the basis that the only man who would fight Hitler was Stalin: that his feelings had been worked onto such an extent that he believed that in helping Russia he would be helping this country and the cause of democracy generally. Whether if he has wanted 'to stop work' he is a type with sufficient moral courage to withstand the inevitable OGPU blackmail and threats of exposure Krivitsky cannot say.

Interview conducted by Jane Archer, January 1940, at the Langham Hotel

The Prime Minister's Brief, 1978

Sir Anthony Blunt
Case History
Anthony Frederick Blunt was born in 1907. He was educated at Marlborough and Trinity College, Cambridge, where he remained as a don until 1937. He then joined the Warburg Institute in London and in 1939 was appointed Deputy Director of the Courtauld Institute of Art, University of London.

2. In August 1939 Blunt enlisted and was commissioned in the Intelligence Corps. In July 1940 he joined the Security Service where he served until October 1945, when he returned to the Courtauld Institute, of which he was Director and also became Surveyor of the King's Pictures. From 1947 to 1972 he was also Professor of the History of Art at the University of London. He retired from the post of Surveyor of The Queen's Pictures in September 1972 but remained in the Household as Adviser for The Queen's Pictures and Drawings, then Adviser on the Drawings only until 1974. He resigned a residual honorary consultancy in November 1978.

3. Blunt was a friend of Philby and Burgess at Cambridge and like them moved in a circle where Marxist sympathies were openly held. After Burgess and Maclean's defection in May 1951 he, like Philby, came under suspicion; he was also the subject of an allegation made to the Security Service by the writer Goronwy Rees that in about 1937 Burgess had told him that he (Burgess) was a Comintern agent, and Blunt was working for him in the same capacity. Blunt was interviewed on eleven occasions over a period of years in the course of efforts to clear up this allegation and the other suspicions about him. He made no admissions of performing any services for the Russians and said that he was unaware that Burgess was working for the Comintern; he had understood before the war that Burgess was an agent of British Intelligence and had given his assistance in that belief. Efforts to obtain, by other means, information which would establish whether or not Blunt had wittingly acted as a Soviet agent were unsuccessful.

4. In the early 1960s an important KGB defector to the Americans, Golitsyn, provided a great deal of information about Russian espionage in Western countries. In dealing with Britain he spoke inter alia of an extensive espionage group recruited in the 1930s and which was said to have five founding members. Members of this network, to which Burgess belonged,

were aware of each other's activities and the defector believed that through it the Russians had achieved serious penetration of British Intelligence. In the detailed investigation which followed, the case of Philby was reopened, leading to his confession in Beirut in January 1963 and subsequent flight. The defector provided no information which implicated Blunt but subsequently an American, Michael Whitney Straight, volunteered to the FBI, who passed the information to the British authorities, that before the war Blunt had recruited him to be 'economist and adviser on policy matters for the International' and that he believed Blunt had tried to recruit others. Straight confessed to the FBI that he had spied for the Russian Intelligence Service whilst working in the State Department and the Department of the Interior from about 1938 to 1940. He was not prosecuted and his evidence could not be used for a prosecution of Blunt.

Straight was appointed Deputy Chairman of the Arts Council of the United States under the Nixon Administration.

5. In view of Blunt's former career in British Intelligence and his friendship with Burgess and Philby it was concluded that it was essential to try once more to establish the truth about his role and in particular whether he answered to the allegations relating to penetration of British Intelligence, or could contribute to their solution. It was expected that he would maintain his denial of any guilty involvement, unless he were offered some inducement to confess. An approach was therefore made to the Director of Public Prosecutions.

6. In April 1964, the Deputy Director of Public Prosecutions (acting in place of the Director, who had recently died) wrote to the then Attorney General, Sir John Hobson. The Attorney was informed that Straight had made an allegation that Blunt had worked for the Russians and that it was the intention of the Security Service to interrogate Blunt for the purpose of obtaining information from him about others who might still be a danger. The Deputy Director told the Attorney that he had authorised the investigating officers, if they felt it necessary in order to obtain the information, to assure Blunt that there would be no criminal proceedings against him in relation to matters which had occurred 20 or more years ago. The Attorney General replied the following day saying that he had no comment to make on what the Deputy Director had authorised.

7. Blunt was interviewed on 23 April 1964, and was confronted with the information given by Straight. This produced no admission from Blunt and, indeed, he described it as pure fantasy. The interviewers then put it to Blunt that if it was fear that deterred him from speaking he could give him 'an absolute assurance that no action would be taken against him if he now told the truth'. Blunt confessed then and both then and in subsequent interviews at which the assurance was repeated, he provided much useful information.

8. In his initial confession he said that he had been recruited for the Third International by Burgess in the 1930s to work for the RIS. He said that his

regular dealings with the RIS ended shortly after his departure from the Security Service in October 1945 but he admitted that he had known of Maclean's intended defection in 1951, and had put Burgess in touch with an RIS officer at the time.

9. In later interviews Blunt admitted to occasional meetings with RIS officers between 1945 and 1947, when he acted as a courier for Burgess, and on one occasion between 1951 and 1956 when he assisted Philby in contacting the RIS. He also explained his role as a talent spotter for the RIS in the 1930s and spoke in detail of the cases of three undergraduates (including Straight) whom he had recruited for the RIS at that time. In addition he described Burgess' work for the RIS and his recruiting activities on its behalf.

10. A Security Service research team, which was set up to investigate the group of five referred to by Golitsyn and related cases, had considerable success aided by Blunt's information in identifying personalities and activities of the network. In one notable instance, where his information and assistance played a significant part, a senior Admiralty scientist was removed from a sensitive post after it had been concluded (although it could not be conclusively proved) that he had been recruited for the RIS by Burgess in the 1930s.

11. However, as more details were uncovered the interrogators felt that while the information Blunt had given in his early interviews had been substantially true, he had not told all he could. Efforts to extract additional information from him have been largely unsuccessful. Blunt's reasons for withholding (he does not himself admit to it) are not known; nor is it clear that the information he is keeping back has security significance. The conduct of his dealings with interviewing officers has throughout been one of apparently trying to assist the Security Service in tracing unidentified Soviet agents while avoiding any statement in circumstances which might lead to proceedings against others which might involve him. He may still be protecting friends.

12. There remains the possibility that Blunt retains some loyalty to the Russians and may even be under a degree of Soviet guidance and control. During an investigation which has lasted with occasional breaks for over twenty years this has been the subject of close examination, but with negative results.

13. The decision not to prosecute Blunt was reviewed in 1972 by the then Attorney General, now Lord Rawlinson, who confirmed that the public interest lay in taking no action. The present Attorney General considered the matter in 1974 and saw no reason to differ; he was also satisfied that nothing had occurred since 1972 which would justify a prosecution. The only firm evidence against Blunt is his confession which, in view of the immunity given in order to obtain it, would not be useable against him.

The forthcoming book

14. Mr Andrew Boyle who has written several previous biographies (of Group Captain Cheshire, Trenchard, Brendan Bracken and Erskine Childers) has

recently completed the draft of a book about the Cambridge spies. From very delicate sources the probable content of the book has become clear. For legal reasons it is uncertain whether Blunt will be named as the 'fourth man' but it is likely that he will be sufficiently described for any intelligent reader to identify him. Boyle's book will also suggest that there was a 'fifth man', a British-born spy for the RIS who was later 'turned' by the CIA and used against Maclean, Burgess and Philby and was then rewarded with United States citizenship and a lucrative United States Government post. This story, which is believed to concern a Wilfred Mann, will be considered in a separate paper. The book after recounting the now well-known history of Burgess, Maclean and Philby and their close friendship with Blunt, suggests that in 1951 Blunt, who still had social contact with former Security Service colleagues, told Burgess on Friday 25 May 1951 that Maclean was to be interrogated on Monday 28 May and that this was the reason for their very sudden decision to defect. There is no evidence to support this suggestion. Blunt did indeed have occasional social contact at this period with the Deputy Director General of the Security Service, Mr G M Liddell, which the latter recorded, but there is no record any such contact between 17 May when the first proposal was made to interview and 29 May when it became certain that Burgess and Maclean had defected. Moreover the decision to interview Maclean was taken at a meeting at the Foreign Office chaired by the Foreign Secretary on 24 May and the date was set for the week beginning 17 June, because of Mrs Maclean's advanced pregnancy, which was expected to end then.

15. Mr Boyle's book is also likely to suggest that Blunt confessed, implicated Philby and was 'pardoned' shortly after he was knighted in 1956. The confession was in fact in 1964 by which time Philby had defected.

Damage assessment

16. Between 1936 when Blunt was recruited into the Service of the Soviet Union and the outbreak of war when he left Cambridge to join the Army, his task was talent spotting and recruitment in the university. His contribution to the infiltration of Soviet agents into our society was considerable.

17. While a member of the Security Service (June 1940 to October 1945) by his own account he passed to the RIS any information that came his way which he considered to be of possible interest to them. It must be assumed that this included information on his colleagues and others in Government service of a kind which the Russians might hope to exploit then or later.

18. For his first three months' service Blunt was concerned with vetting of military personnel and civil servants and he had only limited access to other information of value to the Russians. In October 1940, however, he became personal assistant to the Director of the Counter-Espionage and Counter-Subversion Division and at the end of that year he moved to the Counter-Espionage section where he remained until he left the Service five years later.

In this section he dealt with material concerned with counter-espionage operations against the German, Italian and Japanese Intelligence Services, and was particularly concerned with the use made by those Services of neutral diplomats, including Swiss, Swedes. Spaniards and Portuguese. He handled reports from agents, from decyphered diplomatic cables and from telephone intercepts directed against diplomats serving in the United Kingdom and he was engaged in operations against neutrals' diplomatic bags. He had close liaison with the SIS. He was involved in double agent operations. He would have learned a certain amount about SOE operations. He handled files on some Russians living in or visiting the United Kingdom and would have had access to files on other Russians. He selected targets for surveillance operations. He drafted fortnightly reports on the work of all sections in the Service for submission to the Prime Minister.

19. During Blunt's first nine months in the Service when the Soviet Union were in relations with Germany some of the information Blunt provided may have been passed on to the Germans. This could have led to action against people who were helping this country, though we have no evidence of this. After the Russians were drawn into the war they would have been receiving from him information about our war effort which we would have not wished them to have, and information which may well have been useful to them in their longer-term plans for undermining the West. We know of one example of a Russian suffering as a result of Blunt's activities: Blunt revealed that a Russian source was passing information to SIS and was subsequently told by the Russians that a Soviet departmental official had been 'dealt with'.

20. In summary, where we know that people like Philby and Blake sent many men to their deaths, we have no evidence that Blunt did that, and in the circumstances in which he was operating it seems unlikely. This does not mean that we can regard him as a traitor of minor importance: his disservice to the country was grave.

Other associates of Blunt

21. A note on Philby, Burgess and Maclean is attached as an Appendix. Some of Blunt's other associates are discussed below.

John Cairncross

22. At Cambridge Blunt talent-spotted John Cairncross, who worked as an RIS agent from 1936, when he joined the Foreign Office, until 1952, when he came under suspicion as a contact of Burgess. Cairncross was from 1940 to 1942 Private Secretary to Lord Hankey, the Chancellor of the Duchy of Lancaster and Paymaster General. In 1942 and 1943 he worked at the Government Code and Cypher School at Bletchley and from 1943 to 1945 was in SIS. From 1945 to 1952 he worked at the Treasury (with a secondment of six months to the Ministry of Supply in 1951). In 1952 he resigned from United Kingdom

Government service after he had come under suspicion and from that time he worked in a variety of academic and administrative posts abroad until 1971. In 1964 he was interviewed in the United States and confessed to having been an RIS agent throughout his career. He could not be deported under American law and refused to comply with a formal invitation to return to this country and make a statement under caution. He is now living in Rome. We do not think Boyle's book will mention him.

Sir Dennis Proctor

23. Proctor met Philby, Blunt and Burgess at Cambridge first in 1929 or 1930 and has said that either Blunt or Philby introduced him to Marxism about that time. He said in 1966 that he was still a Marxist.

    Proctor served in the Treasury from 1930 to 1950. He then became Managing Director of a shipping firm but returned to the Treasury in 1953.

    From 1958 to 1965 he was Permanent Secretary in the Ministry of Fuel and Power, then he retired. He was a close friend of Burgess and has said that he discussed official matters freely with Burgess before and during the war. He was and still is friendly with Blunt. We do not think Boyle's book will mention him.

Goronwy Rees

24. Goronwy Rees was at New College, Oxford, from 1928 to 1931 and then became a Fellow of All Souls. He worked as a journalist on the *Manchester Guardian* and the *Spectator* from 1932 until the outbreak of war, when he joined the Army and served in Intelligence. From July 1947 to May 1951 he acted as a part-time consultant in the Political Section of SIS. In 1954 he became Principal of the University College of Wales and since his resignation from that post in 1957 he has been a freelance writer and journalist.

25. Rees has said he first met Burgess in about 1932 and they remained close friends until 1951 apart from a disagreement over Burgess' apparent swing to Fascism between 1935 and 1937. Rees held left-wing views but is not known ever to have joined the Communist Party.

26. In May 1951, very shortly after the defection of Burgess and Maclean, Rees volunteered to the Security Service the information that in 1937 Burgess told him that he was working for a secret branch of the Comintern and that Burgess was one of his sources of information. Rees said that Burgess asked him to help in the work, and that he had agreed to co-operate but was never asked to provide specific information, though he discussed with Burgess whatever he knew. He had broken off the arrangement in 1939 at the time of the Russo-German Pact. Rees said subsequently that Blunt had tried to dissuade him from telling his story to the Security Service.

27. Rees has in newspaper articles (1956), a book (1972) and a TV interview (1978) told the story of his association with Burgess and has told many people

in Fleet Street and at Cambridge about his suspicions of Blunt. It is clear from the context that Rees is the source of many of the allegations and inferences about the 'Fourth Man' in Boyle's book in which he is likely to be mentioned.

The Bentinck Street Associates

28. When Blunt returned from France in the summer of 1940, he stayed at Lord Rothschild's flat at 5 Bentinck Street, W1, and it was Lord Rothschild, then a Security Service officer, who recommenced him for recruitment. Later in 1940 Lord Rothschild sublet the flat to Blunt, who shared it with Tess Mayor (whom Lord Rothschild also recommended for recruitment and who became his secretary; they married in 1946 after his divorce) and Pat Rawdon-Smith (now Lady Llewelyn-Davies). They were joined later by Burgess when he left SOE and rejoined the BBC in late 1940.

   Lord Rothschild, Miss Mayor, Mrs. Rawdon-Smith, Blunt and Burgess had all known one another at Cambridge in the mid-1930s. Blunt and Burgess remained there until 1945, Mrs. Rawdon-Smith left in 1943 on marriage to Richard Llewelyn-Davies, who had stayed for a few months in 1942-43.

29. Mr. Boyle, drawing on information from Goronwy Rees, Malcolm Muggeridge and others, is believed to describe the Bentinck Street flat as the scene of drunken orgies (during one of which Maclean was homosexually compromised) and of meetings of Communist and sympathetic intellectuals. It is thought that nothing will be said in the book to the detriment of Lord or Lady Rothschild or of Lord or Lady Llewelyn-Davies but it is possible that others who knew them will elaborate on their apparently close association with Blunt, especially as Burgess, Miss Mayor and Mrs. Llewelyn-Davies were all in late 1945 employed in the Foreign Office. There have been no security worries about Lady Llewelyn-Davies or Lord Rothschild. The latter was of course fully PV'd [Positively Vetted]. Since 1951 both Lord and Lady Rothschild have volunteered assistance in the Security Service investigations. It was information received through Lord Rothschild which led to the final identification of Philby as a spy. Lord Llewelyn-Davies, though suspected of involvement in the 1930s in the recruitment of the scientist who later joined the Admiralty (see paragraph 10) has denied all connection with the RIS.

Briefing of Ministers

30. Apart from the Attorney General (Hobson) in 1964 Ministers have been consulted on the following occasions.
   (i)   At a meeting in February 1964 attended by the Prime Minister (Douglas-Home), Chancellor of the Exchequer (Maudling), Foreign Secretary (Butler), Home Secretary (Brooke) and Attorney General (Hobson) about Cairncross (see paragraph 22) it is thought that some mention was made of Blunt's involvement with Burgess and Cairncross, although the note of the meeting does not mention Blunt.

(ii)   The Prime Minister (Wilson) and the Home Secretary (Jenkins) were informed about the progress of the Blunt investigation in 1967. The Home Secretary (Callaghan) was informed of the case in 1968.

(iii)   The Home Secretary (Maudling) was informed of the case in May 1971.

(iv)   In 1972 the Attorney General (Rawlinson) was consulted.

(v)   In 1973 the Prime Minister (Heath), Home Secretary (Carr) were informed in detail against the likelihood of publicity in case of Blunt's death.

(vi)   In June 1974 the Attorney General (Silkin) was consulted.

(vii)   In July 1974 the Prime Minister (Wilson), the Lord Chancellor (Elwyn-Jones), Home Secretary (Jenkins) and Attorney General (Silkin) were fully informed.

(viii) In June 1977 the Prime Minister (Callaghan) and the Home Secretary (Rees) were fully informed.

(ix)   All Home Secretaries from March 1964 to date have signed interception warrants on Blunt.

In addition the Attorney General (Manningham Buller) was informed about the investigation of Blunt in 1957 before Blunt was directly implicated and confessed.

31. Mrs. Thatcher has not so far been briefed about the case. It is for consideration whether she should be briefed now since advance publicity for Boyle's book could lead to revelations about Blunt at any time.

Appendix

Burgess, Maclean and Philby

1. In 1962 the KGB defector Golitsyn said that in the 1930s there had been a very important spy network in the United Kingdom which originally had five members, all of whom knew each other and had been at the University together. He knew that Burgess and Maclean were members. He thought that the network had expanded beyond the original five and that it still had some sort of existence even after their defection.

2. Philby was undoubtedly an original member. The fourth was probably Blunt, although there remains some doubt as to whether he was an original member. The fifth is still unknown. James Klugmann, a life-long Communist from his days at Cambridge and a prominent member of the Cultural Committee of the Communist Party, who worked for the RIS before and during the war, when he was an officer in SOB in Italy, is one of the possible candidates. There is no reason to suppose that Boyle is aware of Golitsyn's report. His 'discovery' of a 'fifth man' is merely coincidental; his candidate has no common background with the known four and can be ruled out as Golitsyn's fifth man.

3. There were very few Communists at the universities in the 1920s but in the 1930s the economic slump, the rise of Fascism, the influx of refugee Marxist

intellectuals from Europe and the Comintern's switch to United Front tactics, gave a great impetus to Communism among dons and undergraduates. This situation provided the Russian Intelligence Service (RIS) with opportunities which it did not fail to exploit. It was assisted by the fact that some Communist students were instructed by the Party to become 'moles', that is to sever overt connections with the Party, in anticipation of employment in the Public Service when their abilities, reinforced by Communist discipline, were calculated to take them to positions of influence where they could help to create the Revolution from above. The following paragraphs concern Blunt's immediate companions. Philby, Burgess and Maclean all figure largely in Boyle's book. Though some of this account comes from suspect sources, the general sequence of events is believed to be true

H.A.R. Philby

4. In 1933 Philby completed his degree course at Trinity College, Cambridge. Although not a card-holding member of the Communist Party, he had been closely associated with Communist circles at Trinity. Before taking up his career he went to Vienna, ostensibly to improve his German. Through Maurice Dobb (a Communist then and until he died in 1976) he was provided with the address of Lizzy Friedman. Philby stayed with her in Vienna, married her and brought her back to England in the spring of 1934. Shortly afterwards Lizzy was instrumental in introducing him to a Russian Intelligence Officer who is thought to have recruited him formally for the RIS. In his 1963 confession, which was certainly a mixture of truth and falsehood, Philby claimed that he was told to review his friends for other possible recruits. His first candidate was Donald Maclean and his second Guy Burgess. He may have been responsible for other recruitments then or later.

5. When Philby returned from Vienna his tutor refused to recommend him for the Indian Civil Service because of his left-wing views. He took up journalism and among other activities became associated with Peter Smolka alias Smollett in the formation of a Press Agency. (Smolka, an Austrian Jew, was another Russian spy and probably was recruited in Vienna before he came to the United Kingdom. He joined the Ministry of Information in 1939 and was head of its Soviet Relations branch from 1941 to 1945. He has lived in Austria since 1946 and was *The Times* correspondent from 1947 to 1949 before recovering possession of his family's metal-working business).

6. In February 1937 Philby went to Spain and later became correspondent for *The Times* on the Franco side. In 1940 he joined SOE and subsequently transferred to SIS and by the end of the war he had become Head of Counter Intelligence. After serving in Turkey, he was in Washington at the time of the Maclean investigation. Much of this investigation was concerned with leakages which had occurred while Maclean was en poste in Washington from 1944-1948, and Philby was privy to it. In 1950 Burgess was posted to Washington as an

ordinary Foreign Service officer and lived in Philby's house there. He returned to the United Kingdom in 1951 carrying a warning from Philby to Maclean a few weeks before he and Maclean defected. Suspicion fell on Philby as the source of the warning and he was made the subject of intensive investigation. He was required to resign from SIS because of his early Communist record but his guilt was not established until 1962. He was then outside the jurisdiction. He was interviewed abroad and made a partial confession. A few days later he fled to Russia.

D. D. Maclean

7. Maclean was recruited for the RIS in 1934 shortly before coming down from Trinity Hall, Cambridge, when he was preparing to enter the Foreign Office. As an undergraduate he had been openly left-wing, but after recruitment by the RIS gave no overt sign of Communist views. He operated as a spy throughout a successful career in the Foreign Service, which included postings in Paris, Washington, where he was acting Head of Chancery in 1946, and Cairo. He became the prime suspect in the leakage investigation mentioned above and would have been interrogated if the investigation had not been betrayed by Philby. It is not known what Maclean did in the way of talent-spotting or recruitment during his espionage career.

G.F. de M. Burgess

8. Burgess was a brilliant undergraduate at Trinity College. Cambridge, a convinced Marxist and a member of the Communist Party. After his recruitment by the RIS at the end of 1934 or early 1935 he ceased to be an open Communist, He worked in the BBC from 1936 to 1939 when he joined the section of SIS which later became SOE. From 1941 to 1944 he was again employed by the BBC and then joined the Foreign Office News Department. From 1941 to 1946 he was an outside agent of the Security Service. In October 1947 he became an established member of the Foreign Service (Branch B) and served as personal assistant to the Minister of State, in the Far Eastern Department and finally in the British Embassy, Washington. He was not suspected of being a spy before he defected in 1951.

9. Burgess had direct access to important secrets in the course of his various employments from 1939 to 1951. In addition he had a very wide circle of friends, many of whom were, as he was, homosexuals. Many of his friends reached high places. He was accepted in intellectual circles in Cambridge and London, and particularly at All Souls College. Oxford. There is no doubt that many of his friends wore valuable unconscious sources and be was in a position to give very important assistance to the RIS as a talent-spotter. He made some recruitments for the RIS himself though the full extent of these is unknown. One of them was Blunt. Burgess died in Moscow in 1963.

Blunt and the Palace

Sir Anthony Blunt is a leading authority on art. Before the war he was Deputy Director of the Courtauld Institute of Art. He rejoined the Institute on leaving the Security Service in October 1945 and became its Director in 1947.

He has also been Professor of the History of Art at the University of London and Slade Professor of Fine Art at both Oxford and Cambridge. In 1945 he was appointed Surveyor of the King's Pictures: he was reappointed to his position on The Queen's accession and held it until 1972. Thereafter he held an honorary position as Adviser for The Queen's Pictures and Drawings until 1978. He was awarded the KCVO in 1956.

Given the fact that criticism may centre on the continuation of Blunt in a post in the Royal Household after Goronwy Rees made his allegations in 1951 and the award of the knighthood to Blunt in 1956, it is important to bear in mind the following sequence of events.

(i)   1945. Blunt appointed Surveyor of The King's Pictures. No suspicion about him at that time.

(ii)   1951. Goronwy Rees allegations. Unsupported by evidence. Interrogation of Blunt begun. But no grounds for action.

(iii) 1956. Blunt knighted. An honour invariably given to persons serving in the Royal Household in posts such as Blunt then held.

(iv)   Early 1964. Information received implicating Blunt.

(v)   April 1964. The Queen's Private Secretary (Sir Michael Adeane) informed and told that Blunt was to be seen and invited to confess. [XXXXXXXXXXXXXXXXXXXXXXXXXXXXXXXX]

(vi)   Later April 1964. Blunt confessed.

Against this background it is not too difficult to defend the award of a knighthood to Blunt in 1956. It would have caused surprise if he had not got it and there was no real evidence against him at the time. More difficult to defend is the fact that be continued to hold the post of Surveyor of The Queen's Pictures after he had confessed. Given the fact that he had been promised immunity, no consideration seems to have been given to asking him to resign. The post which he held in the Royal Household did not of course afford him any access to classified information.

The Prime Minister will have noticed the piece in *The Times* Diary of 9th November (copy attached).

2. There have since been some very confidential contacts (which must respected) with the publishers, as a result of which it is clear that:

(a) Andrew Boyle's 'fourth man' is Blunt and that will be clear to readers of the book. He may be named directly as such (the publishers' lawyers have not yet decided): or the fourth man characteristics may be described in some places and Blunt's in others in a way which clearly links them.

(b) Boyle claims there was a 'fifth man' who was an English atomic scientist who worked in the United States on the joint atomic bomb projects, had been recruited by the Russian Intelligence Service and subsequently turned into a double agent by the CIA who used him to pass controlled material to Maclean to pass on to the Russians. The clear candidate from Boyle's description would be Dr Wilfred Mann, who now lives in the United States and the allegations in Boyle's book about him, if true, are new to us.

The book is not expected to be published for some months yet.

3. Sir Anthony Blunt, having read the piece in *The Times* Literary Diary, asked to see an officer of the Security Service. The interview took place on 15th November.

4. Blunt seemed nervous and rather depressed. He said that the piece in *The Times*, coming on top of the TV interview which Goronwy Rees gave on 5th September (in which he reminisced about Burgess and said that he thought there was more to come out about the Burgess/Maclean story) made him think that Boyle's book would unmask him. He asked if the Security Service could recommend someone to give him legal advice. He was told that this could not be done and that he should reach his own decision. In further conversation it became evident that he was not thinking about the possibility of an injunction or a libel action but rather the possibility that he might be prosecuted as a result of the book. The Security Service officer said that he was no lawyer but that it would be surprising if after this lapse of time any private author were able to produce evidence which would be usable in a prosecution. Blunt then asked whether it would be in order for him to write an apologia and leave it with Lady Rothschild in ease of his death. He was told that this was a matter for him to decide. He then went on to ask whether it was in order for him to consult Dennis Proctor, whose judgment he much respected. He was told that this was also a matter for him to decide, so long as he did not seek to discuss matters outside Proctor's knowledge. Blunt then asked if he was named in the House by a latter-day Lipton, what reply the Government would give. The Security Service officer replied that he could not say what Ministers would wish to do. Finally his residual connection with the Palace was mentioned. Although he retired from the post of Surveyor of The Queen's Pictures in September 1972 he has remained as an honorary Adviser for The Queen's Pictures and Drawings and was responsible for mounting the current Holbein exhibition. [XXXXXXXXXXXXXXXXXXXXXXXXXXXXXXXXXXXXXXXXXXXXXX]

5. Blunt told the Security Service that long before the piece in *The Times* had appeared he had arranged to spend a month in Italy. He was leaving yesterday and was due to return on 20th December.

6. I understand that the Prime Minister has it in mind to speak to the Attorney General. I have passed the above information to the latter's Legal Secretary. I have also suggested that Mr. Silkin ought to be prepared to answer two questions

in particular:- (i) the grounds for non-prosecution; and (ii) the seriousness of Blunt's espionage activities.

7. I hope to hear fairly soon a little more about the publishers' intentions and about whether they will let us have a copy of the book in advance of publication.

8. In the meantime we are urgently revising and bringing up to date the contingency material which was annexed to my minute A07423 to Sir Harold Wilson on 3rd July 1974. In particular I think that, given the water which has flowed under various bridges since 1974 and not least the Old Bailey Secrets Trial, it would not now be possible to get away with as brief and uninformative a Parliamentary statement as was then envisaged.

John Hunt
17th November 1978

Ref. A068.

PRIME MINISTER

1. You will remember the concern in the early '60s about penetration of the Security Service and MI6 by hostile intelligence agencies. About that time it became clear that a former intelligence officer had been a Russian agent. There was in particular Blake's confession and Philby's defection. Furthermore a number of Russian defectors (primarily the agent KAGO) provided circumstantial evidence of penetration. Most of this evidence could be traced back to individuals who had already been identified as spies: but there remained a number of leads where cither their origin was not certain or indeed where it seemed possible that the culprit was somebody else. We also had to take into account the possibility that people like Philby might have recruited other members before they were themselves detected.

2. In the course of the subsequent investigations suspicion fell – at different times – on Graham Mitchell, the Deputy Head of the Security Service who retired in 1963 (codename PETERS) and on Roger Hollis, the Head of the Security Service who retired in 1965 and has since died.

3. A thorough investigation into PETERS began in March 1963 (two months after Philby's defection) and was the subject of two reports in July and September of that year, when PETERS retired. Each report concluded, the second perhaps rather less confidently than the first, that he might be a spy; a direct confrontation with him was considered but was not undertaken following submission of the issue to the Prime Minister of the day. Instead enquiries were continued after his retirement and resulted in further reports in March 1964 (which concluded that he was more likely to be innocent than guilty) and May 1964 (which concluded that the evidence was inadequate to support a finding of 'guilty'). The investigation was then discontinued but later, in 1968, it was decided to make one more effort to clear up the case. The upshot was that PETERS was interviewed in August 1970 and the Director General of the Security Service (Sir Martin Furnival Jones who had by then

succeeded Sir Roger Hollis) told him that he was satisfied that he had <u>not</u> been a spy.

4. During the course of these investigations a joint Security Service/MI6 Working Party of counter-espionage specialists had been established to advise the Director General and 'C' on the problems of penetration of their own Services. In 1966, that Working Party produced a report which cast suspicion either at Sir Roger Hollis (codename DRAT) or another (unidentified) individual rather than PETERS. DRAT had by then retired and it was decided to investigate the suspicion of the unidentified individual first, and then to clear up the PETERS case. In consequence it was 1969 before the case against DRAT began to be assembled. This investigation, in the course of which DRAT was interviewed, was inconclusive although the then Director General of the Security Service was of the opinion that DRAT was not a spy.

5. We are thus formally in a position where PETERS was cleared and DRAT is dead. Nevertheless the joint Working Party has remained in existence to assess and review any fresh intelligence that may arise affecting PETERS or DRAT or any other case of suspected penetration of the two Services.

6. Last summer the Working Party produced a more general report on the whole question of penetration of the two Services. The principal conclusions of the report were:-

   (a) Although there was no direct evidence of current penetration, the evidence from the past of undetected penetration was sufficiently strong to require both Services to commit significant resources to continued study in this field.

   (b) The weight of evidence of undetected penetration pointed more at the Security Service than MI6,

   (c) Priority should be given to further work on evidence relating to the period from the mid-'50s until the early '60s.

7. Sir Michael Hanley and 'C' agreed with these conclusions, but they also recommended to me that if in future an investigation of a serious character became necessary which also concerned a member of their Services, it would be in the best interests of all concerned if they could put the facts to an independent person who, while sufficiently versed in security affairs to understand what was at stake and to offer advice on any proposed action, had no direct responsibility for the individual concerned. This seemed a very desirable recommendation in the case of suspected penetration in the area where those responsible for the investigation were investigating their own people: and Lord Trend seemed very suitable for the role proposed.

8. Before I could put this proposition to you however there was an unexpected development. A Mr Stephen de Mowbray, an officer in MI6 but who was formerly a member of the team which bad investigated the PETERS and DRAT cases, came and told me that he continued to have doubts about the conduct of these cases. These doubts, which relate to DRAT rather than

PETERS, derive from a conviction that in both cases (but particularly as regard DRAT) enquiries were pursued with insufficient vigour and that, since they were conducted wholly within the two agencies, they might be thought at best to fall short of complete impartiality and at worst to constitute a kind of 'cover-up' operation.

9. De Mowbray has an air of fanaticism about him which falls to carry much conviction: and it was also relevant that de Mowbray made no allegations about present members of the Security Service or MI6. Nevertheless the seriousness of his suggestion seemed to call for investigation. Accordingly I asked Lord Trend whether, if you subsequently agreed, he would be willing to take on the role proposed in paragraph 7 above and whether, as a 'one-off' assignment he would see de Mowbray and investigate his allegations in whatever way seemed best. Sir Arthur Peterson, Sir Thomas Brimelow, Sir Michael Hanley and 'C agreed that this should be done.

10. At that stage we envisaged that this would not take Lord Trend very long. But over the last 11 months Lord Trend has conducted a most thorough review of the PETERS and DRAT cases (including some 22 visits to the Security Service to study papers and interviews with many of those concerned). I attach a copy of his report. In short his conclusions are –

(a) PETERS was probably rightly cleared,

(b) He found no reason to dissent from the 1971 judgment that the case against DRAT was at least 'not proven' and was not capable of being further pursued unless fresh evidence became available.

(c) While one might wish, with hindsight, that enquiries into DRAT had been started earlier and pressed forward more vigorously, there were no grounds for regarding the investigation as deficient either in thoroughness or impartiality.

11. Following Lord Trend's report, he and I had further talks with de Mowbray. Lord Trend explained his conclusions de Mowbray did not dissent from (a) and (b) and said that he had no fixed view on what the right answer was. He accepted also that there had been no irregularity in the investigation of the two cases, that Lord Trend's investigation had been objective and fair, and that no further post-mortem of the past could now be expected. He did, however, remain concerned that higher authority had not been sufficiently determined to get at the truth at the time and he also expressed the fear that if there had been undetected penetration, our enemies must know of it and might choose to disclose it at a moment convenient to them. He is therefore very anxious to be satisfied about the arrangements for the future. This is not of course strictly his business since his current job in MI6 has nothing to do with counter-espionage. Nevertheless he has, as I said earlier, an air of fanaticism about him and I would like to do whatever is possible to reassure him – both for his own peace of mind and to avoid him pursuing his allegations through other channels. Having said that however I ought to add that we consider it

unlikely that he would alert the Press; his loyalty to the United Kingdom is not in question and he is well aware of the danger of publicity.

12. I don't think anything would fully satisfy de Mowbray other than being put in charge of 'penetration' investigations himself. Lord Trend's investigation has been very thorough and has not put in any doubt the basic conclusions of the earlier investigations. I think therefore that de Mowbray should be told that his complaints will not be further investigated, but that:-

(i) A Privy Counsellor (Lord Trend) will be brought in in the event of any future allegation of the kind in question against a member of the Security Service or MI6.

(ii) Lord Trend will also keep in regular touch with the work of the joint Working Party which remains in being and considers any new evidence about the earlier cases.

(iii) In addition to the Heads of the two Services, the Chairman of the joint Working Party will have independent access to Lord Trend.

(iv) Ministers know of these arrangements.

13. If you agree, the question remains as to how de Mowbray should be given this information, I could do it myself and am of course ready to do so. But I have already seen him twice: and I do not want to give him any grounds for suspecting that his worries have not been brought to the attention of Ministers. For this reason my own view is that it might be most effective if the Home Secretary could spare the time to see him and tell him at first hand the action now proposed. I understand the Home Secretary would be willing to do this.

14. Lord Trend and I can of course supply further background orally if you so wish.

15. I am sending a copy of this minute to the Home Secretary.

John Hunt
5th August 1975

Source Notes

I: The Duke of Windsor
1. Karl von Loesch file at the National Archives, Kew: FO 271/64481.
2. Guy Liddell's Diary, 24 August 1945.
3. Walter Schellenberg's MI5 file: KV2/94–KV2/98.
4. Rudolf Blaum's MI5 file: KV3/412.
5. Eberhard von Stohrer's NARA file: RG 226.
6. Walter Schellenberg's NARA file: RG 263.
7. BRONX's MI5 file: KV2/2098; KV2/3639.

II: CORBY
1. CORBY's MI5 file: KV2/1420–KV2/1427; KV2/14258; KV2/1419.
2. Alan Nunn May's MI5 file; KV2/2212–KV2/26; KV2/2563–KV2/2564. See also FO 1093/41; FO 1093/638.
3. Ormond Uren's MI5 file: KV2/1594–KV2/1598.

In January 1954 Senator William Jenner interviewed Gouzenko at the Seignory Club on Montbello Island on behalf of the US Senate Judiciary Committee's Internal Security Sub-committee. The FBI later reported that thirty-four words of his testimony relating to a spy in London, possibly ELLI, had been removed from the transcript of his evidence, and was omitted from the committee's final report, *Interlocking Subversion in Government Departments*, Part 17, 84th Congress, 1st session, No. 5.

The 137-page transcript of the interview, *Testimony of Former Russian Code Clerk relating to the Security of the United States*, printed on sixty-seven pages, shows that Jenner was particularly interested in Gouzenko's allegation that an assistant to Secretary of State Edward Stettinius was a Soviet spy, but Gouzenko, under cross-examination by the Committee's counsel Julien G. Sourwine, also referred to ELLI:

> I understand that it was never mentioned, and yet this is one of the things when I first came to the Canadian authorities. I mentioned it because it was of extreme importance I believed to Canada too. I mentioned three names, first, or three persons. First the assistant to Stettinius, which I didn't know the real name, yet I thought it was of extreme importance because he was in a position practically to influence the foreign policy of the United States. Then I mentioned Fred Rose, Member of Parliament, which I thought of extreme

importance because he had access to secret sessions of parliament and besides he was more or less a recruiting agent. Then I mentioned also through information when I was in Moscow in general headquarters. I mentioned one agent from whom a telegram would come, was in [name of organization, 2 words deleted]; it talked of a man in [name of same organization, 2 words deleted], which is [name of same organization, 2 words deleted].

This may not – like I say it is up to you to evaluate it but I believe there was such a person because through my hands passed that telegram in Moscow, and I thought maybe it would be of interest to the American authorities because I understand that sometimes they do their work in cooperation with the British authorities.

BY MR SOURWINE

Q: I gather that you are telling us about an agent who was ostensibly [name of same organization, 2 words deleted], who was in fact a Soviet agent?

A: Yes, that is it.

Q: Where does the connection with the United States come in? Was he in the United States?

A: No, he was in London, according to the telegram,

Q: Was he in connection with the United States? Was he in a place to dispose of United States secrets? What is the United States connection with him?

A: Like I said in my previous statements, I thought in dealing with your particular case you would be in a better position to evaluate the importance of that matter because you knew better than I if there is any connection whatever.

Q: Can you identify the agent?

A: It was by cover name, and anyway I gave all this information to the royal commission and I believe it was probably passed over to the FBI. There was also my statement in this respect, more detailed, I understand; I wrote about three pages in respect of that person. He was under the cover name [name, one word deleted], as far as I remember, which is more or less a woman's cover name but it does not mean anything. It might be a man.

Q: You were never able to identify him further than that?

A: There was identification, a further clue; in fact I believe there were more clues than in the assistant to Stettinius. He was one of the five assistants to Stettinius, yet this particular one figured he had a Russian background. This may mean that he was on a commission in Moscow previously or maybe it could be that some of his relations had a Russian background, or maybe he was engaged previously on Russian questions. But from the telegram it was clear and I also described in detail the circumstances under which the telegram came to my attention.

Q: You are telling us that you had no knowledge that this man ever had any direct contact with the United States or operated in the United States?

A: No, no.

Q: Then you are telling this in the connotation that it is information which you have given the royal commission. Have you any reason to believe the royal commission has not made that available to the United States?

A: No, I have not. On the contrary I think it is in the files of the FBI.

The two words deleted were 'British Intelligence' and the single codeword deleted was 'ELLI'. The transcript does not explain why, or at whose request, the deletions were made.

4. Ismail Akhmedov, *In and Out of Stalin's GRU* (Lanham, Md: University Publications of America, 1984).

5. Engelbert Broda's MI5 PF, opened in January 1931, records that his father's apartment at PrinzEugenStrasse 14 had been implicated in the murder of a former OGPU agent, Georg Semmelmann, in July 1931, when Engelbert had been 14 years old. Evidently Dr Ernst Broda's address had been used as a 'live letter-box' by the Soviets, and had been compromised when Semmelmann's assassin, Andreas Piklovic, had been apprehended, searched, and found to be carrying incriminating letters, KV2/2349-2354.

6. See Henry Hemmings, *Maxwell Knight* (London; Penguin, 2017), p. 195.

7. See Paul Broda, *Scientist Spies* (London: Matador, 2011).

8. Alex Tudor Hart's MI5 file: KV2/1603–KV2/1604.

9. Edith Tudor Hart's MI5 file: KV2/1012–KV2 1014; KV2/9091; KV2/1603–KV2/1604.

III: Klaus Fuchs

1. Klaus Fuchs' MI5 file: KV6/1603–KV6/1604; KV2/1245–KV6/1270. Also CAB 301/108; PREM 1297; PREM 2799.

2. Rudolf Peierls' MI5 file: KV2/1658–KV2/1663.

3. Jurgen Kuczynski's MI5 file: KV2/1874–KV2/1877; KV2/1679; KV2/1871–KV2/1880.

4. Charles Moody's MI5 file: KV2/2793–KV2/2797.

5. Ursula Beurton's MI5 file: KV6/41–KV6/45.

6. Alan Foote's MI5 file: KV2/1611–KV2/1616

IV: Konstantin Volkov

1. Cecil Barclay had been SIS's wartime representative in Moscow, while George Hill had acted as a liaison officer for SOE.

2. Volkov Letter: see Nigel West, *Historical Dictionary of Cold War Counterintelligence* (Lanham, Md: Scarecrow, 2007).

3. Kim Philby, *My Silent War* (London: MacGibbon & Kee, 1968).

4. Gordon Brook-Shepherd, *The Storm Birds* (London: Weidenfeld & Nicolson, 1988).
5. Vasili Mitrokhin and Christopher Andrew, *The Mitrokhin Archive* (London: Allen Lane, 1999).
6. Christopher Andrew, *The Defence of the Realm* (London: Allen Lane, 2009).
7. Ben Macintyre, *A Spy Among Friends* (London: Bloomsbury, 2015).
8. Chapman Pincher, *Their Trade is Treachery* (London: Sidgwick & Jackson, 1982).
9. Peter Wright and David Greenglass, *SpyCatcher* (New York: Viking, 1985).
10. Keith Jeffery, *MI6: The History of the British Secret Intelligence Service 1909–1949* (London: Bloomsbury, 2010).
11. John Costello, *Mask of Treachery* (London: William Collins, 1988).
12. David Mure, *Master of Deception* (London: William Kimber, 1980).
13. Anatoli Golitsyn, *Checkmate*, unpublished memoirs.

V: BARCLAY and CURZON

1. All the VENONA texts are available on the US National Security Agency website www.nsa.gov
2. Cedric Belfrage's MI5 file: KV2/4004 – KV2/4012. Belfrage's confession, 3 June 1947: FBI Silvermaster file, 65-56402 serial 2583. See also web. archive.org/web/201303064446/http://education-research.org. The FBI's codename for Cedric Belfrage was 'Robert Fisher'.
3. Trudie Reint, FBI Silvermaster file, 65-56402 serial 1862. While working at the US embassy in Moscow, Trudie was employed to teach German to a young Foreign Service officer, Tyler Kent, who would be arrested in London in May 1940. He was sentenced to seven years' imprisonment. According to Paul Willetts in *Rendezvous at the Russian Tea Rooms* (London: Little Brown, 2015), Trudie Rient was associated in Moscow with another US embassy employee of Czech origins, Jack M. Marsalka, later regarded by the FBI as a Soviet espionage suspect and member of the Silvermaster group. He served in the State Department from 1934 and 1944, but was discharged 'due to doubts about his loyalty to the United States' and then taught at the University of Pittsburgh and Yale, where he was fired for 'unacceptable teaching'. He and his wife Milada were active in CPUSA front organizations, such as the Women's International League for Peace and Freedom. She died in 2000 and her papers are lodged at the Swarthmore College Peace Collection, Pennsylvania. Jack Marsalka died in June 1983 in Prague at the World Assembly for Peace.
4. James MacGibbon's MI5 file: KV2/1670 – KV2/1683. See also Hamsih MacGibbon's *Maverick Spy* (London: I.B. Tauris, 2017).
5. MI5's file on the molehunt: KV6/143; The HOMER investigation is documented at FCO 15827; MI5's file on CURZON: KV2/4140.
6. Jacob Moness's New York address, that of the Moness Chemical Company at 426 Broome Street, had been on a list seized from a Soviet cipher clerk, Anton

Miller. When the FBI raided on 16 May 1927 they found it unoccupied. A search of the empty premises revealed documents suggesting the Moness family was involved in espionage and that Jacob's wife Rachel Garsov and their daughter Pauline had fled to Paris some two months earlier, in March 1927, apparently in fear of having been compromised by the arrest of another Soviet agent, Ethel Chiles. Jacob Moness had been born in Libau, Latvia, and had subsequently lived briefly in England and Germany before emigrating to the United States. His sudden disappearance from New York had been prompted by the conviction in London on 2 May 1927 of Ethel Chiles. In fact, by that date Ethel Chiles had been in custody for nearly six weeks but she had stubbornly refused to help her Special Branch interrogators establish her true identity. She had been arrested in Dover on 15 March, having disembarked from the Calais cross-Channel ferry with a British passport identifying her as Chiles, but an alert Special Branch officer had recognized her as Kathe Gussfeldt, alias Edith Blaser, a German who was already well-known to his colleagues. She had previously been in England in February 1924, ostensibly to attend the International Workers Relief Committee (IWRC) meeting in Manchester, and three months later she had visited Glasgow for a similar political event. However, on the latter occasion she had switched clothes with a travelling companion in a railway carriage and thereby had successfully evaded police surveillance. Later in the year, in October, she had entered Britain for a third time, and had been granted an extension to her visa so she could attend another IWRC conference. Upon her departure it had been noted that she was carrying a false German passport, and an order had been issued that she would be barred from re-entry. Special Branch had maintained a rather incomplete record of Gussfeldt's subsequent movements and had spotted her in Paris in September 1925, and on a voyage to Quebec from Cherbourg later the same year. She was then seen in Brussels where she attended a meeting organized by the League Against Imperialism. Immediately following her arrest in Dover Gussfeldt had been escorted to Victoria Station where she had been met by Inspector Charles Frost who collected her suitcase from the left-luggage office. When searched it had been found to contain a mass of incriminating material, much of it written in secret ink.

The only link that could be established between Gussfeldt and Moness was handwriting found on a questionnaire recovered from an unlit stove at the Broome Street office. Evidently Moness had been tasked to acquire certain American military publications by Gussfeldt, and this had been enough to ensure her deportation to Germany, but only after she had served a sentence of two months imprisonment. Because of incriminating entries found in her diary she became the subject of a lengthy investigation conducted in London by MI5's Captain Hugh Miller. Her notes, written in a secret ink of the type used by the Germans during the Great War, showed that she had been in contact with the French spy, Jean Cremet, and an American espionage suspect

Robert Switz. She was also found to be carrying a photograph of herself with Willy Munsenberg, the prominent German Communist and founder of the Communist Youth League. There were also a series of poems which, when analyzed, suggested that after her arrival in Canada in September 1925, she had visited New York the following month. Thereafter, little was known of her movements until her arrest in Dover when she declared herself to be a steno-typist and interpreter who intended to travel to Holland, Germany, France, Switzerland and Belgium for her health. She also claimed that on another visit she had translated a report of a British trade union delegation to Russia. When the police traced the origin of Gussfeldt's British passport it was discovered to have been issued on 1 March 1927, following an application made in London a few days earlier. The referee who had authenticated the applicant was a physician, Dr Gerald Gateley of Bow. He had apparently certified that she had been born at Garston in Liverpool and was presently resident in Rendlesham Road, Clapton, a poor district in London's East End. When challenged, the doctor had denied any knowledge of 'Ethel Chiles'.

7. William Ewer's MI5 file: KV2/1017.
8. Freddie Kuh's MI5 file: KV2/984.
9. Moura Budberg's MI5 file: KV2/979–KV2/981. See also Deborah McDonald and Jeremy Dronfield, *A Very Dangerous Woman* (London: OneWorld, 2015).
10. Goronwy Rees's MI5 file: KV2/3102–KV2/4106.
11. The choice of BARCLAY as a codename for Burgess had an unfortunate effect years later when it was reported that the distinguished diplomat Sir Roderick Barclay had been considered an espionage suspect.

VI: PEACH

1. The redacted passage relating to Lizzie Friedman may have concerned her affair with an SIS officer, Tony Milne, who failed to declare the relationship. Tony's elder brother Tim had been Philby's schoolfriend at Westminster and colleague in Section V. Tony had joined SIS in 1944 from SOE, for whom he had had served in North Africa and Greece, and retired in 1969. She also conducted an affair with a British diplomat, Sir Michael Stewart.
2. Lizzie Philby's third husband was Georg Honigmann. His MI5 file: KV6/113–KV6/114.
3. The redacted passage refers to Philby's SIS secretary and mistress, Esther Whitfield. Her statement is at KV2/4103.

VII: Exposure

1. Vladimir Petrov's MI5 file: KV2/3440–KV2/3488. See also David Horner, *The Spycatchers: The Official History of ASIO* (Sydney: Allen & Unwin, 2014).

Bibliography

Adamson, Iain. *The Great Detective*. London: Frederick Muller, 1966.

Albright, Joseph, and Marcia Kunstel. *Bombshell*. New York: Random House, 1997.

Andrew, Christopher. *The Defence of the Realm: The Authorized History of MI5*. New York: Alfred A. Knopf. 2009.

——, and Oleg Gordievsky. *KGB: The Inside Story*. London: Sceptre, 1991.

——, and Vasili Mitrokhin. *The Mitrokhin Archive: The KGB in Europe and the West*. London: Penguin. 2002

——. *The KGB and the World: The Mitrokhin Archive II*. London: Penguin. 2006.

Ball, Desmond, and David Horner. *Breaking the Code: Australia's KGB Network 1944-50*. St L NSW: Allen & Unwin. 1998.

Barros, James. *No Sense of Evil: The Espionage Case of Herbert Norman*. New York: Ivy Books. 1987.

Batvinis, Ray. *The Origins of FBI Counterintelligence*. Lawrence: University Press of Kansas, 2007.

Belfrage, Cedric. *The American Inquisition*. New York: Bobbs-Merill, 1973.

——. *The Frightened Giant*. London: Secker & Warburg, 1957.

——. *Something to Guard*. New York: Columbia University Press, 1978.

Benson, Robert Louis, and Michael Warner, eds. *VENONA: Soviet Espionage and the American Response 1957I*. Washington, DC: NSA & CIA, 1996.

Bentley, Elizabeth. *Out of Bondage*. New York: Ivy Books, 1988.

Bly, Herman O. *Communism: The Cold War and the FBI Connection*. New York: Huntingdon House, 1998.

Borovik, G. *The Philby Files: The Secret Life of the Master Spy Kim Philby*. Boston: Little, Brown, 1994.

Bowen, R. *Innocence Is Not Enough: The Life of Herbert Norman*. Vancouver: Douglas & McIntyre, 1986.

Bower, Tom. *The Perfect English Spy*. London: Heinemann, 1995.

Brook-Shepherd, Gordon. *The Storm Petrels: The Flight of the First Soviet Defectors*. New York: Harcourt Brace Jovanovich, 1977

——. *The Storm Birds: Soviet Postwar Defectors*. New York: Henry Holt, 1989.

Burke, David. *The Spy Who Came in from the Co-op: Melita Norwood and the Ending of Cold War Espionage*. London: The Boydell Press, 2008.

Burt, Leonard. *Commander Burt of Scotland Yard*. London: Heinemann, 1959.

Cairncross, John. *The Enigma Spy: The Story of the Man Who Changed the Course of World War II*. London: Century, 1997.

Carter, Miranda. *Anthony Blunt: His Lives*. New York: Macmillan, 2001.

Cecil, Robert. *A Divided Life*. London: Bodley Head, 1988.

Cockerill, A.W. *Sir Percy Sillitoe*. London: W.H. Allen, 1975.

Constantinides, George. *Intelligence and Espionage: An Analytical Bibliography*. Boulder: Westview, 1983.

Cookridge, E.H. *Secrets of the British Secret Service*. London: Sampson, Low, 1947.

——. *The Third Man*. London: Arthur Barker, 1968.

Costello, John. *Mask of Treachery*. New York: William Morrow, 1988.

——, and Oleg Tsarev. *Deadly Illusions*. New York: Crown, 1993.

Dallin, David J. *Soviet Espionage*. New Haven: Yale University Press, 1955.

Deacon, Richard. *The British Connection: Russia's Manipulation of British Individuals and Institutions*. London: Hamish Hamilton, 1979.

——. *A History of the British Secret Service*. London: Frederick Muller, 1969.

Driberg, Tom. *Guy Burgess*. London: Weidenfeld, 1956.

——. *Ruling Passions*. London: Jonathan Cape, 1977.

Elliott, Nicholas. *Never Judge a Man by His Umbrella*. Stroud, Wiltshire: Michael Russell, 1991.

Ellis, C.H. Dick. *Transcaspian Episode*. London: Hutchinson, 1963.

Epstein, Edward Jay. *Deception: The Invisible War Between the KGB & the CIA*. New York: Simon & Schuster, 1989.

Feklisov, Alexander. *The Man Behind the Rosenbergs*. New York: Enigma Books, 2007.

Foote, Alexander. *Handbook for Spies*. London: Museum Press, 1964.

Gazur, Edward. *Secret Assignment: The FBI's KGB General*. London: St. Ermin's Press, 2001.

Gordievsky, Oleg. *Next Stop Execution: The Autobiography of Oleg Gordievsky*. London: Macmillan, 1999.

Gouzenko, Igor. *The Iron Curtain*. New York: E.P. Dutton, 1948.

Hamrick, S.J. *Deceiving the Deceivers: Kim Philby, Donald Maclean, and Guy Burgess*. New Haven: Yale University Press, 2004.

Hart, Jenifer. *Ask Me No More*. London: Halban, 1998.

Haynes, John, and Harvey Klehr. *Venona: Decoding Soviet Espionage in America*. New Haven: Yale University Press, 2000.

——, and Alexander Vassiliev. *Spies: The Rise and Fall of the KGB in America*. New Haven: Yale University Press, 2009.

Holt, Thadeus. *The Deceivers: Allied Military Deception in the Second World War*. New York: Skyhorse, 2007.

Hornblum, Allen M. *The Invisible Harry Gold: The Man Who Gave the Soviets the Atom Bomb*. New Haven: Yale University Press, 2010.

Jeffrey, Keith. *MI6: The History of the Secret Intelligence Service 1909-1949*. London: Bloomsbury, 2010.

Klehr, Harvey. *The Secret World of American Communism*. New Haven, CT: Yale University Press, 1995.

Kuczynski, Ruth. *Sonia's Report*. London: Chatto & Windus, 1991.

Lamphere, Robert. *The CIA-KGB War*. New York: Random House, 1986.

Lownie, Andrew. *Stalin's Englishman*. London: Hodder & Stoughton, 2015.

Macintyre, Ben. *A Spy Among Friends*. London: Bloomsbury, 2015.

Martin, David C. *Wilderness of Mirrors*. New York: Harper & Row, 1980.

Miles, Jonathan. *The Nine Lives of Otto Katz*. London: Bantam, 2011.

Modin, Yuri. *My Five Cambridge Friends*. London: Hodder Headline, 1995.

Moorhead, Alan. *The Traitors*. London: Harper & Row, 1952.

Mure, David. *Master of Deception: Tangled Webs in London and the Middle East*. London: William Kimber, 1980.

Mure, David. *The Last Temptation*. London: Buchan & Enright, 1984.

Peake, Hayden. 'OSS and the Venona Decrypts', *Intelligence and National Security*, Vol. 12, No. 3 (July 1997).

Peierls, Rudolf. *Bird of Passage*. Princeton, NJ: Princeton University Press, 1985.

Penrose, Barrie, and Simon Freeman. *Conspiracy of Silence*. London: Grafton Books, 1986.

Perry, Roland. *Last of the Cold War Spies: The Life of Michael Straight*. New York: Da Capo, 2005.

Philby, Kim. *My Silent War*. London: MacGibbon & Kee, 1968.

Philby, Rufina, and Hayden Peake. *The Private Life of Kim Philby*. London: St. Ermin's Press, 1999.

Pincher, Chapman. *Their Trade is Treachery*. London: Sidgwick & Jackson, 1981.

Polmar, Norman, and Tom Allen. *Spy Book: The Encyclopedia of Espionage*. New York: Random House, 2004.

Powers, R.G. *Secrecy and Power: The Life of J. Edgar Hoover*. New York: Free Press, 1987.

Purvis, Stuart. *Guy Burgess: The Spy Who Knew Everyone*. London: Biteback, 2015.

Radosh, Ron, and Joyce Milton. *The Rosenberg File*. New York: Holt, Rinehart, and Winston, 1983.

Rees, David. *Harry Dexter White*. New York: Coward, McCann & Geoghegan, 1973.

Rees, Goronwy. *A Chapter of Accidents*. London: Chatto & Windus, 1972.

Report of the Royal Commission, Australia, 1956.

Report of the Royal Commission, Canada, 1946.

Sawatsky, John. *Men in the Shadows: The RCMP Security Service*. Toronto: Doubleday, 1980.

——. *For Services Rendered: Leslie James Bennett and the RCMP Security Service*. Toronto: Doubleday, 1982.

Smyth, Henry D. *Atomic Energy for Military Purposes*. Princeton, NJ: Princeton University Press, 1945.

Stockton, B. *Flawed Patriot: The Rise and Fall of CIA Legend Bill Harvey*. Washington, DC: Potomac, 2006.

Straight, Michael. *After Long Silence*. New York: W.W. Norton, 1983.

Trevor Roper, Hugh. *The Philby Affair*. London: William Kimber, 1968.

Weinstein, Allen. *Perjury: The Hiss-Chambers Case*. New York: Random House, 1987.

——, and Alexander Vassiliev. *The Haunted Wood: Soviet Espionage in America—the Stalin Era*. New York: Modern Library, 2000.

West, Nigel. *Historical Dictionary of British Intelligence*. Lanham, MD: Scarecrow Press, 2005.

West, Rebecca. *The New Meaning of Treason*. New York: Viking Press, 1967.

Whitaker, R., and G. Marcuse. *Cold War Canada: The Making of a National Insecurity State, 1945- 1957.* Toronto: University of Toronto Press, 1994.

Wright, Peter, with Pail Greengrass. *Spycatcher: The Candid Autobiography of a Senior Intelligence Officer.* New York: Viking Penguin. 1987.

Younger, Kenneth. *Changing Perspectives in British Foreign Policy.* Oxford: Oxford University Press, 1964.

Index